Madame Langlois' Legacy
A Culinary History of French Colonial Louisiana

Jon G. Laiche

Technical Support Services, Inc.
Franklinton, Louisiana
2021

Copyright © 2021. Jon G. Laiche
Copyright © 2021.
Technical Support Services, Inc.

All rights reserved. No part of this publication may be reproduced, distributed, or transmitted in any form or by any means, without prior written permission.

Technical Support Services, Inc.
21373 Dutch Road.
Franklinton, LA 70458 USA.
www.tssi-no.com

Publisher's Note: This work contains non-fictional historical material and includes historical recipes. Other parts contain works of historical fiction. Included therein are names, characters, places, and incidents that are a product of the author's imagination. Locales and public names are sometimes used for atmospheric purposes. Within the fiction sections, any resemblance to actual people, living or dead, or to businesses, companies, events, institutions, or locales is completely coincidental.

Book Layout © 2020 BookDesignTemplates.com

Madame Langlois' Legacy/ Jon G. Laiche -- 1st ed.
ISBN 978-0-9907378-8-9

10 9. 8. 7. 6. 5. 4. 3. 2.

Table of Contents

DEDICATION 5

A NOTE TO THE READER 6

STATEMENT ON THE ORIGINS AND PROVENANCE OF THE IMAGES INCLUDED IN THIS BOOK 7

ACKNOWLEDGEMENTS 8

1 1722 -FRENCH AND INDIAN BREAD 9

2 1722-FRERE GERARD DISCOVERS SAGAMITE 17

3 1724 - SUZANNE COMES TO NEW ORLEANS.. 25

4 1724 - GERARD'S PLAIN COOKING 37

5 1725 - COUNTRY COOKING 53

6 1725 - FRERE GERARD'S POTAGER 61

7 1727 - GRITS AND GRILLADES 69

8 1727 -THE 3 SAUCES MERES.......................... 77

9 1729 - A VOYAGE UP THE BAYOU 85

10   LATE 1729 - FRERE GERARD DISCOVERS THE PACCAN... 93

11   1729/30 - FRÈRE GERARD AND THE NATCHEZ INDIANS 99

12   LATE 1720's – MAKING SAUSAGE ON THE COTE DES ALLEMANDES.................................... 109

13   EARLY 1730's – MARKETS, MARSHES AND MEAT 119

14   1730's – A VISIT TO THE URSULINE POTAGER 127

15	EARLY 1730's – SOME CALAS IN THE FRENCH MARKET	139
16	1730's - A BOUCAN FOR PENTECOST	145
17	1730's – THE HOUMA VISIT	151
18	1730's – A SMUGGLER'S PARADISE	161
19	1733– HUNTING IN COLONIAL LOUISIANA	181
20	1738 – A VISIT FROM NATCHITOCHES	197
21	1740 – COFFEE, CHOCOLATE AND WINE	211
22	1740's SUZANNE COOKS FOR CHRISTMAS	223
23	1740's - THE ILLINOIS COUNTRY	235
24	1747 – THE ENGAGEMENT PARTY	245
25	EARLY 1740's – SHRIMP, ALLIGATORS AND TURTLES	257
26	1750's - A COLONIAL MARDI GRAS	269
27	300 YEARS AGO - EVERYDAY EATING IN NEW ORLEANS	281
28	1790's THE EMERGENCE OF A CREOLE CULTURE; GISELLE'S KITCHEN	291
RECIPE INDEX		299
BIBLIOGRAPHY:		303
ABOUT THE AUTHOR		313

DEDICATION

To my big brother, Robert C. Laiche. Here's to the man who taught me how to shoot a bow, how to fence like Cyrano, how to mop a barroom floor like a sailor.

Bobby was, like the man he inspired me to be, a fountain of useless and ancient information. I was in my twenties before I beat him in a game of chess, a game I learned lying on his bedroom floor listening to Marty Robbins and the Kingston Trio. He never stopped reading, so I never stopped reading. He wrote poetry. I write history. He always played the jester but was way cleverer than he let on.

Bobby passed on in early June of 2018, just as Beth and I were editing the final draft of our manuscript celebrating the Tricentennial of our city. I was wondering to who and how I would dedicate the book. This book is as much a product of his inspirational genius, as much as our labors and research. It is only fitting that it be dedicated in love to his memory.

Thanks for everything, big brother.

A NOTE TO THE READER

In 2015 The Petticoat Rebellion was published containing many of the same chapters and recipes as will be found in this volume. Madame Langlois' Legacy is a complete revision of those original chapters. Mistakes have been corrected, new images have been added, and quite a few new recipes have been included.

Madame Langlois' Legacy also includes many new chapters and recipes as well. It brings the story of Creole Cuisine into the "American" period of the Louisiana colony to 1803 and just a bit beyond. New readers to this concept will find a wealth of information about the French colony of Louisiana as well as a comprehensive culinary history of the region in the eighteenth century. It is hoped that they will also enjoy the tales of Frère Gerard and Tante Suzanne as they live out their lives bringing the unique creation of one of America's most famous regional cuisines into existence. Readers of The Petticoat Rebellion will find loads of new "history" and many more tasty recipes to try out for their enjoyment.

By the way, Madame Langlois was Bienville's housekeeper who took twenty-two poor girls - shipped to Louisiana from the streets of Paris - and taught them how to deal with all the new foodstuffs they encountered here.

I hope you find many hours of enjoyment delving into the story of French Louisiana and digging into the meals and memories of the kitchen folks and others who gave Creole Cuisine to the world.

BON APPETIT!

STATEMENT ON THE ORIGINS AND PROVENANCE OF THE IMAGES INCLUDED IN THIS BOOK

The images used in this book come from essentially three sources:

1. The authors' own photographs, taken during the course of research for this work between 2013 and 2020.

2. Public Domain photos and images from the British Library collection found at:
https://www.flickr.com/search/?media=photos&text=British%20Library&max_taken_date=-1893348001
(see note below).

3. Public Domain and/or "No Copyright Restrictions" photos and images found on the Internet in general.

NOTE: The Flickr British library collection:
In December of 2013 The British Library generously made available to the public literally over one million images 1,020,418 to be exact.
See the announcement at:
http://blog.flickr.net/en/2013/12/16/welcome-the-british-library-to-the-commons/
The million plus images are FREE and in the public domain. Use them as you will. They can be found at http://www.flickr.com/photos/britishlibrary/
This work is licensed under the Creative Commons Attribution-Non-Commercial-Share Alike 3.0 Unported License.
To view a copy of this license, visit: http://creativecommons.org/licenses/by-nc-sa/3.0/ or send a letter to Creative Commons, 444 Castro Street, Suite 900, Mountain View, California, 94041, USA.

ACKNOWLEDGEMENTS

The genesis of this work goes back to my retirement from teaching in 2010. I t has been a long and gratifying journey and now thanks must be given to all who have made this work possible

At the beginning. In a cohesive neighborhood in the center of New Orleans, there existed in the 50's and 60's a community of friends and family that formed my intellect and moral character. As scion of a HUGE extended family, 16 aunts and uncles, and 45 first cousins, there was a sense of community, history and belonging like no other.

Next, I must express thanks to my teachers and professors, who taught me how the past can inform a life of scholarly seeking and understanding. Especial gratitude must be extended to Gerald P. Bodet, Thomas Schlunz, Joan Johnson, Father Stephen Duffy, and Robert Gnuse for molding this quest and world view into a body of knowledge that was the rich soil that nourished the flowering of this work.

I cannot forget the local librarians, Lynne Moore, Gayle Atkins, Kathy Soulier, who were always there with a helping hand, a wise recommendation, and the granting of access to both common and obscure works to fill the attached bibliography.

And finally, my incredible life partner and wife, Elizabeth, who has supported my impecunious academic lifestyle for the past 45+ years and fed and housed our family through all my ups, downs, and fantasies. The woman who never hesitated to call my "baby" (this book) ugly and putting my loquacious storytelling in line so "normal" people would know what I was trying to say. Thank you, Beth, for being you and keeping me on the straight and narrow.

Finally, of course, all of the errors in fact and omission herein are mine alone. If you take issue with anything here, I would appreciate your input and recommendations. (nola1718@tssi-no.com)

1
1722 -FRENCH AND INDIAN BREAD

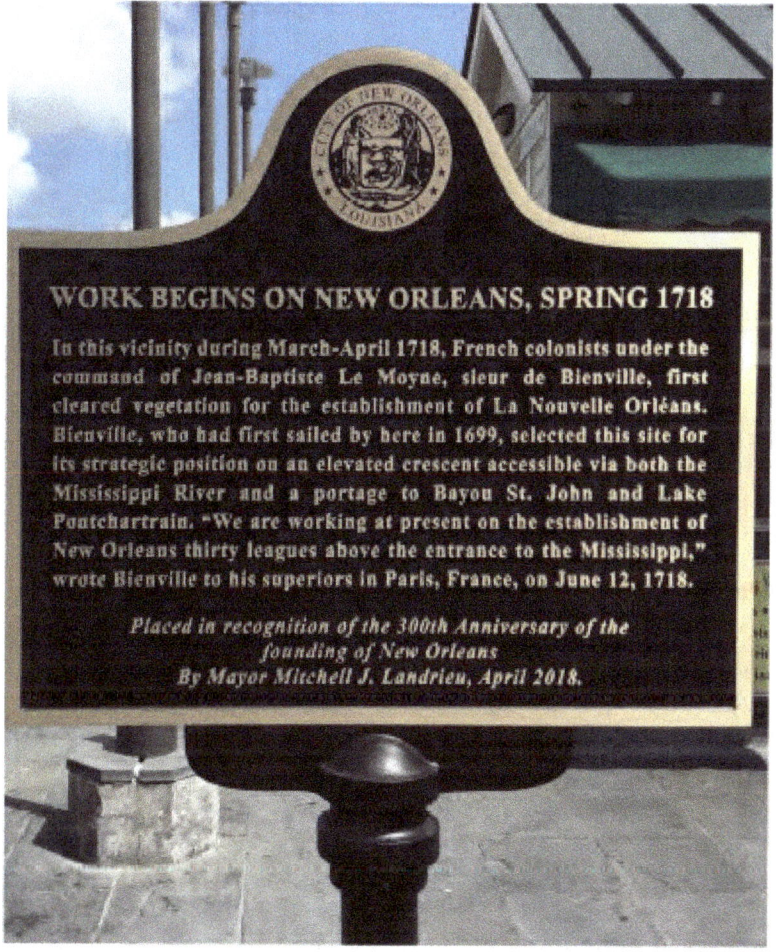

We arrived in the New World at the beginning of September 1722, on Dauphin Island. Father Bruno led our small group onto the island. My legs wobbled as though a ship deck was still beneath my feet instead of marshy land, but after weeks on the swaying ship, I was grateful for land of any kind. Relief would be short-lived, though, as we would soon board a small boat to take us to Fort Louis at the town of Mobile. From there, we would begin our preparations to leave for the new capital at New Orleans.

This New World was unlike anything I had ever experienced. While completing the thousand tasks associated with the upcoming trip, we watched with fascination the atmospheric antics of our new surroundings as the wind tossed the water about in the Mobile Bay and rushed the clouds across the sky. At that time, we didn't know that a few hundred miles to the south, violent storm winds were whipping the seas into a froth, and the storm was moving our way.

A few days later, as we prepared to leave the coast and head to the capital, the storm fell upon us. September 11th dawned with a somber black veil to the south, and within just a few hours, fierce winds and rain pounded the coast with unbridled fury. We were on the eastern end of a violent hurricane that swept across the coast.

Huddled together in a frightened group, we listened to its howling like some sort of demented beast. It slammed into Biloxi, leveling everything in its path. New Orleans fared no better. The hurricane virtually destroyed all the buildings there before continuing as far up as the Natchez settlement where it finally quieted into a nasty squall.

What a welcome to the New World! But the Lord Almighty never sends us a misfortune without some meaning. By wiping out the feeble huts and barracks at the new capital, the storm gave us a clean slate upon which to build a new city on the river.

Naturally, our first task upon reaching New Orleans was to provide ourselves some shelter before the blood-thirsty insects called mosquitoes ate us alive. Insects seem to be the real rulers here, and many were delighted to dine on us. So bad are these tiny but vicious mosquitos that Natives used them as punishment for major crimes, staking out a person at dusk to be stung and dined upon all night! Despite the heat, we kept most of our bodies covered to escape the terribly itchy welts caused by these tiny devils. We had to set smudge pots around our camp each evening, as it was the only way to discourage the little devils and get some much-needed sleep.

Despite the oppressive heat, the multitude of bugs, and the overall strangeness of the place, there was much work to be done. My part of setting up housing for the Capuchin Order was the kitchen, and later, to start our potager. I set about my labor with a full heart and a sense of excitement in finally building our future in the New World.

As part of the job, I also had to feed my Capuchin Brothers and the few workers we rounded up to help us rebuild the settlement. This combination of being newly arrived, the emotions surging through us at the loss of the town and its rebuilding, and the general lack of food supplies, set me quite a task.

Chargement d'un navire

To sustain the work effort until a supply chain could be established, I decided to heed the holy Psalmist, "Here is bread, which strengthens man's heart, and therefore is called the staff of life" (Ps.104), and Isaiah in Ch. 30 also says, "Brown bread and the Word of the Lord are good fare," so upon this sage advice, I set up the bakery first.

From the local sauvages (The French term for Native Americans - did not necessarily connote 'savage') I acquired a strange flour made of ground corn, and from the Germans up the river, we got some rice. With a little conversation among the earlier settlers, and some guidance from our Native neighbors, I was able to supply our community with a steady supply of bread.

And so, with bread in our bellies, and an abundance of courage to season it with, and hope for a prosperous future, we began our life in New Orleans.

RECIPES

FRENCH AND INDIAN BREAD

This experiment began on a rainy June day. Bread baking in the rain can be a slightly different procedure. On a rainy, humid day, you must reduce the liquid added to the batter/dough as the bread absorbs moisture from the air in the rising stage. How much to reduce by? Only the day, the weather, and experience will know.

- 2 cups of rice
- 1 tablespoon yeast
- 1 cup of buttermilk
- 2 cups of cornmeal/flour
- 2 eggs
- 2 teaspoons of cooking oil or melted lard or butter or bear fat
- Salt to taste

To begin, boil 2 cups of rice in about 3 or 4 cups of water until mushy- about 20 to 30 minutes. Dissolve 1 tablespoon of yeast into 1 cup of buttermilk. In a casserole* dish, blend the buttermilk/yeast into 2 cups of cornmeal/flour along with 2 eggs and 2 teaspoons of cooking oil or melted lard or butter or bear fat. Mush the rice into a paste and mix with the corn batter. Add salt and any other flavorings you wish. Set to rise.

After about 2 hours, the experimental pan of bread had only risen about ½ inch. Nevertheless, it was placed into a "hot" oven † and baked for 30-35 minutes. Test with a toothpick, as you would test cakes or brownies, when the toothpick comes out clean, the bread is done.

Author's Tasting Notes:

The bread came out very light and fluffy, almost like an angel food cake. It had a pronounced corn flavor. Overall, it was very good. This experiment used hardly any flavoring agents. I didn't put salt in it for fear of inhibiting the yeast. Served with dinner, its basic neutrality, allowed for the addition of various toppings, such as:

---Brown sugar: excellent
---Steak gravy: very good

---Lemon sweet & sour sauce: different
---Salt: very good

*For this trial I used a 9 x 13 glass casserole pan (3.7 quarts). An earthenware casserole size vessel would be more authentic.

† A "hot" oven is normally 450° to 500° F.

YOUR TRICENTENNIAL MEMO

There was a great deal of "strangeness" to be dealt with by those brave enough to come to the fledgling New Orleans, and many challenges to be met in stocking their kitchens and building their new gardens, which the French called a potager (po-ta-shay). Like Frère Gerard - the fictional French Brother in the story above - who came to the New World to spread the word of God, these pioneers faced a multitude of issues they had never even dreamed of at home in France.

One of the major changes for the colonists was not only the general lack of food, but the uniqueness of what was available. Frenchmen had known rice as early as the 8th century and while there are records of it being sold at fairs in Champagne in the 14th century, it was not a staple on the French table, as most Europeans ate barley, wheat and rye. Indian corn or maize was virtually unknown to the colonists.

While corn meal is a common ingredient in today's kitchens, it was a very strange ingredient for Frère Gerard in the1720's. A recipe discovered in a journal written by Dumont (see Bibliography) - one of the first French explorers of Louisiana - describes how one had to go about converting the hard kernels of corn into a flour meal.

That original and detailed recipe is described by Dr. Shannon Dawdy (see Bibliography) as "… an excellent colonial bread created with a combination of African labor and Indian and European technology." Quoting Dumont, she writes:

> "*Dried corn kernels are soaked overnight, after which the Negres ou Negresses pound them into flour using a pestle and sift the flour in basket sieves made by local Indian women, which are works of perfection. The resulting coarse flour is then mixed with cooked rice and the sticky dough is placed in a French casserole dish to air-leaven and bake in a hot oven. He also describes a more familiar version of southern cornbread, a half-and- half mixture of corn and "French flour," made when*

wheat was available."

Zecher, Dawdy, et. al. Dumont de Montigny, 414-15.

This new flour may have been strange to the newcomers, but it was gratefully received as a deterrent to hunger, and in the decades to come, would become one of the mainstays of Southern cuisine.

2
1722-FRERE GERARD DISCOVERS SAGAMITE

I set about building our first kitchen, but while trying to stock it I encountered an immediate and most serious problem. In simple terms, there was very little food to be had in the area.

Although the "town" had been here for some three years, most of it had blown away in the hurricane that had greeted our arrival, and the food stores provided by the Company were woefully inadequate. Hardly anything had been planted so far, and what had was barely enough to feed the owners of the gardens. The closest farms were two leagues away at the bayou settlement. All others were leagues away in the Biloxi and Mobile settlements where they had been established for some 20 years already.

My only option was to adventure out into the town and the immediate neighborhood to see if I could scrounge up anything with which to stock my kitchen. A bit risky, considering the many ruffians and Natives in the area and my inexperience with such folks, but I had no other choice.

The next morning, I gathered some of our trade goods - a few knives, a small pot, and some strings of beads - and set out at sunrise, heading up the road through a damp fog, toward to the Bayou St. John settlement to visit the farm families and the trading post there. I managed to get a few eggs, a small collection of herbs, and a couple of sacks of the odd meal they grind from the local grain called maize.

On the way back home, I fell in with some Natives from the local Tchoupitoulas settlement where the bayou meets the river and learned of the delectable fare they traded in - bear oil and meat, nuts and berries, wild game and fish - so much available that starvation no longer seem to loom over our heads. I left their company with some salt and a basket of nuts, and a promise to trade with them as soon as I could manage it.

Back in the town, I caught the fragrance of ripe fruit, and discovered a treasure trove of wild fruit trees scattered around the colony. With childish delight, I set about gathering plums, berries and even a few pears. Many did not make it into my bag! The orange trees, limbs bending toward the earth with their bounty, offered so much fruit that I had to fashion a bag out of my apron to carry them. With fingers sticky with berry juice, I wandered around the streets, letting my new home take root in my soul.

Once home, I laid out and contemplated my treasures. I scratched my head, wondering what I could do with these ingredients. The biggest mystery were the sacks of grain. As far as I knew, and I knew very little, no one in the colony had managed to produce a harvest of wheat, rye or barley in this New World, at least not along the lower Mississippi. However, most of the people I had talked to during my expedition were familiar with this grain that sat on my table.

Growing up in the forests of northern France, I had heard talk of it but had never really seen or used it. As far as I knew, maize was mostly a grain grown around the Mediterranean countries and used mainly for decoration or to feed farm animals. Here in America, I was given to understand that it was a common dish among the Natives as well as the colonists who had been here for some time.

For new arrivals, like those in my community, it was quite a new experience. Most of our French compatriots here in Louisiana had originally come from New France, where they had grown up eating this common American grain. I had managed to make an edible thought somewhat unusual bread from the grain, but nothing else. If I was to learn anything about cooking corn, I would need considerable help... and I knew just where to get it.

I went back to the Natives who had built their huts at the edge of town next to the river. They are an interesting lot full of wonderful and exciting stories - at least, exciting to me - and after inevitable small talk, I excused myself from the men and sat down with the women. I felt my face flush with embarrassment as they teased me about my manhood, then teased me even more as my face blushed red, but still I managed to ask them how to go about preparing this new grain in an appetizing fashion.

All teasing ceased the moment we began discussing their cooking skills. Every time I reflect upon what the Native ladies taught me that day, I must smile. The preparation we discussed was called sagamité (sag-uh-my-tay). It is prepared with either whole kernels of corn or corn grits, a coarse grind of the corn kernel, along with herbs and flavorings, according to whatever was available. It was a New World variation on what we call porridge in the Old Country. Buoyed by this simple solution to my immediate problem, I headed back home to try my hand at different recipes.

My very first sagamite meal consisted of this boiled corn grits, flavored with a robust cheese and a handful of savory herbs. I then baked this mush in the oven, where it puffed and spilled over the sides. The dish turned out quite well and proved to be a filling and satisfying meal for my brothers. It soon became a staple in my Presbytère kitchen.

RECIPES

1718 SAGAMITE

Prepare a pot of corn meal or grits as usual. Pour into a pie dish or baking pan. Add: (any or all of the available below).

- 4 green onions, snipped into 1/8-inch (or smaller) bits
- 2 tablespoons chopped chives
- 3 toes garlic, smashed, peeled, and chopped
- 1/2 stick butter
- 1/8 teaspoon cayenne pepper, or to taste
- Salt to taste
- 4 ounces shredded Gruyere or other semi-hard cheese
- 3 teaspoons sesame seeds

Thoroughly mix the herbs, seasonings, and cheese into the corn meal or grits and bake for at least 20 min. in the 375° oven. Keep an eye on the dish during the last five minutes as the grits may begin to "souffle" and overflow the pan. Once you have mastered this simple recipe, you have mastered Sagamité. Your imagination is now free to roam the markets and fill in this culinary blank canvas with whatever takes your fancy.

YOUR TRICENTENNIAL MEMO

Indian corn (maize) ground into flour, meal, or grits was the staple foodstuff that French explorers and settlers encountered as they spread their colonial influence among the Iroquois and Huron nations of what would become New France or French Canada in the 17th and 18th centuries. One great advantage of any flour or meal (be it corn, wheat, rye, oats, etc.) is its unending variability.

Over the millennia, humanity has added just about everything under the sun to the basic mix of flour, water, fat, salt, and sometimes yeast or soda. The Natives of the northeastern American woodlands and, as it turns out, the Gulf Coast and its piney woods hinterland, used their ground corn, or sagamité, no differently. Even the LeMoyne brothers, - French Canadian landed gentry who explored the Gulf Coast and the Mississippi's gulf delta - were no strangers to sagamité.

It was often an ice breaker and a medium of gift exchange in their first contacts with Louisiana Natives. As a testament to its versatility and ubiquity, Iberville writes in his journals as leader of the Louisiana expedition (1699-1704) (see Bibliography) of sagamité prepared with the native plums and of the same dish prepared with wild game meat and bear fat. It easily covers the entire sweet-savory spectrum.

You will, no doubt, encounter many recipes that call for boiled corn flour. Research has shown that the extent or size of the "grind" was solely an accident of the milling or grinding equipment and the upper body strength of the miller. In the 1700's, it was likely that the corn used to boil for sagamite was of a coarser texture, as finer flour was probably not available at the time. It was the coarser grind that was called grits, and still is today.

We must admit a bit of sardonic irony in choosing the cheese and herb presentation in Frère Gerard's story. A gleeful chuckle cannot be avoided when in recent years local (New Orleans) casual dining establishments add their "new specialty" of roasted cheese grits to their upscale menus, as this meal has been around for at least 300 years.

Prof. Richard Campanella* of Tulane offers a linguistic and geographical study of sagamité which we, in turn, offer here for your consideration. He states on p. 472, "There are, after all, only so many ways to render corn edible…". Frère Gerard's preparation of sagamité can easily be placed aside the descriptions contained in his paper. While sagamité was most often prepared with large corn kernels, there is reason to maintain that this is not the only way to go.

Many of the original sources, both in our research and Prof. Campanella's also describe the dish made with ground corn. Corn meal and sometimes even wheat flour were used in preparation of the porridge. It is not unreasonable to include grits among these options. Like gruel, broth, soup, or jambalaya, what the Natives called sagamité is almost universal among

Eastern Woodland Indians, a one-pot meal that can really use any type of grain.

Prof. Campanella's descriptions of this ubiquitous corn preparation needs to be included here to complete the coverage of this versatile and convenient recipe.

> "*Linguists trace sagamité to the Algonquin Indian word ki-jagamite, which the philologist Father Jean André Cuoq translated to mean l'eau est chaud - the water is hot - in his canonical 1886 Lexique de la Langue Algonquine. Cuoq noted that "It is from this misheard word that the word 'sagamité' comes from, which can be compared to the 'little hot water' of the English." Algonquins apparently applied the term to hot broths regardless of ingredients, and broadly to the manner of cooking in which ingredients were immersed in boiling water-a method that usually rendered a one-pot soup or gruel.*"

(Campanella, 2013, p. 466)

> "*Grace King interpreted 'sagamity' as 'hominy cooked with grease and pieces of meat or fish' and speculated that it represented the original of the Creole jambalaya, in which rice has since been most toothsomely substituted for corn.*"

(Ibid., p. 471)

> "*Sagamité resembles a wide range of modern New World corn dishes, including New England's succotash and hasty pudding, the South's cornbread and hush puppies, the Acadian macaque choux ...*"

(Ibid., p. 472)

It is important to note that the word sagamité refers not only to the food but also the methods of preparing it. Obtain some corn grits, add your favorite herbs and flavors, and enjoy this wonderful dish like those Louisiana Natives, the old French settlers, and their Creole descendants, who never make it twice the same way.

* Campanella, Richard. "Geography of a Food, or Geography of a Word? The Curious Cultural Diffusion of Sagamité." in Louisiana History: The Journal of the Louisiana Historical Association. Fall, 2013, Volume LIV, No. 4. pp. 465-476.

3
1724 - SUZANNE COMES TO NEW ORLEANS

Maman never said much about how she came over here to the New World. In the last years of her life, she would sometimes voice her memories of being a young girl living along the east Senegal River and watching her brothers, cousins, and friends work the rice fields and herd the cattle. Before the Europeans came, her father's world was the great sophisticated kingdom of Mali. Her world was torn apart, and she suffered much as a young girl when dragged away from her family in Africa and sold into slavery in the New World. I remember hearing her quiet crying sometimes in the darkest hours of the night.

I am proud of my heritage, which in many ways fashioned me into the chef I am today. From early on, my Maman would try to recall the good times in her life, mostly about her times in the kitchen with her own Maman. She told me stories of her homeland, the foods they cooked, the gardens they grew.

Her beauty, goodness, and her own fame as a good cook earned her a place in her "master's" kitchen, and eventually, a place in his heart. In the eyes of government and church, they could not marry, nonetheless they lived as man and wife as much as any other couple on San Domingue. In a sure testament to their love, all her children, myself included, were born free.

My happiest memories are when Maman taught me many of those kitchen skills she had learned as a child or developed while living here in the West Indies. During moments in the kitchen as we went about washing dishes, cleaning up, and getting ready to cook the next meal, she would sometimes sing a song from her childhood or tell a story or share a memory about her mother and father. I treasure those times and was able to share some of her homeland memories with my brothers and sisters.

Planting time on a San Domingue Plantation

    As a child in the kitchen, I was first in charge of cleaning up. As I washed the dishes and pots Maman would say "let me show you how my Maman did it" or "come on down to the stream with me and I'll show you how to clean the towels like we did when I was a girl." She would tell me stories of her uncles and about the river she lived on and some of the grand heritage of her family, and how in her homeland, women were treated as equals.

    Maman taught me all that she knew about running a kitchen and planting a garden, about planting the ngombo seeds - called okra in the New World - for the best crop, but it was her creative use of herbs and spices that fascinated me. "Taste this," she would say, as she offered me a bit of chicken flavored with coconut and a dash of nutmeg, or a slice of pork dusted in ginger, "and tell me what you think." I cannot recall one time when I thought it was anything but delicious.

    I learned how to get the most flavor from the rare spices and herbs she bartered from the traders, and how to make the pot-au-feu, a simmering pot of water kept on the hearth into which all scraps went, making a delicious stock for soups and sauces. She taught me how to make sumbala, the fermented seasoning mix added to most recipes in her African homeland, and how to make the mirepoix, that blend of vegetables and spices used by the French. Maman had a way of mixing together all the different foods from different places, creating something new and wonderful.

In 1705, when the Master moved us to Mobile in the new Louisiana colony, Maman found even more ingredients to work with. Maize, large ocean fish, and waterfowl, the likes of which I had never seen before, all became transformed into wonderful meals in her kitchen. As those early years in Mobile passed by, my gifts for managing and preparing all things food manifested itself.

Under Maman's watchful eyes, I grew in experience and organizational skills until, at the age of 20, I was the chef de cuisine at the big house on the farm, where I was very happy. But the only certainty in life is change. It wasn't long after these events that I was off on a new adventure and a new life.

When Maman passed, Papa missed her so much that he passed soon after. With the plantation inherited by my oldest brother, my younger brother and I decided to adventure to New Orleans, where we both found employment at the house of a rich officer, Major Francois Philippe de Marigny de Mandeville, I as a cook, and my brother as the stable manager.

Everything in the new capital was in a state of flux. When I arrived, the Major had just begun to build his new home at the corner of Chartres and Ursuline. Besides doing the marketing, the cooking, and cleaning, I, along with entire household staff, was engaged in building a new kitchen and planting a new potager.

This situation gave us the freedom to install the latest and best hearths and ovens, and even a new row of brick fireboxes topped by individual burners. As usual, the kitchen was placed behind and some distance from the main house. The big hearth, which contained the cranes, trivets, and various iron supports, was the centerpiece of the kitchen. Into the walls of the hearth were built several baking ovens, and just outside the door and under a shed was a fire pit for outdoor cooking and boucane. I had never seen such a kitchen!

The kitchen garden containing herbs and vegetables was placed alongside and behind the kitchen. Between the kitchen complex and the main house was a wide covered walkway so the food could be brought back and forth to the dining areas with a minimum of effect by the weather. Fronting this walkway was a cabin where I kept the preserved food and where herbs hung from the ceiling and vegetables and fruits were allowed to dry. Between the potager and the kitchen building we placed the requisite small smokehouse of the household for smoking our sausage, game meat, and the hams we occasionally got from the Illinois country upriver.

Now, looking back over the past 20 years - coming from the islands to Mobile Bay, migrating to New Orleans, meeting my best friend, Frère Gerard, and discussing with him the ways of kitchens and cooking - I can see much change in the way we cook our food. Many of the ingredients Maman told me about are not available here in the New World. On the other hand, there are many ingredients here that dear Maman had never heard of.

By and large, the actual ways of cooking have not changed very much, but the ways ingredients are combined and prepared has changed. So here in the new colonial capital, it is new ideas along with the new or different foodstuffs found here that Frère Gerard and I love to experiment with. Strange fish from the river, waterfowl aplenty, massive oak trees full of huge acorns, and large succulent oysters... one of my favorites.

For the past 2 years, Frère Gerard and I have shared many cups of coffee on the levee, or in our kitchens. I have taught Frère Gerard much and shared many recipes with him, and in turn, he taught me not only the art of stretching ingredients, but how to barter with the traders and smugglers that come up the swamps and bayous, and how to select the best ingredients. Often, I think of Maman, and I bless her for sharing her great knowledge, and teaching me the ways of a cook. But Maman's greatest lesson to me, unspoken as it was, was not to give up. Her physical beauty was only exceeded by her determination to end her slavery and make the best of her life as it was.

She did that, and so much more, for here I stand, a free woman of color, and the respected chef of the Marigny household. Maman would be proud.

RECIPES

Compared to our pioneer forbearers, cooks today have it way too easy. An old French proverb states that "chefs prepare the food; the fire cooks the food". This old saying comes into sharp focus when making or creating certain recipes. So many basic ingredients are at our fingertips when we moderns stroll through today's supermarket. Here I am speaking of the really basic stuff, like flour, sugar, milk, spices, canned fruits, vegetables, and meat, etc. Eighteenth century chefs, like our fictional characters Gerard and Suzanne, would have had to create similar ingredients from scratch before they even approached the creation of the dishes and meals that have come down to us through the centuries.

A good example of this idea is simple basic custard. Essentially, slowly cooking or baking a mixture of eggs and milk until it thickens into custard sauce goes back at least to ancient Rome. Adding flavors and sweetening are as time honored as the custard itself. In the Creole Americas of the eighteenth century a particular variation called Flan became popular. To the basic milk and egg mixture, Caribbean Creoles added the native coconut to the mix. To wit:

FLAN (serves 6)

- 4 eggs
- 1 can sweetened condensed milk
- 1 can coconut milk
- 1 can whole milk
- Coconut flakes
- Caramel sauce
- 1 cup sugar
- 1/4 cup water

Blend all flan ingredients together. In a separate pot, make the caramel sauce by adding 1 cup of sugar in a small pot with 1/4 cup of water. Bring to a boil over high heat. Stir once and reduce the heat to medium and cook about 5 minutes or until the syrup turns a caramel color.

Preheat oven to 375°. Pour a layer of caramel sauce into ramekins or a large mold, then gently top with flan mixture. Place all the ramekins in a large roasting pan, then add hot water to the roasting pan until the water comes halfway up the sides of the ramekins or the mold. Bake 40 to 45 min.

Easy right? In the eighteenth century, though, there was no canned milk or coconut cream. Cooks back then would have boiled down milk right from the cow until it lost about 1/4 to 1/2 of its water. For what we moderns call condensed milk, they would have added sugar (brown, unprocessed) or sugar syrup. To get the coconut cream, requires boiling together scraped coconut meat with the juice from the coconut. (1 to 1 ration for coconut milk, 4 to 1 scrapings to juice for coconut cream). All we have to do is buy a can of each off the grocery shelf. Never discount the usefulness of the lowly sous chef.

HOMEMADE SWEETENED CONDENSED MILK

In a heavy bottomed saucepan, pour 2 cups of whole milk and ⅔ cups of sugar. Heat it on a low heat until the sugar has dissolved. Bring the mix to a simmer over medium low heat. Do not stir once the mix starts to simmer otherwise it can crack and crystalize. Let it gently simmer for about 35-40 minutes, or until the milk has darkened to an almost grey color, has reduced by half and thickened slightly. If some foam forms on top, gently skim it off with a spoon. When ready, remove from the heat and pour into a jar to cool. Let the condensed milk cool completely before putting on the airtight lid.

ROASTED PORK CHOPS WITH ACORN DRESSING

Begin by making a pan of cornbread according to your usual recipe. While the cornbread is baking, slice a pork roast into thin slices or use six thin sliced pork chops. Marinate the pork chops in a mixture of herbs-de-Provence, some sort of nut oil like walnut oil, and red wine vinegar, and salt. Let them steep for a couple hours.

- Pan of cornbread
- 1/2 a cup of crushed pecans
  (NOTE: if you are brave, use 1/2 cup of crushed acorns, but acorns are full of tannins which are very bitter. Before using acorns, research how to prepare them for consumption)
- 4 to 5 toes of garlic
- 6 green onions
- 1/2 of a chopped red bell pepper

In a baking dish, mix together the cornbread and the crushed pecans. Finely chop the garlic onion and bell peppers add them to the dressing. Poor a little of the marinade into the dressing and mix well. Top with the pork slices. Seal the pan tightly with some aluminum foil put it in a moderate oven for an hour or two until the pork is cooked through. Serve with baked potatoes, white or sweet, and a vegetable or salad of your choice.

YOUR TRICENTENNIAL MEMO

As Suzanne was growing up in her family's cuisines (French word for kitchen) in San Domingue and Mobile, French America was turning its eyes south. Having been in Canada for over 100 years by the late 17th century, France, or rather the government of Louis XIV, was seeking imperial expansion on the North American continent as well as in the Caribbean islands.

As was the case in most of the Crown's ventures, the geopolitical policy that historians call "the balance of power" required that the French government should equalize this balance with Britain and Spain in America. The streets of the New World were said to be littered in silver and gold, and though many people were dragged to the colony against their will, many more came willingly, hoping to find their fortunes.

As it turned out, Louisiana's wealth was never found in furs or gold or silver. By the mid-eighteenth century, based on agricultural, forestry, and trade-based resources, Louisiana had become an epicenter of trade. The colony also achieved its geopolitical goals of establishing a French presence on the Mexican Gulf and connecting New France (aka Canada) to the Caribbean, all the while driving a wedge between Spain and Britain in the New World.

The connection with the Caribbean also aided in a process not especially noticed by the colonial powers at the time, but one that proved to be a major influence on the world today. The so-called "Columbian Exchange" laid the biological and agricultural foundations of modern society. Simply stated, the "Exchange" was the movement of crops and other products of farm, field, and forest around the world following the great trading networks of Early Modern Europe and the explorations of the world's continents.

This exchange continues today to influence foodways around the world. Specifically, in the French Louisiana context, it is the very stuff of creole cuisine. Primarily adding sugar and coffee to colonial Louisiana larders, it also introduced all the vegetable and spice resources to 18th Century French and Louisiana kitchens that we take for granted in our foodie culture today.

The growth of sugar production in the West Indies and eventually Louisiana also inadvertently provided another rich contribution to New Orleans's Creole cuisine. This contribution did not come without a price however, since here the discussion turns toward that awful "peculiar institution." Economically, sugar equaled slaves. This horrible institution led to a heavy influx of Africans to the New World, and they brought with them their ingredients and methods of cooking that became Louisiana's Creole culture.

It is worth noting that the entire African Creole experience in Louisiana was markedly different, at least through the 18th century, than the African experience in the rest of the American colonies. Two factors combined to create this difference. First, most of the slaves France imported came from the West African territories that had been some of the most civilized areas of Africa at the end of the European Middle Ages. In fact, these territories and kingdoms were considerably more advanced than their European counterparts. The population of these former powerful kingdoms were significantly culturally advanced. They provided many skilled laborers as well as substantial numbers of (what we call today) professional people such as doctors, scholars, and managers.

The second factor was the official French policy toward slavery called the Code Noir. By no means a justification for any form of slavery in modern eyes, the Code Noir was extremely liberal for its day. It allowed individuals to purchase their freedom, to be (relatively) easily freed by their masters, and to earn money through their own efforts. It allowed slaveowners to arm their slaves for military and hunting purposes. It even allowed for some limited cultural activities by the enslaved such as worship, song, and dance. Taken together these two factors created an African population that, by 1800, had evolved into a significant and distinct social division in America. In no small way, this also had effects in the Creole kitchens of New Orleans and the Louisiana colony.

The kitchens of Louisiana are only one small example of a larger phenomenon that altered the European culinary landscape. The 18th century, especially in France, saw an explosion of exploration, change, and invention in the kitchen that did nothing less than create new and modern ways to acquire and consume our meals. This massive expansion of wealth (at least for the proverbial one percent) created by colonial activity was combined with the slow development of new cultural classes and systems. As the bourgeois population grew more influential, cafés, restaurants, and the production of cookbooks and a more specialized food literature began to change the culinary landscape of Europe and her American colonies.

While building kitchens from scratch, our mythical cooks, Gerard and Suzanne were able to incorporate the latest technology and equipment into their kitchens, most notably brick fire boxes (one burner stoves), and large hearths with built-in ovens in the wall. Most of the other equipment had been around for centuries. In these "modern" kitchens, the cooks were able to use all the local, imported, and smuggled foodstuffs available to create a new style of cooking… Creole cooking.

Without doubt, most of the cooking done in colonial New Orleans and Louisiana was by Africans, especially in the more prosperous homes. Although the local Native Americans were not especially noted as household cooks, their food products and ingredients - game meats, fish and seafood, sassafras as filé, persimmons, pecans, other local fruits and nuts, as well as beans, maize, and squash - were commonly used. Add to these native cultural influences the French traditions, foodstuffs, and methods, a cook in 18th century New Orleans would have been a considerable cultural force.

French Louisiana provided little fur or silver, and no gold. The government in Paris may have often wondered "why are we there anyway?" But, then as now, there does seem to be awfully lots to eat!

4
1724 - GERARD'S PLAIN COOKING

Some years prior to our arrival in Louisiana, the Mississippi Company had been busy sending new émigrés to New Orleans and beyond. After all, a colony is not worth much if there are no settlers to build the houses and plant the gardens. Two groups of these newly imported people, the Africans and the Germans, were destined to play an important, indeed a crucial, role in my job of providing good food for my brothers, our guests, and neighbors.

The first group to influence my New World cooking experiments were the Africans that the company provided to serve the planters and merchants of New Orleans. Sent as slaves, theirs was a hard lot, but they persevered in their fate, and some were eventually able to buy their freedom, or earn it in some other fashion from exceptionally kind owners.

The Africans brought with them the techniques, skills, and even some Native foodstuffs from that dark continent. Some of these folks were lent to our community to help us build our chapel, home, and the other requisites for our community life, and when certain of them discovered that I was in charge of the kitchen, they were generous to me in their help and advice.

One of the vegetables the Africans introduced me to was okra, an edible pod containing all of its seeds, with a most pleasant flavor and aroma. The African word for this plant was ngombo*, and we discovered together that the plant grows well in this new and unusual climate. They taught me to dry out the pods in the front of the fire, which eliminates the pod's naturally slimy nature while keeping its savory flavor. I also learned how to use it in stews and soups, or season and bake it with onions and pork strips.

Along with okra, the Africans also brought rice from their low-lying country along the Senegal and Gambia Rivers. The company directors, in their wisdom, had directed the ship captains to take along a quantity of rice with which to feed their unfortunate cargo, but also to supply their needs in their new home. However, it was the other group I mentioned, John Law's Germans, who would be responsible for making this staple available in our larders.

Monsieur Law's plans for New Orleans and Louisiana included the development of agriculture. To this end, he - or rather his company - had appealed to the German peoples occupying the newly French districts along the Rhine. After many adventures up the Mississippi, Alsatians and Lothringians from these districts were finally settled several miles above the capital, where the land becomes less of a swamp and is more suited for farming.

We call this area the Côte des Allemandes. These hardworking farmers were soon producing enough food to ship their surplus supply of vegetables, meats, and grains to the levée markets here at New Orleans. These supplies not only provided for our immediate survival but laid the foundations for household gardens around the town, including my own potager.

A year or so after we had arrived in New Orleans, I had the unusual and distinct pleasure of meeting a lady of African descent who was not only a free person but one of some substance as well. We visited the markets together on a daily basis, as we still do today, to see what we could add to our larder. As I remember, it was on one of these visits that I first encountered this remarkable woman who would turn out to be the lifelong friend she remains to this day.

Tante Suzanne, as everyone calls her, is the chef de cuisine of the Marigny household over on Ursulines Street.

She moved here from Mobile several years back, but originally grew on up the island of St. Domingue. It was there she learned and developed her fabulous skills in the kitchen. Further perfected at her plantation home north of Mobile, her cooking prowess knows no equal in the city and perhaps even the entire colony of Louisiana.

I cultivated her friendship at first for selfish reasons, that being to increase my own culinary talents - may the Lord forgive my weakness - but quickly realized that she, also, was enlarging her perspective on the culinary arts through association with me. Our two situations complement each other very well. Where she opens my eyes to the arts of high cuisine, my cooking stresses the fundamentals of feeding a large group of people in the simplest, most economical way possible. We are indeed a couple of companions who fit together hand-in-glove and have developed a fast friendship.

Today, as we shared a cup of coffee on the levee, we talked of a wide range of topics - government, politics, our families - but what we love best was talking about food. Things seem to have settled down to everyday activities, of which both of us are glad, leaving us both more time to cook, talk, and just sit on the levee drinking coffee.

"Frère Gerard," Suzanne said, "you frown too much today. What are you pondering?"

This particular morning, I had been working out the menus for the next few weeks to feed my fellow brothers at the

Presbytère, as such planning allows me to take advantage of the markets, the fluctuations of the seasonal produce, any upcoming holidays, and the needs of my larders and pantries. As always, my prime planning and cooking tool is the dietary requirements laid down in our order's doctrine, St. Benedict's Rules, where simplicity and plain cooking are the guiding spirit.

"I frown because I am supposed to cook simply and plainly, in accordance with our Rules, but what had been simple and often obvious at home in northern France is anything but simple in this New World of Louisiana."

The swamps, forests, bayou, lakes, rivers, and even an ocean less than 40 leagues away offer a multitude of food that the brothers back in France had never considered in their Rules. Thankfully, Benedict's Rules are very adaptable to a wide variety of locales and climates. My recurring dilemma, however, had been balancing the European ideal of plain cooking with Louisiana's emerging notion of plain cooking. Whereas porridge, soups, vegetables, wheat bread, and an occasional bit of cheese are served as a typical European monastery's meals; beans, maize, rice, and seafood are much more plentiful and common fare in lower Louisiana.

"I must admit," I said, "adapting the plain and simple European monastic diet to the erratic food supplies we encounter here is somewhat a challenge, but isn't that what makes one a pioneer?"

Those early days were a trial in many ways. Never knowing where the next meal was coming from, or even if there would be a next meal, could be vexing at best. Food shortages, supply disruptions, and even eruptions of violence made for frightening times. We all feared for the very existence of the colony when the Natchez tribe rose up against the dishonest treatment by a less-than-scrupulous French commandant, killing the men and holding the women and children as prisoners. But as it turned out, Monsieur de Bienville was able, as always, to get control of the situation.

As a result, the Company, which had governed Louisiana throughout the 20's, decided to pull out of this economically unstable situation. The Crown once again took control of Louisiana, and showing remarkable judgment, placed Monsieur de Bienville in the governor's chair. With such stability, the building of New Orleans re-commenced on strong footing.

"My first days here were not easy," I told Suzanne. "My first task was scratching around for the seemingly non-existent food supplies, and we sometimes went hungry, surviving on a few donated eggs, some corn flour, and local vegetables that the Natives would help find and prepare. Fortunately, soon other sources of food began to appear."

She listened quietly as I explained how the local Natives were often in or near town and traded with us, and they were always willing to teach us how to cook these sometimes-strange native foods. Along with the game and fish that the natives supplied, the three sisters - maize, beans, and squash that the Indians plant together allowing each to grow better than if planted alone - became part of our everyday fare.

Eager to learn, as well as to eat, I told her how I had quickly learned how to make a large pot of corn grits, the Indians called sagamité, to which could be added anything and everything that could be found in the kitchen or the gardens. At that time, Tante Suzanne had not heard of sagamité, and we spent a fun afternoon of cooking, and I must say, she composed her first pot with all the diligence and pride of a musician composing a delightful concerto!

Within a couple of years our first gardens began to bear crops providing fruits and vegetables. By the mid-twenties, these, along with a variety of meats from professional hunters, fisherman, and Natives, provided a simple but steady diet as we continued to build New Orleans. Some of the dishes from those early days prior to Suzanne's arrival, are still part and parcel of my dinner catalogue.

RECIPES

FIRST YOU MAKE A ROUX

This is the crucial and essential start to the classical gumbo and many other recipes. The "soup" is not really like a soup at all. The roux is the base that creates a dish somewhere between a soup and a stew.

Preferably in a heavy iron pot, like a cast iron skillet with high sides, heat up a measure of oil into which you will stir in an equal measure of flour. Plain lard and plain wheat flour works just fine. As the oil heats, chop, slice, or dice whatever vegetables are going into the dish and have them in a bowl ready to add to the roux IMMEDIATELY to stop the cooking.

After the oil is heated, the skill to making a good roux is to cook it very low and very slow until it has achieved the desired color. Add the flour slowly, and stir, stir, stir. The roux must be constantly stirred to prevent the flour from sticking to the bottom of the pot.

IF THE ROUX BURNS, THE DISH IS DESTROYED AND YOU HAVE TO START OVER!

The color of the roux ranges from ivory or eggshell to a shade of tan or brown that will ultimately set the color of the sauce you are aiming for. Once the roux is thoroughly blended and the desired color is reached, remove it at once from the heat source and stop the cooking by mixing in the chopped vegetables.

Madame Langlois' Legacy · 43

    Now proceed with whatever recipe you are preparing. One last note on quantity. The usual minimum is one tablespoon each of oil and flour. This amount is used as the base for other more complex sauces. If you are making a big pot of gumbo or stew, or the like, you can use as much as a cup of each oil and flour. TIP: if you want to reduce the "greasiness" of a said sauce or gumbo, go with a ¾ oil to 1 flour ratio and then adjust to your taste as your cooking career goes forward.

OKRA GUMBO

- Roux
- 2 cups of rice
- 1 pound okra pods, sliced about 1/4 inch thick
- 1 medium onion, 3 celery stalks, 2 small bell peppers, (= the Trinity)
- 2 cayenne peppers
- 4 carrots
- 1/2 cup flour, enough stock to balance the roux,
- Water
- Seasoning meats (here you decide whether you will make seafood gumbo or chicken gumbo)
  ---For seafood gumbo, use 3 or 4 gumbo crabs, 2 pounds shrimp, alligator sausage, 1 pint of oysters.

---For chicken gumbo, use a 5 pounds chicken (cut up) and 1 pound Andouille sausage or smoked sausage
- Gumbo Filé
- Salt and Pepper

The above ingredient list is only a starter guideline. Every gumbo cook has their own recipes. Gumbo's charm is that it is a lot like the old folktale of "stone soup". The essence of the poor peasant's stone soup is simply that you make a pot of soup from whatever you have on hand to throw into the pot of boiling water. And so it is with gumbo, which is also sometimes humorously called the "clean out the fridge" meal.

YOUR TRICENTENNIAL MEMO

WHERE TO PUT THE CAPITAL?

From first landfall in 1699 at Dauphin Island off of Mobile Bay until the mid-teens of the 18th century, the LeMoyne brothers Pierre and Jean, were too busy founding a colony and exploring "Lower Louisiana" to worry too much about building a new capital city. Later, in 1714, after Antoine Crozat became proprietor of Louisiana, the search for a suitable spot to situate the capital commenced.

By that time, both Biloxi and Mobile had been well-established, Natchez and Natchitoches had also been founded, and all were fully functioning towns. A small settlement had also sprung up at the source of Bayou St. John, and during those first decades, Iberville, then Bienville, set up a fort on the banks of the Mississippi just below English Turn.

French and Indian relationships in the region and explorations between the rivers, bayous, and Lakes Maurepas and Ponchartrain offered the most likely possibilities for a capital city. Other locations were also considered, including Natchez, Biloxi, and Bayou Manchac. Indeed, Manchac was named the capital, on paper at least, several times between 1719 and 1722. After 1717, all of these spots and settlements became active contenders for the establishment of the new capital of Louisiana.

Discussions regarding the placement of the capital caused much hemming and hawing. Angry words flew back and forth, accusations were laid one against the other by the players involved. The controversy was partly fueled due to the faraway managers of the colony in Paris, who in their infinite wisdom had split the administration of Louisiana among three offices. The first was the office of governor, held by La Mothe de Cadillac at this period. The second was the commandant or military commander, held by Bienville at this time. The third was the chairman of the Colonial Council, during this era held by one Monsieur Marc-Antoine Hubert.

Partisans in Mobile and Biloxi each wanted the capital and its economic resources in their town. Harking back to the original voyage up the Mississippi in 1699, Bienville had always had a certain spot in mind. That spot was a portage from the source of Bayou St. John to the river by which the great river connected to Lake Ponchartrain and then to the Gulf. This, of course, would be the ultimate site of the new capital at New Orleans.

In 1717, the final decision came with a change in the colony's administration. Now under control of John Law's Company of the West and once again with Bienville in the commandant's chair, the top of that "beautiful crescent" was chosen. In March of 1718 Bienville and fifty convicts showed up where the Mississippi takes its last major turn to the south before heading into the Gulf. Here was the portage that Bienville and his brother were shown when they first entered the river in 1699.

The workers began to clear a spot where a new town, to be called New Orleans, would be built. By autumn about a half dozen temporary huts made from cypress and palmetto had been set up. Local colonial politics, as noted above, then created a stalemate for the next four years. While the new town both formally and physically existed, it never really got past this temporary stage until everything changed in 1722.

As the clearing and building continued in the new "capital" during 1719, the Chief Engineer for Louisiana, Pierre Le Blond de La Tour, and his second, Adrien de Pauger, arrived in the colony. These two added their voices to the "capital" controversy, La Tour favoring Biloxi, Manchac, or even Natchez, and Pauger favoring New Orleans. The two engineers maintained a courteous but strained relationship throughout.

In March of 1721, La Tour sent Pauger to the portage city to draw up plans for the city. It was almost a pro forma mission, seemingly designed to get Pauger out of La Tour's hair. The result, though, proved to be the first plans of the new city laid out as a grid pattern and expressing the new architectural and urban planning ideas of the French Enlightenment.

In May of 1722, New Orleans finally achieved its official status as the new capital and the rebuilding of the city began in earnest. Implementation of the plan really got underway after the storm of September 1722 which, for all intents and purposes, gave the engineers a clean slate upon which to build the city. Coincidentally, at the same time, some Capuchin monks arrived in Louisiana to assume religious leadership of the colony.

Welcomed by a fierce hurricane, the newly arrived Capuchin monks landed at a New Orleans that had been wiped clean. After a few years of lean times and getting established as the local clergy for the colony, things began to come together in late 1724, and construction on the new Presbytère and Church began. Quite naturally, the community's cook would have been heavily engaged in the building of a new kitchen and planting a new potager. From the culinary standpoint, the only remaining piece to the puzzle was a local market.

(NOTE: The reader can access a full and well-written account of this "great capital controversy" in Villiers du Terrage, Marc de, Baron 1867 -1936. Warrington Dawson (Tr.). A History of the Foundation of New Orleans, 1717-1722. Ville Platte, La. Provincial Press, 2003. Original published in the LHQ VOL. III, #2 (April 1920) pages 157-251.)

THE CAPITAL AS MARKET TOWN

Towns and cities have many functions. In addition to centralized places of worship and governmental administration, towns are gathering places for a population to promote common safety and, most importantly, function as the economic foundation which establish organized ways of trade and exchange. An old adage speaks of "food, clothing, and shelter," all of which may be found in relative abundance in a town.

To Europeans in the 17th and 18th centuries, the New World was a blank slate upon which they could build communities, not shackled by the age-old bonds of custom and inequality found in the Europe. Professor Lawrence Powell, in his treatise on early New Orleans, "The Accidental City," makes a good case for this notion and carries it further into a consideration of New Orleans as an example of a city and culture based on the Enlightenment principles that were sweeping Western Europe into the Modern Era.

In the case of colonial Louisiana, with its dismal reputation of starvation and woe, it is imperative to remember the historical axiom that any city, any civilization, or any culture requires one and only one precondition to exist: economic surplus. To build such an enterprise, in this case a colony, requires that the people, and the society, must meet a fundamental need. Put simply: "They Had to Eat." People do not build cities, create cultures, and conquer a new land when they are hungry, and while there certainly were times of scarcity and want, the French colonists in Louisiana did, over time, establish a system by which they fed themselves.

As trading and supply systems slowly coalesced, the population fed themselves through the 1720's and 30's using time honored methods of hunting, fishing, gardens, and the markets where these goods were exchanged. The journals of Iberville record that, upon first landing on the coast that would become Louisiana from Mobile Bay to the mouths of the Mississippi and Barataria Bay, first contact with the Natives usually included the exchange of some food items, especially the corn grits dish called sagamite. As the French settled this coast and moved up the Mississippi valley, relations with the local Native Americans were generally on a friendly basis.

During Louisiana's first two decades, it is well attested that often French soldiers and even settlers were sent to the various Indian towns, villages, and settlements to be fed while the trading and supply systems mentioned above were being formed. Those first twenty years saw the building of Mobile, Biloxi, St. John's Village, Natchez, the Arkansas Post, and Natchitoches, first as forts, or as the French referred to them "posts", and then as trading centers for the locals.

Indeed, the settlement of the new country was based on establishing trade with the natives and setting up local production, not only of food supply, but also of animal pelts and skins, lumber and other building supplies. These years also saw the organization and creation of the "concessions" or plantations for the aristocratic investors back home in France. The creation of marketplaces at these towns and posts was the natural result of all this economic activity. It was no different, and indeed it was part of the plan, as New Orleans came into existence in 1718.

Typical Caribbean market stall

The famous French Market on the New Orleans waterfront would have to wait to come into its real existence until the Spanish administration of the 1780's and 90's. Nevertheless, after 1720, there was always a market on the levee at New Orleans.

During the 1720's the streets of the town themselves were popular market venues. This same decade also saw the beginnings of what would eventually become Congo Square in the rear of the town, serving the dual functions of assembly place and market. The vendors in these unregulated markets - Native Americans, German farmers from the Cote des Allemandes upriver, African slaves, local hunters and fishermen - all supplied food and other goods both legally and not-so-legally sourced from their farms, villages, forests, and waterways.

Some food also came from the "Company" or the government at home. However, by the 1730's, fifty to seventy-five percent of the Louisiana food economy was based on a supply chain of smuggled goods. Trade with the Spanish, with the Caribbean Islands, and less so with British, all of which was illegal, was quite common.

Barataria Bay began its long tradition of pirate fame by dealing in these shipping lanes, as well as supplying quite legal fish and seafood to the capital city. Taken together, all of these sources of proteins, carbohydrates, and vitamins depict quite a different scenario than the traditional picture of the starving Louisiana colony. And it was in the markets of New Orleans, Mobile, Biloxi, and the other French settlements that the rich and varied origins of Creole Cuisine were found.

The many challenges created by the pioneer market economy of the new Louisiana colony were particularly vexing for those individuals whose work and lifestyles were symbols of a proper Christian approach to living. It is well known that the pendulum of life in a monastery in Europe swung from the sacred to the profane, but in all probability, the reality of the situation was probably somewhere in the middle. In general, French clerics have a bad reputation among historians and the literati. New evidence from Caillot's Journal point to a laisséz-faire attitude among the clerics of New Orleans in the 1720's.

On the other hand, official Capuchin records point to a group of men trying desperately to do their job in the most trying of circumstances.

By the 1730's and 40's, New Orleans had finally moved away from constantly being on the brink of starvation. At that same time in France, the middle classes were rising to level of prosperity that allowed them to indulge in more lavish dishes. Cookbooks were actually being published during this time. One such cookbook was first produced in the 1690's by François Massialot, Chef de Cuisine to Louis XIV. Readers will find examples of this cookbook throughout this volume. This actual real cookbook is folded into the tales of Frère Gerard and Tante Suzanne and provides examples of actual 18th century French recipes.

In New Orleans, the Ursuline and Capuchin convents were in receipt of lots of different food items. The selection, if not the quantity, of food - meats, grains, vegetables, herbs, and spices - was almost as complete and varied as we find in today's modern grocery stores. Trade with Native Americans and with the colony's hunters and fishermen was as lively as ever. African cooks were usually in control of most of the city's and plantation's kitchens. From within this colonial fricassee arose New Orleans' Creole cuisine.

Driving this new market economy was the rise of the middle class in France among the bourgeoisie, and in England, among the gentry or "country squires." In the French, English, and Spanish colonies of North America, old class divisions and old aristocratic traditions were being shattered daily by the realities of frontier life. Such a social revolution could hardly escape even the supposed cloister of a monastery kitchen, especially in a frontier society like early Louisiana. This atmosphere of liberty, combined with the reality of doing whatever was necessary to survive, would have gone a long way to experimentation in the kitchens of the Presbytère, a Commandant's household, or most of the bourgeois kitchens in French New Orleans.

What, then, faced those clerical settlers, as well as the kitchen staffs of the early bourgeois households? Was it 'same old, same old', that is porridge and bread every day with a bit of fish, cheese, or meat thrown in once in a while? Was it this standard monastic fare with an occasional lavish dish on the special occasions? Was it meat, rice and vegetables stewed together every day? Was it a combination of all of this? The last was probably the closest to reality.

In England and her North American colonies, these centuries were the age of the yeoman farmer. In New France and Europe these same years saw the rise of the middle merchant class in the towns and suburbs. While this is not the place to discuss the revolutions that arose from this new set of philosophies and ideals, it is worth mentioning that those revolutions, for all intents and purposes, ultimately ended the rule of the old aristocracies both on both sides of the Atlantic. The fundamental ideals and philosophies of individualism and freedom became a new way of life, especially in America, but also in the Western European countries.

In the culinary sphere, these new, and revolutionary ideas served as a background to the development of cooking and dining, especially in colonial French Louisiana. The rise of cookbooks in the mother country during this era supports this idea. Almost everyone learned how to cook simple meals. Those with enough resources were able to hire someone else to cook their meals for them. It is no accident that the 18th century saw the rise of restaurants and cafes, along with the cuisines, high and low, that were served therein.

5
1725 - COUNTRY COOKING

Il fait chaud!!! (It is hot!) Not that July in Louisiana is ever cool, but one would think that after three years of these tropical summers in this mosquito-infested swamp, a person would finally be able to accommodate the weather. Nevertheless, the work of the Lord goes forward, and the new church is finally being built in the town's center.

Father Raphael and his fellows in the regular clergy have made good headway into the conversion of our heathen, savage neighbors. We have regular, if not overlarge, attendance at our Masses. None of this is my doing though, for I am just a lay brother in service to our brotherhood of friars and priests. Like Blessed Pascal before me, my parish is the kitchen and the potager, my congregation are the vegetables, fruits, and herbs, as well as the game, fish, and meat we manage to acquire to feed our little order of Capuchin friars.

But, *mon Dieu*, today's heat nearly suffocated us all! As a lay brother - promised to serve but not to study - I am normally allowed outside of the convent to do the marketing, and gather what news there is to be had in Nouvelle Orleans. This time of year, though, there is not much news, either good or bad.

This morning I left the house early to get the marketing done before the afternoon sun baked us all into dust. Everywhere I looked, my gaze fell onto piles of Indian maize. My mind buzzed with possibilities for interesting recipes. It has been a good year for maize, and I procured several bushels to take home. I knew I had a good portion of good salt pork sealed in barrels in my storeroom, and when combined with the fresh corn and some spices, it would make an excellent corn stew.

Always on the lookout for herbs and spices to add interest to my meals, I stopped along the levee to see what little treasures made it to market and was not disappointed. After my arrival here some short seasons ago, I quickly learned that in this marketplace of river and wilderness, one does not ask too many questions about how the wonderful spices and sweet-smelling herbs had come to our riverside market.

I was able to replenish my supplies of rice, beans, squash and sugar as well as two varieties of those wonderful spicy peppers that sometimes even grow wild in our lush climate. The small green peppers are sweet to the taste with just a hint of fire, while the tiny red finger-shaped ones will set the mouth ablaze, make a grown man cry, and clear one's nose, all within a few heartbeats.

Lastly, before leaving the market, I saw some of the Indians from the coast, and bought a few pouches of salt from them. At home, my potager will yield up some onions, a head of celery, and a garlic to add to the pot.

Obviously, using the beans, corn and squash together makes the wonderful Succotash dish which my Tchoupitoulas neighbors had taught me. This time, however, I was planning to try out a new recipe.

A close friend of mine in the city, Tante Suzanne, had often exhorted me to combine the Indian beans with German Coast rice to make a filling and nutritious meal for little money. She had been amazed that I had never heard of this, as she had literally grown-up eating beans and rice. These victuals were part of her mother's African heritage and had become an everyday dish among her family. After returning from the marketplace, and using simple cooking methods, it was easy to prepare Suzanne's dish for my Presbytère with even enough left to share with our servants and neighbors.

Yes, this would be a wonderful dish!

RECIPES

CORN AND PORK STEW
(Cajun Macque Choux)

- 6 ears corn, silk removed and washed

- 1/2 pound crisply cooked bacon (Colonials would have used salt pork in this recipe, especially in summer, but bacon works just as well
- 1 pound of cubed pork
- 1 small, finely chopped onions (sweet if possible)
- 1 small bell (green) pepper, diced
- 2 or 3 stalks of diced celery
- 1 toe garlic, minced
- 1 or 2 handfuls wheat flour (if available); rice flour is the next choice, and cornmeal can be used as the last resort
- 1 cup water
- Bacon drippings
- 1 tablespoon of butter

Cook and crumble bacon. In same pan, brown the onion and pork cubes. Melt butter or fat in a large stew pot, add the bacon drippings. Finely chop the onions, bell pepper, celery, and garlic; add to the pot and sauté over medium heat for 8 minutes. Cut the corn kernels off the cob. Fold in corn and cook an additional 15 minutes.

While the corn is cooking, cut your pork into bite size pieces. Do NOT discard the fatty bits, (remember, fat = flavor). Add the remaining ingredients and simmer for approximately 30 minutes. If you feel you need a "soupier" stew than cooking down the juicy corn provides, add the cream at the end and heat through. Serve over hot cooked rice.

Frere Gerard would have prepared this dish when he returned from the market and let it sit in the coolest place he had available until suppertime, OR he would have waited until the sun began to set to cook the stew. After all, it was July!

Modern Adaptation:

Corn - If freshly shucked corn is unavailable, frozen is an acceptable substitute, and canned will work. If using canned corn, use 2 cans (14.75 ounces each) of whole and 1 can cream-style (14.75 ounces).

- 2 tablespoons butter
- 1 medium onion, diced
- 1 medium bell pepper, diced
- 1/4 cup diced celery
- 1 clove garlic, minced
- 8 ears of corn, shucked (about 4 to 5 cups)
- 1/4 of a 10 ounce can of diced spiced tomatoes
- 1 teaspoon salt
- 1 teaspoon Worcestershire sauce
- 1/4 teaspoon cayenne
- 1/2 teaspoon black pepper
- 1/4 teaspoon granulated garlic
- 3/4 teaspoon sugar

- 1/2 cup heavy cream
- 12 ounces crawfish tails, cooked and peeled
- 3/4-ounce pimentos
- Cooked rice

    Melt butter in a medium sized pot. Add onions, bell pepper, celery and garlic and sauté over medium heat for 8 minutes. Fold in corn and cook an additional 15 minutes. Remove about 1/4 of the corn mixture from the pot and puree it in a food processor. Return the pureed corn to the pot. Add the remaining ingredients and simmer for approximately 8 minutes. Serve over hot cooked rice.

CLASSIC RED BEANS AND RICE

- 1 to 2 pounds dry red kidney beans
- 1 pound of sausage (beef. pork, what have you)
- 1/2 pound of pickled pork
- 1/2 of a large onion
- 1/2 fresh cayenne pepper
- 1 large clove of garlic
- 1 small green bell pepper
- 5 or 6 stalks of celery
- 1 teaspoon of file' powder
- 1/2 tablespoon of salt
- Ground black pepper to taste
- 1 tablespoon dark brown sugar
- 4 tablespoons oil
- 2 bay leaves
- 1 cup of flour

    Soak the dry beans overnight in plain cool water in a large pot. Chop up finely the Creole Trinity, (bell peppers, onions, celery), and about four or five toes of garlic. Add the oil, salt, pepper, sugar, bay leaves, and file'. Sauté lightly for about 45 minutes on low to medium heat.

Slice the sausage or meat of your choice into 1/4 to 1/2 thick slices and add to seasoning mix, stir frequently. Add some pickled pork, cook on low/medium heat for about 90 minutes, stirring frequently.

Modern Adaptation:

In a large soup or gumbo pot soak dry beans overnight in plain cool water. Make sure there is enough water to let the beans expand and re-hydrate, top off if need be.

Chop up finely the Creole Trinity, (bell peppers, onions, celery). Set aside in a large frying pan over low heat. Mince about four or five toes of garlic and add to the pan.

Add the oil, salt, pepper, sugar, bay leaves and file', and sauté lightly for about 45 minutes on low to medium heat. Slice some smoked sausage, andouille, or meat of your choice into ¼ to ½ thick slices and add to seasoning mix, stir frequently. Rinse off and add some pickled pork, cook on low to medium heat for about 90 minutes, stirring frequently.

COOKING THE BEANS

Add about a half-gallon of water to the beans (soaked earlier) place over medium heat. Cook for about 2 hours, stirring occasionally. Remove about one cup of beans add the flour and smash the mixture into a paste. Add the paste to the meat mix, cook for about 30 minutes. Add the meat mix to the beans, cook for 1 hour. Serve over boiled white rice.

Suggestions:

Serve with homemade cornbread crumbled on top and fresh thin-sliced buttered French bread baguettes to use as a spoon!

YOUR TRICENTENNIAL MEMO

During the last years of Frère Gerard's life in the colony, another group of Frenchmen arrived in Louisiana. They had come from Acadia, being forced from their homes by the British. In 1710, during Queen Ann's War, the British in New England gained control of French Acadia, renaming it Nova Scotia.

For the next 50 years, a state of war existed in the province between the French Acadians allied with the native Mikmacs and the British occupiers. By the late 1750's, the Acadians were finally being rounded up and shipped overseas to other British ports in America.

During this period some Acadians arrived in French Louisiana, where their name was shortened to "A 'Cajuns" and finally into "Cajuns". They eventually settled in the bayous to the west and south of the capital city. The corn stew described in the recipe above was adapted by these Acadians, or Cajuns, into a one dish meal still popular all across south Louisiana.

6
1725 - FRERE GERARD'S POTAGER

Finally, after about a year and a half in the little shack that served as our original home, we moved to larger quarters in some former barracks at the corner of Rue Chartres and Rue St. Ann. These were directly across the street from where the new church and Presbytère were being built. The larger space also allowed for a real chapel to be installed as well as an adequately sized kitchen.

As the winter of 1724-25 waned, I could not wait to finally begin digging a real garden. I approached Pere Raphael and requested to place the potager across the street directly behind the site of the new Presbytère in the rear of the square that had been reserved for our use. I reasoned that, since plans for the new Presbytère were already being drawn up, it would be counterproductive to dig a garden on the river side of Rue Chartres and only have to dig a brand new one on the opposite side in a season or two. Pere Raphael commended me on my foresight and instructed me begin as soon as the weather allowed. I could not help but to grin with pride... an action I later confessed.

Together we paced off a large plot bounded by the Rue St. Ann, Rue Royal, and what was proposed to become the central Rue d'Orleans. The front of the property facing the Rue Chartres, of course was left open for the soon-to-be built residence.

I set to work, watching the glow of the sun as it rose and set across the property and laying out the garden plan. In late winter, right before Ash Wednesday, I transplanted some of city's many orange trees creating the line of the garden along Rue d'Orleans then turning the corner at Rue Royal to mark the potager's western boundary. Between the orange trees, I planted some plums and sassafras as well, rewarding my hard work with thoughts of how wonderful their flowers would smell in the spring. Finally, on the eastern (Rue St. Ann) edge, I planted a low hedge, so as not to interfere with the morning sun.

Lent began to merge with Eastertide, and time came to decide what to plant and where to plant it. As the winter progressed, I had the entire space dug over, weeded, dug again, manured, hoed and chopped up and made ready for the seeds and sets.

As a boy in the monastery at Charleville, the friars had put me to work in the kitchen and garden. The two are natural companions and complement the production of one to the other. As all things within monastery walls, not much space is given to ornament (excepting the church, of course). Occasionally, various fancy foods and dishes are prepared in our kitchens, these are usually reserved for traveling noble guests, local dignitaries, and high feast-days. So, now as the one in charge of the garden and kitchen, I made it a point to make both serve their proper, everyday roles.

Of primary concern in laying out a potager is accessibility. After all, one cannot go tromping through the lettuces to get to the beans, or through the potatoes to dig a cabbage or a few onions, so paths through the potager are of great importance. The actual vegetable beds should be no wider than one can reach into halfway, to easily harvest the dinner's ingredients without disturbing the other plants.

Another chief consideration of plant placement is the nature of the vegetable plant itself. For instance, the high stalks of the Indian maize should not block the sun from the low growing plants like cabbages, lettuce, strawberries, etc.

As April faded int May and Pentecost approached, our new potager had taken form. The paths between all the sections of the potager are all 2 to 3 *pieds* wide and will soon be graveled. On a fine day at the end of April, Pere Raphael and the community joined me in a blessing ceremony. So now we only await God's blessing and the magic of His natural creation to do their work, and our kitchen will now be provided with a steady stream of good, fresh food. The sun warms the soil, and the gentle spring rains nourish the ground, and the Capuchin friars have, with the grace of Our Lord, set the first permanent roots of their Presbytère and potager.

As the potager matured during the summer, I have made many trips over to the garden, gathering the vegetables as they ripened. During that first summer, the Louisiana heat and frequent rains - by the grace of God - produced a bumper crop for the brothers' table. So much in fact, that we always had plenty to share with the poor of the city and the travelers who were passing through.

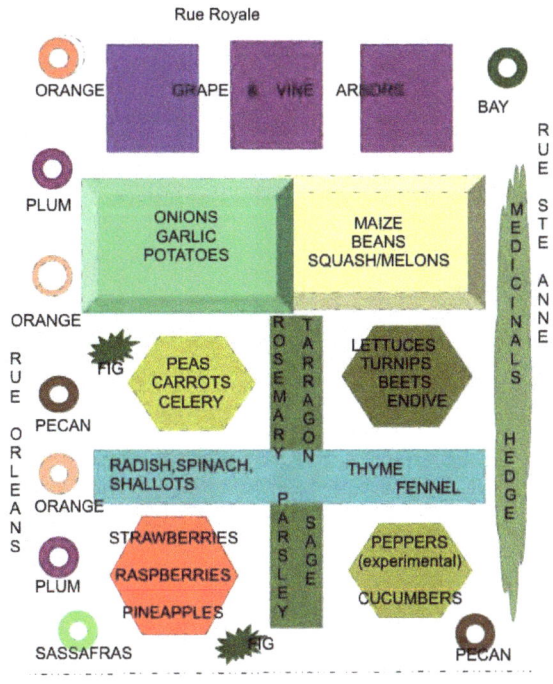

The goods from the garden were a welcomed change from the many days of eating French and Indian bread. I decided to expand the kitchen's repertoire. In the market that day, I was looking for something different. During my shopping, I encountered several of my African acquaintances, along with their women from across the river. The ladies were discussing (arguing?) about their best okra recipes. I joined in and soon was devising a new combination of foodstuffs which were both abundant, cheap, nutritious, and quite filling.

Along with my usual supply purchases, I increased the amount of rice I usually bought, procured a goodly supply of okra, and gathered several bunches of onions, both to plant and to cook. Some of the okra would be set aside for seeds to grow in my own garden.

Now that the community's hearth was nearing completion, I unpacked some large earthen casserole platters and began my trial of an okra/pecan casserole.

RECIPES

OKRA/PECAN CASSEROLE

Modern Adaption:

This is an adaptation for modern (21st Century) kitchens.

- 12-18 pods of fresh okra (or one 15 ounce can of sliced okra)
- Salt and black pepper
- 1 cup of rice
- 1 small onion,
- 1 small bell pepper,
- 2 or 3 stalks of celery
- 5 or 6 toes of garlic
- 1 tablespoon olive oil
- 1 cup of coarsely chopped pecans

- Cayenne pepper to taste
- Several pats of butter (up to 1/2 stick).

    Begin by slicing and roasting 12-18 pods of fresh okra (or one 15 oz. can of sliced okra) for 15 minutes in a hot oven, 425°. Season with salt and black pepper. This process dries the okra out and eliminates the sticky slime that stewed okra generates. Prepare one cup of rice as though you were cooking it for an ordinary meal. Finely chop a small onion, a small bell pepper, 2 or 3 stalks of celery, and 5 or 6 toes of garlic. Sauté in olive oil until tender and cooked through.

    When done, add the rice and okra, and mix thoroughly. Place the mixture in a casserole dish (glass or earthenware). Mix in one cup of coarsely chopped pecans, cayenne pepper to taste (if you are not sure of the cayenne, start with 1/4 teaspoon and adjust with experience). Top with several pats of butter (up to 1/2 stick). Bake at 350° for about 20 minutes. The longer the casserole sits, the more the flavors meld.

YAM, ONION AND SWEET PEPPER CASSEROLE

- 2 large yams (sweet potatoes)
- 1 large sweet (bell) pepper - red or yellow preferred
- 1 small onion
- Additional seasonings of your choice (sliced turnip, garlic, etc.)
- Salt
- 2 tablespoons sesame seeds
- 1 stick butter

    Parboil two medium sweet potatoes, then slice them, skin included, about 1/2 inch thick. Slice a small green pepper about 1/4-inch-thick. Slice 1/2 small onion even thinner. Put a layer of sweet potato in the dish, then a layer of pepper, then a layer of onion, salting each layer as you go. Add your extra seasonings to each layer.

    Top with sesame seeds. Slice butter into generous pats and place on top. Bake in a 350 degree oven for at least an hour. This will make a wholesome and nutritious side dish for 4 to 6 people.

YOUR TRICENTENNIAL MEMO

A 1730 plan of the city indicates that the Presbytère occupied the whole square - Chartres, St. Ann, Royal, and Orleans. The potager in the rear filled most of the space.

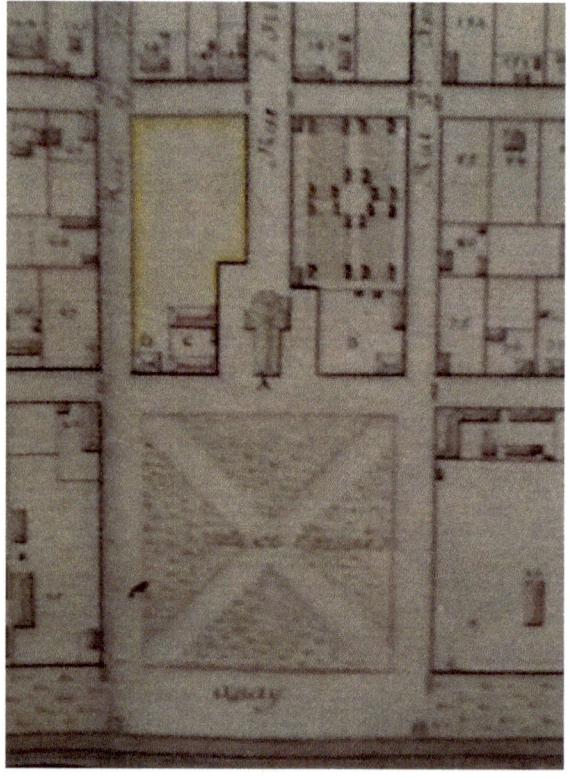

Notes from the following original sources illustrate the establishment of the Capuchin Presbytère and Potager during the 18th Century.

Madame Langlois' Legacy · 67

"Finally, on February 27, 1725, de la Chaise notified the Directors ... that work on the house for the Capuchin fathers had been started and the framework was already set up by that date. {Fr. Raphael to Capuchin Superior in September of 1725),

"We have here as yet neither church nor parsonage,"

"By the early part of 1726, the Capuchin's house was completed and they occupied it..."

Baudier, Roger. *The Catholic Church in Louisiana.* New Orleans: A.W. Hyatt Stationery Mfg. Co. Ltd., 1939. pp. 81-83.

An excerpt from the plaque on the present day Presbytère building at St. Ann and Chartres in New Orleans reads:

"Construction begun through the generosity of Don Andres Almonester/Roxas, was halted when he died in 1798. The building remained unfinished, only one story high, until it was completed by the Wardens of St. or Presbytère, the building was rented to the city for use as a courthouse and {finally} sold to the city in 1853."

Apparently, the Capuchin residence survived until the great fire of 1788, after which the Spanish replaced it with the beginnings of the present-day Presbytère.

7
1727 - GRITS AND GRILLADES

Pere Raphael was in an expansive mood. After five years of struggle, pain, hardship, and illness, after losing several of our brothers to disease in this New World, after the trials of starting a mission to bring the Gospel, the Church, and the simple comfort of having a priest or brother to provide support and spiritual guidance to Louisiana's Natives and settlers alike, we at last had a place to live. Our mission now had a church and Presbytère wherein we could call our home and headquarters.

When we arrived in our new "city" after the hurricane of September 1722, there was not much of a city to inhabit. For years, my kitchen was our only chapel. From our first poor hovel of three rooms, we set out on our ministry. By 1724 we moved to somewhat larger quarters in the abandoned barracks along the eastern side of the town square (at that time, a mere patch of grass on the river in the middle of city).

From these more adequate quarters, we were able to begin building our new home. Near the beginning of Lent in '26, we moved into the Presbytère, and I finally had a real kitchen to cook in, with space outside the backdoor for the potager. Through '26 and into '27, the work on the church proceeded. Forgive my pride, but the sagamite from my kitchen gave sustenance to the workers, as well as my brothers who guided their efforts.

And now, as the church neared completion, Pere Raphael called me into his presence. The governor, the Company director, and other of the local gentry were to be invited to a celebration dinner in the spring of 1727. Among the guests for that evening were Governor Perrier, Commissioner De La Chaise, Pere Raphael, Mesdames de Villemont-Rivard, Dubreuil, and Caron. It was still the middle of Lent, but plans were already being put into place.

"Gerard, I need you to begin thinking about the Easter season," he started, "I am hoping to see our new Church of St.

Louis dedicated towards the end of April. The 24th seems a good day to do it. It's about 2 weeks after Easter, still in a period of good weather, and not too many distracting holidays. I need you to plan a dinner for the night before. Something really special to honor our local dignitaries, and to get this special celebration started. Prepare a suitable feast to set off these special events on good footing. Do you think you can handle it?" he winked.

I felt such excitement that for moment, I could find no words. "Reverend Father," I calmly responded, even though my mind was already in a flurry, "thank you for this honor and I already have some ideas for such an occasion."

Earlier this year, a small group of Ursuline Nuns had arrived in the city and their work went far to alleviate some of our burden. Occasionally, a supply ship would arrive with and news of our homeland and supplies bringing some relief to our perennial food shortages. On one such ship, a kind friend in Paris had sent along a true treasure for our kitchen. It was a copy of a new book, Le Nouveau Cuisenaire Royal et Bourgeois by François Massialot, the chef de cuisine for His Majesty at Versailles. This remarkable volume contained all sorts of techniques and recipes for cooks, humble and high, to use in their labors.

For the upcoming celebration, I turned to this tome and soon found the perfect dish. What's more, this particular grillée could be served with some local foods, making a new and unique dish for Louisiana. The meal would begin with a green salad of early lettuces and herbs from the potager. A dressing of olive oil and vinegar would serve. Some fine wheat and rice loaves with good butter would follow with a soup of shrimp, oysters, crab, and German sausage. The main course would be Monsieur Massialot's Cotelettes de Veau Grillées served over some of the finest ground sagamite. This would be accompanied by a few bottles from our home province of Champagne. All would be followed by strawberries, oranges, pecans, topped with fresh cream from the German Coast. Coffee, chocolate and Brandy would wash everything down.

I had to pray for patience, as I could hardly wait!

RECIPES

GRITS AND GRILLADES

An old recipe for Veal Grillades from the Massillot Cookbook of 1699. It can be interpreted it to be perhaps an original preparation from which the now famous Creole Grits & Grillades (pronounced gree-odds) dish originated.

Cotelettes de Veau Grillées

Cotelettes de Veau grillées.

Coupez un carré de veau en cotelettes & les parez proprement sans être trop longues mettez-les mariner une heure avec sel, gros poivre, champignons, persil, ciboule, une petite pointe d'ail, du beure un peu chaud ; ensuite vous faites tenir la marinade après les cotelettes en les panimant avec de la mie de pain, mettez-les griller à petit feu en les arrosant avec le restant de la marinade ; quand elles seront cuites de belle couleur, servez dessous une sauce d'un jus clair avec deux cuillerées de verjus, sel, gros poivre, vous pouvez encore les servir sans sauce. *Hors d'œuvre ou Entrée.*

F ij

Original Author's Translation:

Cut a square of veal into chops and adorn (dress) them cleanly without being too long, put it in to marinade for one hour with salt, pepper, mushrooms, parsley, leeks, a small point of garlic, and little hot butter; then coat the chops in breadcrumbs to help seal in the marinade. Put them on the grill with a small fire, sprinkling them with the rest of the marinade; when they are cooked to a good color, serve under the sauce of a clear juice with two spoonsful of verjus (aka sour grape juice) OR juice of unripe grapes, salt, coarse pepper. Or you can serve without sauce.

Modern Adaptation:

Cut a square of veal into chops and adorn (dress) them cleanly without being too long: Buy some veal chops or another cut of beef, like a flank steak or a London Broil, and slice into thin strips across the grain.

… put it in to marinade for one hour with salt, pepper, mushrooms, parsley, leeks, a small point of garlic, and little hot butter; "then coat the chops in breadcrumbs to help seal in the marinade". Marinate the meat in the above (chopped fine) ingredients mixed into a glass or two of red wine (enough to cover the meat), then coat the meat with breadcrumbs of your choice.

Put them on the grill with a small fire, sprinkling them with the rest of the marinade; when they are cooked to a good color… Grill or fry the meat about 4 to 5 minutes on each side.

… serve under the sauce of a clear juice with two spoonful's of Verjus (aka sour grape juice) OR juice of unripe grapes, salt, coarse pepper. OR marinade as directed but cook the meat down in a tomato sauce of choice for an hour or two and serve over grits.

Today's grits & *grillades* is usually made from either veal or beef round steaks, but really a "grillade" can be simply translated as a piece of fried meat. Also, as French cuisine did not fully adapt to the tomato until Napoleon's time or later, the inclusion of a tomato sauce may be seen as a true Creole adaptation of the early 19th century.

YOUR TRICENTENNIAL MEMO

Note: Most of the "Tricentennial Memo's" found in this volume treat primarily of culinary history. On occasion, entries such as this one following are pure and documented HISTORY. A commemoration of the New Orleans Tricentennial has to include these notes on the establishment of the religious community and the parish church (later Cathedral) of New Orleans, or it would be failing in its concept. In this context also take note of the peculiar nature of French Catholicism found in the Tricentennial Memo section of Chapter 22. [as well as the notes on the Natchez Indians.]

From 1718 through most of 1722 the new city of New Orleans was nothing more than a collection of rough buildings and huts trying to eke out an existence. During these same years, the powers-that-were had been arguing back and forth as to whether or not it should be the new capital "city" of the colony. Also, in the summer of '22, a group of Capuchin friars from Champagne arrived at Mobile to take over the ministry of Louisiana.

As the year progressed, the capital question was mostly settled in favor of Bienville's new town. At the beginning of September, as the brothers prepared to leave for New Orleans, a hurricane slammed into the northern Gulf Coast. For the first time (and certainly not the last), the city at the crescent and much of the Gulf Coast were wiped away.

Ironically, when the brothers finally made it to the city, they had a clean slate upon which to build the spiritual foundation of French Louisiana. The earliest plan of New Orleans (de la Tour & De Pauger, 1722) marked out a place in the center of town for the square and the church.

As the engineers, inhabitants and workmen began to rebuild the city, their first concern, quite naturally, was the construction of necessities such as houses and warehouses. Construction of the ecclesiastical complex was finally begun in 1724. The first building laid out was the priest's house or the Presbytère. Finally, after waiting more than two years, the community would have a decent base of operations.

Since 1718 (even before the Capuchins arrived) there had been three or four makeshift places of worship. The first was a shack in St. Ann Street between Chartres and Royal. This site, destroyed in the 1722 hurricane, eventually became the kitchen garden (potager) of the Presbytère.

After that there was a "half a wretched warehouse" on Toulouse near the river (mentioned by the traveler Charlevoix in 1722). This was also the first housing for the Capuchin mission. Next, the barracks at St. Ann and Chartres was given over to the brothers. Here they set up house and a chapel space while awaiting their permanent housing. Finally, the church construction was started sometime around 1726.

It took over two years to build the Presbytère and church, using heavy timbers, mortise and tenon joints, with local brick for the foundational piers and to fill in between the timbers. It was "...so substantial a building that the planned buttresses were unnecessary. The brick walls were covered with chamfered planks." (Huber & Wilson, p. 6.)

The church itself followed the traditional cruciform layout of ecclesiastical buildings in Europe. The main and central entrance faced the town square. There were also two wings or transepts about two thirds of the way toward the rear of the building (usually pictured with two more entrances in the earliest drawings). Inside the nave was: "112 feet long by 32 feet wide by 24 feet high. Outside in the tower and steeple were 2 bells and a clock (striking only the hours)." (ibid.) The original church only had one belfry or tower.

Inside the church the pews were laid out reflecting the stratified class structure of the colonists. In front, closest to the altar, two l-shaped pews were provided for members of the Superior Council and staff officers. The Governor and the Intendant sat near the altar in two armchairs. Eighteen pews for the worshippers were auctioned off to the highest bidder, showcasing a "considerable rivalry among the parishioners." Everybody else attending Mass, following European practice, stood or knelt on the floor behind the pews.

From the earliest period, the church also had an organ and choir. Father Raphael, the Superior of the local Capuchins, dedicated the church shortly before Christmas of 1727. Pauger's building lasted until 1763, at which time it was pretty dilapidated. Services were temporarily moved to a nearby warehouse, while repairs were made. This building the lasted until burned down in the Good Friday Fire of 1788.

8
1727 -THE 3 SAUCES MERES

When I was a young man in Champagne, just coming into my own in the cloister's kitchen in Charleville, old Brother Kitchen - whose real name was Frère Bernard - pulled me aside one day.

"Gerard," he said, "you have tended the fires, cleaned the hearth, and cultivated the potager since you came here as a lad four Easters ago. Along the way, I have watched you as I have minded all the boys in my charge. Your actions, your obedience, and of most importance, your questions have proven to me that you, of all my charges, have the promise to succeed me one day."

Needless to say, I was most pleased with myself upon hearing this, so pleased that I had to confess the sin of pride at my next confession. In any event, Frère Bernard took me under his wing and began to teach me his recipes and, more importantly his methods, in the preparation of meals for our convent.

At first, I made the soups and the porridges. He let me begin to bake the breads and even to prepare some simple meals for the Abbot and other senior friars. Finally, after many months of this constant practice, he let me join him in preparing the daily main meal for the convent at large. On most days we ate mostly soups, porridges, cheese, and bread. On high feast days, we added some meat to the mix by way of stews and sometimes even a fricassee. Of course, we cannot forget fish and other seafood on Fridays and Fast Days, especially during Lent.

Finally, on those rare occasions when we received a visit from the bishop or local dignitaries or more infrequently, the duke or his nobles on a journey, we got to practice all the culinary arts we so often heard about but never experienced.

For instance, before the death of our dear King Louis the Great, his court at Versailles was a showcase for the best cooks in the kingdom. One of these, Chef de Cuisine Francois Massialot, wrote a book which gave an outline, a history, and the methods of preparing - literally - food for a king. The book also included methods of service - table settings, plates, goblets, and so on - and descriptions of ingredients to use and the method to prepare the ingredients. The foods ranged from the straightforward and simple to the elaborate.

Our librarian at Charleville managed to get a copy of this work which Frère Bernard would consult prior to our occasional high feasts. From this book and his trips to the markets around town, Brother Kitchen was able to put together a large repertoire of recipes and methods which he used when the occasion arose and which he now included in his training of this humble acolyte.

It has been said that French cooking in general, is largely defined by the use of sauces. Frère Bernard was careful to teach me the three Sauces Meres {Mother Sauces}, so called because they are base for pretty much all the sauces that come into use. They are the Sauce Espagnole, the Spanish or brown sauce; the Sauce Allemande the German or white sauce; and the glace or glaze.

Along with these three traditional bases, and usually included within, is a method that I brought to Louisiana and that I have since heard may be unique to our style of cooking in the colony. The method I speak of has become somewhat of a lighthearted turn of phrase among my fellow cooks at the market. When sharing recipes, we often say "first, you make a roux." As the Sauces Meres becomes the basis for many a local dish, the roux is usually the base for the Sauce Mere. Why separate the identity of these two? Because a roux is often used by itself as the base of other dishes such as gumbo, étouffée, fricassees and the like, whereas the Sauce Mere is the crowning glory of a particular dish.

RECIPES
LES SAUCES

FIRST YOU MAKE A ROUX! The basic ingredients and method for making a roux is above in Chapter 4 on plain cooking, gumbo, and the founding of the capital.

Example of a chocolate-colored roux (author's photo)

The color of the roux ranges from ivory or eggshell to a shade of tan or chocolate brown that will ultimately set the color of the sauce you are aiming for. Once the roux is thoroughly blended and the desired color is reached, remove it at once from the heat source and stop the cooking by mixing in the chopped vegetables.

Example of the 'Trinity' or mirepoix (author's photo)

Now proceed with whatever recipe you are preparing. One last note on quantity. The usual minimum is one tablespoon each of oil and flour. This amount is used as the base for other more complex sauces. If you are making a big pot of gumbo or stew, or the like, you can use as much as a cup of each oil and flour. TIP: if you want to reduce the greasiness of a said sauce or gumbo, go with a ¾ oil to 1 flour ratio and then adjust to your taste as your experience grows.

Modern Adaptation:

Here are some 21st Century variations. As you become more adventurous, vary the oil and flour to get a variety of tastes, for example, olive, peanut, canola, corn oils. If you really want to create an authentic 18th Century roux, use bear fat (believe it or not it's available on the Internet). Flour from various grains work fine as well. Corn flour (most authentic), white wheat flour (also available in colonial Louisiana, but pricey), other grains or nut flours (more modern) can all be used. It's up to you and your imagination.

To achieve the desired color, depending on the dish, you will get the roux to a shade of tan or brown that will set the color of the sauce. Think in terms of peanut butter, café-au-lait, milk chocolate, dark chocolate, etc. regarding the color. The lightest color for the Sauce Allemande will be an ivory or eggshell.

Once the roux is thoroughly blended and the desired color is reached, remove it at once from the heat source and stop the cooking by mixing in the chopped vegetables. These are known in French cuisine as the mirepoix. In Creole and Cajun cooking, mirepoix has come to mean the old Holy Trinity, that is onions, green peppers, and celery, then made into a 'Divine Quadrivium' by adding garlic. The French often add carrots to the mix as well.

After you have mastered the roux, proceed to the other Sauces Meres as follows:

Le Sausse Espagnole;
From Massailot's Cookbook (translation by author):

Madame Langlois' Legacy · 81

> **Perdrix sauße à l'Espagnol.**
>
> Il faut faire rôtir vos Perdrix. Etant rôties, prenez-en une, & la pilez bien dans le mortier : après il faut passer cela avec de bon jus. Il faut aussi avoir pilé les foies de Perdrix, quelques morceaux de truffles, le tout bien passé avec de bon jus, en sorte que le coulis soit un peu lié ; remettez-le dans un plat. Prenez une casserole, avec deux verres de vin de Bourgogne, une gousse ou deux d'ail, deux ou trois tranches d'oignon, un peu de clous de girofle ; des deux verres de cette sauße, il faut qu'il n'en reste qu'un : si le plat est grand, augmentez davantage de vin & de coulis. Vôtre sauße est nt cuite, passez-la par un tamis dans une casserole ; versez-y le coulis dedans, le tout bien assaisonné. On y met un peu d'essence de jambon, & on fait cuire le tout ensemble. Dépecez vos Perdrix, & les mettez dans la sauße, & les tenez chaudement. Auparavant que de servir, il y faut presser deux ou trois oranges.

Author's Translation:

   While roasting the partridges, take one and crush well in a mortar. Make a puree with the juices of birds being cooked. Then take the liver of the fowls, some pieces of truffles (or mushrooms), bind a little to strengthen the puree; set aside in a platter. Take a casserole, with two glasses of Burgundy wine, one or two pods of garlic, two or three slices of onion, and a bit of cloves: for two glasses of this sauce. Reduce the sauce to only one glass.
   If the platter is big, increase the wine and the puree. when the sauce is cooked, pass through a sieve into the casserole; pour the purée inside and season well. Add a little *d'essence de jambon* {ham or pork stock) and cook the whole mixture (make a

reduction). Cut up the partridges (poultry or whatever) and keep hot. Prior to serving, if you prefer, add two or three oranges

LA SAUSSE d' ALLEMANDES

From Massailot's Cookbook:

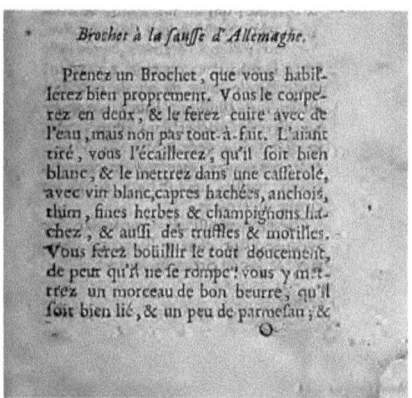

Author's Note:

Take a pike (or any good fish) which you have prepared (i.e., cleaned, filleted), etc., cut in half and cook it in water, but not all the way. Let it cook until just turning white and put it in a casserole, with white wine, chopped capers. anchovies, thyme, fines herbs, and chopped mushrooms, also some truffles and morrells. Now boil gently taking care it does not break apart. Put in some good butter, blended well and a bit of parmesan, and make ready your platter, garnish as you wish.

LE GLACE

Excerpts From: "The Picayune Creole Cookbook"

Below is a cut & paste excerpted from the Times-Picayune Creole Cookbook (6th Edition, 1922) detailing the method for making glacé - A HUGE AMOUNT of glacé! It is basically a aspic or beef jelly that is used as a base for other sauces, sort of like a cold can of consommé.

- 6 pounds of beef
- 5 pounds of bones
- 2 calf's feet
- 1 large herb bouquet
- 1 stalk of celery
- 3 large carrots
- Salt and pepper to taste

    Glacé is the foundation of all sauces for roasts, filets, etc. In other words, it is Liebig's Beef Extract, which every housekeeper may make and keep on hand for gravies for meats.

    Roast five pounds of the rump of the beef. Take five or six pounds of bones of beef and two calf's feet. After roasting the beef well and brown, but rare, chop it in small pieces, and put in a pot with two gallons of water. Add to this the bones and calf's feet, all raw. Then add a large herb bouquet, and one stalk of celery and three shredded carrots. Let the whole come to a boil.

    As the scum rises, skim, and then season with salt and pepper to taste. Let all boil till reduced to one quart. Strain this, and it will make a jelly or glacé when cold. Do not add any flour or grease. The savvy Creole cook considers it little short of a crime to add flour to the gravies of roast or broiled beef. Use the glacé for thickening Sauce Espagnole.

Author's Note:

    This foundational cookbook for Creole and Cajun cooking* also provides clear directions for the other Sauces Meres, which bring Massailot's 17th Century recipes somewhat more up to date. Somewhere between the methods of Massialot and of those excerpted above from the early 20th century would be the styles created and refined by Frère Gerard and his contemporaries. The chief idea to take away from these ramblings on sauce is that the "sauce" remains foundational to most Creole cuisine.

The simplicity of these methods and the availability of their basic ingredients to 18th Century New Orleans' cooks are beyond question. In recreating these recipes and methods the modern Louisiana chef need only remember one major caveat: there is no evidence that tomatoes were available to French colonial cooks in Louisiana (until at least after 1740).

*The Picayune. The Picayune's Creole Cook Book. New Orleans, LA: Picayune Job Print, 1901. (Reprint, Kansas City: Andrews McMeel Publishing, LLC, 2013. American Antiquarian Cookbook Collection).

9
1729 - A VOYAGE UP THE BAYOU

We left before dawn, while haunting mist still hung in the air. It would only take an hour or so to get to Bayou St. John, but once there, we still had 2 or 3 hours of rough travel ahead of us. The endless hours of steamy heat of the past five months were gone, and a welcomed chill tempered the air, at least for a while. Although October had come in all its glory, it would still warm up by the noon hour, but at least the steam was gone from the air, replaced now by the cool mist that brushed the ground. When the sun set, the air would cool off again, providing some very pleasant hours of sleep.

My companions, two of the Natives from our destination, and Herr Lothar Bayer, a farmer from the Côte des Allemandes, met me in the new village square which our Presbytère fronted. Soon the fifth person of our party - Sister Therese, a young novice who was a nurse-in-training - joined our gathering. The Tchoupitoulas group would certainly be grateful for any of the ministrations the young sister could provide, but she, too, would benefit from learning some of the healing methods and herbs used by the Natives.

The Ursulines, an educational order back home in France, were sent to this new colony and originally tasked to ministering to the health needs of the new capital. It was therefore incumbent upon the good sisters to learn as much as they could about the illnesses that afflicted this swampy land and administer to the medical needs of both the French and the Native populations, and being devoted to God's service, they did not look askance at the needs of the Africans in our town. Sister Therese was preparing to assist in these efforts.

My reason for going was obvious. It was harvest time, and I was acting in my office of procurer to gather as much fresh food as possible to cook now and to put up for the winter months. I could not hide my excitement, and I am sure they all considered me a bit strange for being so enthusiastic about a difficult and tiring a trip that they considered a chore.

Morning twilight had just turned the eastern sky indigo when we left the back of town and proceeded up Bayou Road. In all the excitement and frustration that comes with constructing a new colonial capital in the middle of the swamp, it is often forgotten that a French settlement had been at our destination for ten years before our governor, Monsieur de Bienville, decided once and for all to place the new city, La Nouvelle Orleans, where the trail from the three bayous' confluence meets the great river.

It is only a little more than a league from the new city to the bayou settlement. The road is mostly good but crossing the few ancient bridges across the lowest points - simple log affairs that predate our arrival by possibly centuries - set my nerves on edge. At times, the swamp waters pressed close to the road, giving it a somewhat gloomy and, Lord forgive me, supernatural aspect. Thankfully, the trip went quickly, and by the time the October sun was shining through the cypress and palmetto gloom, we had arrived at the Village de Ste. Jean.

The trading post was the only building of substance in the village. The inhabitants were already up and about their business when we arrived. A few folks from the surrounding farms were also filtering in to lay in some supplies for their homesteads. Our only business this morning with M. Lavigne was to hire two pirogues and a bateau - small boats used by the locals to traverse the swamps - which would be our main transport for the food acquired from our trading with the Tchoupitoulas.

We loaded Sister Therese and her medicine bag into the larger bateau, while one Native got into each pirogue. I clambered into one and was hardly bothered by how low the strange boats rode in the water as I was raised on a lake where boats and waterways were almost my natural habitat. Herr Bayer stepped into the other. Even though a trip up the sluggish bayou in fine weather hardly strained our seamanship, we lashed the bateau to each pirogue, providing extra safety for the young sister.

Our passage through the bayou was swift and pleasant, and even somewhat entertaining. Waterfowl splashed around us in great numbers as they attended to their own breakfast.

Beaver, muskrat, and mink also frolicked about in their watery feast. We joined God's creatures by breaking bread and some cheese which we munched on between our turns at the paddle.

Arriving at the Tchoupitoulas village, we were met with a joyous fanfare, as though we were long-lost voyagers from the East Indies, rather than merely from downriver a few leagues. Our Tchoupitoulas companions found their families and immediately disappeared into their warm and welcoming homes.

Sister Therese set about at once talking to the village women, discovering who was sick, and what sort of symptoms they showed. Herr Lothar had arranged with M. Lavigne at Ste. Jean to keep a pirogue until he returned later, to continue his trip back upriver. From the trade goods he acquired at the New Orleans market, he was able to get from the Indians here some seeds for the spring, and some wild beef (buffalo) to take home.

His people had come to Louisiana before we friars had arrived. These Rhenish colonists were settled upriver where the land dried out a little and began to rise towards the higher ground towards the north. On that strip of land along the river, now called the Côte d'Allemandes, these industrious farmers of the Rhineland had carved out numerous small farms and began producing vegetables and rice. They also raised some livestock to feed themselves and the capital. It is not too far off the truth to say that they, along with the friendly Natives like the Tchoupitoulas of this village, saved our capital and most of the colony itself from starvation on more than one occasion.

For my mission, I traded for beans, corn, and squash. I wished to make a dish I had heard about since arriving at New Orleans. At the Levee Market for the past few years, I had often heard a story, which seemed to me to be just a little made up. In any event I was intrigued by this succotash stew that was spoken of in this story. Along with the vegetables needed for the succotash, I also traded for some fresh fish to cook shortly and to salt down for later use. After all, I needed a large supply of salted fish to keep on hand for Fridays. Then, after spending the rest of the day talking with the Tchoupitoulas and even announcing some of the "Good News" to them, Sister and I retired for the night and returned early next morning to our abodes in the capital.

After seeing Sister Therese safely back to her convent, I stopped at the Levee for a bit more trading. From the Africans there I procured various peppers, and from the Germans I got some garlic and onions. I also found some sesame from the East Indies/Caribbean trade from certain folk who do not wish to be named. My own potager at the Presbytère provided more varieties of onions and peppers and finally, from my pantry was the salt, black pepper, and fat. Tomorrow the brothers will eat fish and succotash.

RECIPES

TCHOUPITOULAS SUCCOTASH

The Three Sisters of the Soil: corn, squash, & beans (and a little rice on the side)

- 1 tablespoon spoon fat or olive oil
- 2 cups fresh maize (corn), cut off the cob
- 1 small onion
- 1 large red bell pepper, chopped
- 2 garlic cloves, minced
- 1 small hot chili pepper, diced
- 2 small summer squash, chopped
- Black pepper and salt to taste\
- 2 cups Indian beans
- 1/2 cup chicken or vegetable broth

Soak the beans in the broth for an hour or two. Place a large sauté pan on high heat until very hot. Add 1 teaspoon of the fat, the corn, peppers, and onion, then sauté until the vegetables start to brown and caramelize slightly. This should only take about 5 to 7 minutes.

Add the remaining fat, squash, salt, black pepper and garlic. Cook for another 3 minutes on medium heat. Add the broth and beans. Simmer until all the vegetables are tender. It should take about 5 minutes. Yields: 5 one-cup portions.

YOUR TRICENTENNIAL MEMO

In those early days, the village at Bayou St. John was simply a settlement where three bayous met. Here in lower Louisiana, there are dozens of what people in France would have called a creek or stream. Louisiana however, especially around New Orleans, is flat country, a perennial flood plain.

While these local streams do move water, they simply drain the countryside from one low spot to another. They move with incredible slowness as well, so slow that there is always stagnation here and there along the way. Three of these streams - or as the Natives call them, bayous - meet at the Village. The largest, St. John moves almost due north to the huge lake that

Bienville named Pontchartrain and connects the sea to New Orleans.

Another, called Bayou Sauvage, or sometimes Chantilly, moves east, north of the city and flows into the same lake through a dense swamp. The bayou where we rowed our little flotilla is called Tchoupitoulas, after the Native group which live where the great river carved the bayou through its bank. From the village to the river and the Tchoupitoulas settlement is only about two, or at most three leagues from Village Ste. Jean.

Most Orleanians associate the Tchoupitoulas (pronounced Chop – ah – too – less) Indian group with the street that runs along the river through most of Uptown New Orleans. Others include the land across the river between the two small towns of Westwego and Waggaman, where the old Tchoupitoulas Plantation house is situated (originally Cedar Grave plantation house renamed after the Tchoupitoulas Plantation after the plantation immediately across the river at the site of the Native settlement; this misnamed site was formerly a restaurant and now a reception venue). Both have connections to the Natives who were here in the early eighteenth century.

The surest link today to these Native forebearers is the site of old Bayou Tchoupitoulas. After a crevasse created the bayou distributary that was later known as Bayou Metairie and now Metairie Road, Native peoples eventually settled the area. This was the village that Frère Gerard and his companions visit in the story above.

The Tchoupitoulas people were active and productive neighbors of the French at New Orleans at least in the early days of the settlement. Below is an excerpt from an article in the Louisiana Historical Quarterly, written by a man who claims to have known some Tchoupitoulas when he was a little boy. Take it as you will.

> *"The overall picture of the Native population is enhanced by the presence of another local bayou connected to Bayou St. John from the west (and, indeed, is really one of Ste. Jean's sources). Today, Metairie Road more or less traces its route. In colonial times, it was called the Tchoupitoulas Bayou, because it led to the country (settlements) of the Tchoupitoulas Indians. These people lived along the Mississippi in today's Jefferson Parish."*

> "The Indians of the Tchoupitoulas Village were gradually driven away by the white settlers and moved over the lake in the neighborhood of Mandeville, there joining other tribes. Every winter, however, some of them would come back and camp on a piece of ground called Terre Haute, in the rear of the Tchoupitoulas Plantation, where there was a large grove of magnolias. There the Indians would remain until Spring when they would return to their village near Mandeville. These visits continued until the United States Government had the tribes removed to the Indian Reservation. I remember that, as a boy, I visited the Indians on several occasions at Terre Haute, and saw their huts, which were built of palmetto leaves. The reason given by the Indians for coming from over the lake, was that the winters were less rigorous on this side, but the real reason, no doubt, was that the older Indians who had inhabited the village of the Tchoupitoulas were drawn back to the neighborhood where they, in their youth, had been accustomed to hunt and fish without interference from the whites; then again their descendants also desired to visit the hunting grounds of their ancestors."

> *LHQ 1924; V7, #2, p.314 ff.*

10
LATE 1729 - FRERE GERARD DISCOVERS THE PACCAN

It was a fine September day. Autumn had showed itself early this year, and it was a pleasant change. Today the air felt drier and cooler. Instead of waking up in a pool of sweat, I had to cover myself with my robe this morning, as I tumbled awake before Matins.

After morning prayers, I prepared the breakfast for the brothers of our little community. It was a simple affair of maize porridge and some of my now regular French and Indian bread. On market days, I was relieved of clean-up duty by one of the novices so that I may take advantage of the early morning coolness to walk down to the levee to secure provisions for the next few weeks.

Our little community had been in the capital now for a few years. Speaking as "Brother Kitchen," it had been a tough year. Food supplies were constantly low, and we often lived on a diet of maize, thin soup, and bear fat. Sometimes an egg or two would be generously donated. But as the year progressed, things slowly got better. The small temporary potager I had hastily planted eventually began producing some small onions, garlic, and shallots as well as some herbs to flavor our plain fare. Other gardens around the city also began to produce.

The German communities upriver were also able to ship some rice, milk, eggs, and produce to the capital on occasion. Even our native brethren occasionally offered us in trade some of the game and fish they had secured from the Lord's bounty of forest and river. And now, it was harvest time once again, and I looked forward to reaping the bounty of our labors and lining the pantry and larder for the winter months. Personally, one of the greatest joys I discovered in opening up this new land, apart from the opportunity to spread the Word of God, was the discovery of all the different plants and animals which provided food and healing herbs to us.

In many ways these native foods were much different from the victuals of our homeland. America abounds in grains, vegetables, fruits, nuts, herbs, and spices which were new to our European palates. A wide variety of heretofore unknown game and fish were also to be found here, to be examined, cooked, tasted, and shared. I did not know it this morning, as I prepared to go to the Levee Market, but I would find a new one today.

Much of the land in and around the new capital, New Orleans, is flat and swampy. Closer to the river, the lakes, and the innumerable streams (bayous), the land actually rises several feet higher. This rise allows for long strips of good forest. Here, game, birds, and some productive trees can thrive. M. de Bienville and his brother M. d'Iberville - God rest his soul - upon their arrival found and noted many of these trees producing wholesome fruit, berries, and several types of nuts.

Marking the beginning of the new season, many Indian women and even children had been gathering what looked to my French eyes like, baskets of walnuts. I thought they would be a good addition to the Presbytère pantry, so I asked one of the children if I might try his wares. I broke away the outer shell to find a pretty brown nut with a much thinner skin than our walnuts at home. I popped the nut into my mouth. Dieu soit félicité!!! The nut melted like butter in mouth. I say like butter because the taste was nutty and buttery at the same time! What is this delicious little wonder?

The boy informed me, that in his tongue it was called a paccan. I bought up several bushels of these toothsome morsels and began to formulate great plans for them. The next day, between Terce and Sext, when I would normally be busy in the potager, I left the Presbytère and traveled upriver along the natural levee. As I moved farther away from the town, I encountered a wide variety of trees growing along the bank. A bit away from the bank itself, past the willows and cottonwoods, I began to see the oaks, the gums, and to my great pleasure, some paccan trees, their nuts scattered among the undergrowth.

Hopefully anticipating such a find, I had brought along a large basket. I spent the rest of the morning happily gathering the bounty which our Father had graced this beautiful new world. Returning home with my treasure, I was already planning the wonderful meals these gifts from the Almighty would provide.

RECIPES

PECAN PRALINES

Before going any further, we must talk. New Orleanians are very proud of their culinary heritage, some say even going to the edges of provincialism. The nuts required for this recipe are known as PA-CAWNS in this region, a PEE-CAN are those brightly colored portable toilets one sees along parade routes or at construction sites. On the streets of the Quarter, in candy shops, and even some bakeries, natives and newcomers can always be identified by a simple test. If someone asks to purchase a 'PRAY-LINE', listeners know for certain that this individual is most certainly an outsider, a newcomer, a tourist, a come-here person, or maybe even a real Yankee! Among the natives of the city and region, the confection universally loved by all is a 'PRAW-LEAN'. Now that this most essential matter is settled, we can move on to creating some.

- 1 pound brown sugar
- 1/2 pound fresh Louisiana pecans (peeled and coarsely chopped)
- 2 tablespoons spoon of butter
- 4 tablespoons of water

In a good-size pot, melt the sugar and butter, and bring to a boil. Add water as needed to keep the mixture syrupy.

Once a good hot syrup is boiling, add the pecans and mix well. Using a large cooking spoon, pour the mixture out onto a marble slab or your kitchen counter covered with wax paper. Factors of the spinning earth and universal gravity will shape the mass into a nice circle. Let it cool completely before taking a bite or risk a severe burn in the oral regions.

This is the traditional New Orleans style praline. Variations include using almonds, peanuts, walnuts, etc. Traditional European pralines are various nuts or nougats rolled in sugar. An old New Orleans variation rolls whole or halved pecans in a beaten egg white and water mixture and then coats them with sugar.

The above recipe/method is an adaptation of the recipes found in: The Picayune. The Picayune's Creole Cookbook. New Orleans, LA: Picayune Job Print, 1901. (Reprint, Kansas City: Andrews McMeel Publishing, LLC, 2013. American Antiquarian Cookbook Collection.)

PECAN RICE

- Pecan oil
- Salt
- Pepper
- 1 cup rice
- Chopped pecans

As recipes go, this one is not too complicated. The most difficult part is cooking the rice. The simplest method is boiling one cup of rice in a 2 qt. or larger pot of water for 8 to 10 minutes. For this version, add a tablespoon of pecan oil to the boiling water. When done and rice is poured in a strainer, add salt and pepper and chopped pecans and mix well. Enjoy!

YOUR TRICENTENNIAL MEMO

Native to North America, from Mexico to Illinois to the Gulf Coast to just east of the Alabama/Mississippi line, the pecan is America's only native nut. Native Americans took advantage of the pecan's extensive nutritional value beginning about 8,000 BCE. It was then that Native Americans began to shift from hunter/gatherer to farming as a means of food production. Pecans are forest trees and as such would have been classed as a 'gathering' source of food, from then even through today.

Sometime along the way, Native Americans also began to modify this function by locating pecan trees along their migration routes as well as their temporary and/or established villages. So, by the time the Europeans began to arrive in significant numbers along the northern Gulf Coast, the pecan was an ancient and valued component to the Native American diet.

"Although pecans are native from NE Mexico to Mobile Bay, they were more common in the forests of the Mississippi Valley including its eastern and western tributaries. As this was the center of the French colonial empire below the Great Lakes, it should come as no surprise that the quintessential and non-savory use of the pecan in the evolving Creole cuisine would take the form of the praline.

Some form of candy-coated nut snacks travelled over the Atlantic with the French empire builders and settlers in the late 17th century. A widely-known origin legend maintains that the form of nut-centered candy was first concocted by the cook working on the estate of Marshal

> de Plessis-Praslin (1598–1675), a soldier of France during the era we most often associate with the Three Musketeers."

> McWilliams, James. *The Pecan; A History of America's Native Nut*. Austin: University of Texas Press; 2013. First Edition.

During this era the French American empire was growing. It was when the French arrived to colonize the Mississippi Valley that the North American praline began to transmute away from its Continental origins. Even today, in Europe a praline is entirely different from the ones a person can buy in the New Orleans Vieux Carré.

From its beginning as sugar-coated almonds in the French countryside, the European praline has remained essentially unchanged. Although there have been slight variations in the type of nut used as well as the composition of the coating. One of the more distinct versions is the Belgian praline, which in the USA is called a chocolate with a soft center. Made from ground nuts (walnuts, hazelnuts, almonds, etc.) and mixed into a creamy paste then covered in chocolate, it is similar to the perennial Valentine or Mother's Day box of chocolates.

As the 18th century wore on, and especially after 1730 when the food supply lines began to stabilize, the New Orleans Praline came into its own. Cooks like our imaginary Gerard and Suzanne, using the simplicity of sugar and water and the plentiful pecans of south Louisiana, slowly but surely began to evolve the candy that would soon be ubiquitous throughout the streets of the Old Quarter.

11
1729/30 - FRÈRE GERARD AND THE NATCHEZ INDIANS

I couldn't help but laugh at Tante Suzanne's reaction when I mentioned my admiration of the Natchez Indians. "Those awful people?" she said, her eyebrows dropping into an angry scowl. "I would not say such nice things about them, after what they did."

"They are interesting people," I said, "and if you knew the whole story of what happened to them at the hands of us Frenchmen, you would understand. Not the killing of course, but they were treated terribly and had every right to be outraged."

I was showing her how to make persimmon/walnut bread with cherries, a recipe I learned from the Natchez back in 1726 when I visited their camp on the levee outside of New Orleans and telling her the story of my visit.

"To be honest, I invited myself to their camp. I wanted so bad to taste some of their cooking; I had heard it to be 'interesting.' Knowing they would have a communal meal that evening, I took several pounds of fresh shrimp from the Presbytère's chill box to add to the communal pot, as well as for trading. I gathered a large basket of cabbages, celery, okra, and beets, and a few implements that I could afford to spare. With Etienne's help, we lugged it across town and up to the Natchez camp for an evening of feasting and barter."

"And your trading went well?" Suzanne asked, still frowning.

"I got a good quantity of fresh deer meat for some of my vegetables and iron fishhooks, and a sturdy coiled pot to store my butter in. I had hoped to obtain a good mortar and pestle -- I was told they were common in every Natchez Indian hut -- but I had no such luck. We ate a fish stew made with alligator gar and drum, cooked with wild onions and with the most delicious mushrooms I have ever eaten. My shrimp were an excellent addition to the stew, and the Indians seemed pleased with them. I even got some recipes, including this bread we are making." Tante Suzanne laughed. "Ah, Frère Gerard, I know you well. You wanted more than just trade and recipes and a good meal, no?"

 I just smiled back in agreement. One hears much about them, and I confessed to being curious, not only about their food, but about their religious and ceremonial practices, their construction of large mounds of earth at their ceremonial meeting places, their smoking of the calumet pipe to create an almost spiritual bond of friendship between people, even their beliefs in the gods of nature and of the great benevolent creator, Coyocop-chill.

 I had first heard the story from an old trapper, of Coyocop-chill's conquest of the evil spirits in the world, and of the creation of the first man and woman, which sounded remarkably like our account of Adam and Eve. The Natchez, however, were not forthcoming on this subject and would not discuss it, so I learned little else. I later had the opportunity to read Le Page du Pratz's 1725 narration on their ceremonial practices, but there is still much to know about their religion.

 "I did however discover something interesting," I told her. "Every full moon, they have a feast and a ceremony, with each moon focusing on a different animal, fruit or vegetable. They are quite remarkable. They adapt to any surrounding and climate, and know not only what is good to eat, but what plants can be used as medicines as well. Since there is now so much bad blood between us, we will never know many of their secrets of healing, and this is very sad."

 Suzanne sat across from me, watching as I prepared the mix for the bread. "You were treated well by them?"

 "They were not kind as we consider kindness to be. These Natives are very stoic and do not tend to show emotions of any kind, at least not to us, but they were kind to me in their fashion, making sure I had a good place at the gathering and was well fed, and part of the fire-talk."

 When I told Tante Suzanne of arriving at the camp and seeing the women in fine woven skirts but no covering on their chests, and the men splendidly decked out in buffalo robes of the best quality, she wrinkled her nose a bit.

"No, you do not understand, my friend. These robes were magnificent! So clean and well prepared... I'm sure that even your Monsieur Marigny would love to have one such as that for the couch in his library. He certainly would not need brandy to warm him up if he had such a robe."

"And the naked women?" she said with a naughty twinkle in her eyes.

"I do recall having kept my eyes averted every time a woman came into my view and was grateful for the evening when they threw shawls over their shoulders to avert the evening chill.

"Inevitably, the fire talk turned to hunting. The Natchez are farmers, with both men and women tending and harvesting the crops, but the men still hunted and seemed very much to enjoy the sport of it. There was much bragging and displays of their hand-crafted hunting goods and weapons. I was particularly interested in seeing their bows, which I was told were made of the native acacia wood, with arrows that use garfish scales as tips. What an inventive use of their natural surroundings. Nothing goes to waste."

With the bread finally in the oven, Suzanne made us some strong coffee, and surprisingly, wanted to hear more about the Natchez. We spent a pleasant afternoon that day, two good friends cooking and talking in Monsieur Marigny's spacious and well-appointed kitchen. Surely this day was a little preview of heaven!

RECIPES
PERSIMMON BREAD

Original 1730's Recipe:

- Choose bear or vegetable oil or butter or lard
- Sweet cherries, ripe

- Persimmon pulp
- 4 duck eggs (preferred choice)
- Spices
- Pecans or walnuts
- Corn flour
- Honey or brown sugar

Grind the corn flour well, into a powder. Cut and scrape out the flesh of two large persimmons, mash it well, combine with the corn flour.

To this mix, add two handfuls of ripe pitted cherries and blend together. Add the 4 eggs and a small quantity of grease or oil, beat well. Add nutmeg (or other spices), sugar (or honey), and chopped nuts. Form into a large loaf, smear it entirely in butter or oil. Bake in a hot oven until a knife poked in the middle comes out clean.

Author's persimmon bread (tastes very similar to banana bread)

Modern Adaptation:

Since we rarely cook these days with bear oil and corn flour tends to be gritty, try this modern version

- 1 stick unsalted butter
- 1/2 cup vegetable oil
- 1/2 cup persimmon pulp
- 1/2 cup chopped cherries
- 1 1/2 cups brown sugar
- 1 3/4 cups all-purpose flour
- 3 medium eggs
- 2/3 teaspoon baking powder
- 1 teaspoon baking soda
- 1/2 teaspoon salt
- 1 teaspoon cinnamon (can substitute cloves, nutmeg or use them all if desired)
- 1 cup chopped pecans or walnuts

Preheat oven to 350°. Melt the stick of butter in microwave or in a saucepan over low heat.

In a large bowl, blend the sugar, oil, eggs, persimmons, cherries, and butter. In another bowl, add all other ingredients together and mix well.

Stir the dry mixture into the wet mixture slowly, making sure there are no lumps in the mix. Grease and flour two loaf pans, then fill and place in pre-heated oven.

Bake 45 minutes to 1 hour. The bread is done when a toothpick inserted in the middle comes out clean.

If desired, dust powdered sugar and sprinkle some extra cherries on top. Another good idea is to wrap the finished loaf in cheesecloth lightly soaked in brandy for a few minutes before serving.

YOUR TRICENTENNIAL MEMO

Note: Most of the Tricentennial Memos found in this volume consist primarily of culinary history. On occasion, entries such as this one following are pure and documented history. Although the following does contain agricultural information about the settlement at Natchez, this information is not its primary focus. A commemoration of the New Orleans Tricentennial has to include this chapter on the Natchez Natives, or it would be failing in its concept.

From 1700 to 1730 the Natchez Tribe and the French settlers along the Mississippi were usually on friendly terms. However, there were several incidents during these three decades where both French and Natchez being, shall we say, high-spirited folk, caused a little trouble for each other. Generally, though, until the final uprising in 1729, both the French and the Natchez benefitted from their mutual friendship.

The first documented historical contact with the Natchez Indians occurred in March 1682 when the Rene-Robert Cavalier, Sieur de La Salle expedition descended the Mississippi River. Following La Salle's meeting of the Natchez Indians, French and English explorers, priests, and military personnel made frequent visits to the Natchez area.

(Paraphrase of ...) http://mshistory.k12.ms.us/index.php?id=4

Later, when the Iberville expedition arrived on the Gulf Coast in 1699, the commanders already had a good idea of what to expect. Lasalle and other explorers, as well as some of the couriers de bois, had been active in the lower Mississippi for 20 years before Iberville confirmed the mouths of the Mississippi. As part of this confirmation, Iberville's agenda included meeting with several nations of Native Americans that the earlier explorers had mentioned. Navigating up the river during the winter of 1700, he met with and established relations with the Indians below the mouth of the Red River, then made it up to the Houma settlements by early March.

On March 11, Iberville and his party, including brother Bienville arrived at the Natchez town. Iberville described what he saw:

> "We proceeded to [the chief's] hut, which is erected on a 10-foot mound of dirt carried there, [the hut is] 25 feet wide and 45 feet long. Close by it are eight huts. Facing the chief's is the temple. These form a ring, somewhat oval shaped and enclose a public square about 250 yards wide and 300 long. Close by flows a little creek, . . . [There are also] about 400 more huts, within an area of 8 leagues along the banks of the small creek that waters the country. From the river landing, one

climbs a hill about 150 fathoms high, a sheer bluff covered with hardwood trees.

Once on top of the hill one discovers a country of plains, prairies, full of little hills, with clumps of trees in some spots, many oak trees, and many roads crisscrossing, leading from one hamlet to another or to huts. It is a country of yellowish soil mixed with a little gravel as far out as a cannon shot, where the gray soil begins, which appears to me to be better. This countryside is very much like France."

(Iberville's Journals, p. 120 ff)

Another early description of the Natchez area is given by one of its early settlers. Antoine le Page du Pratz arrived in Louisiana in 1718, just as New Orleans was being cleared and built up. He settled in the village at Bayou St. John but resolved to move to a less damp and more healthful environment within a few months after he arrived. Du Pratz's Native concubine, when she found out they were considering a move upriver was quick with her pleased response.

"Thou art going, then, to that country; the sky is much finer there; game is in much greater plenty; and as I have relations, who retired there after the war which we had with the French, they will bring us everything we want. They tell me that country is very fine, that they live well in it, and to a good old age."

{Du Pratz continues the tale:} *"At last we arrived at the Natchez, and we put on shore at a landing-place, which is at the foot of a hill two hundred feet high, upon the top of which [is] Fort Rosalie. This is on the east side of the Mississippi and appears to be the first post on that river which we ought to secure. When you are upon the top of this hill, you discover the whole country, which is an extensive beautiful plain, with several little hills interspersed here and there, upon which the inhabitants have built and made their settlements. The prospect of it is charming."*

Typical Natchez hut. after Du Pratz

"I found upon the main road that leads from the chief village of the Natchez to the fort, about one hundred paces from this last, a cabin of the natives upon the roadside, surrounded with a spot of cleared ground, the whole of which I bought by means of an interpreter. I made this purchase with the more pleasure, as I had upon the spot, wherewithal to lodge me and my people, with all my effects: the cleared ground was about six acres, which would form a garden and a plantation for tobacco, which was then the only commodity cultivated by the inhabitants."

"I had water convenient for my house, and all my land was very good. On one side stood a rising ground with gentle declivity, covered with a thick field of canes, which always grow upon the rich lands; behind that was a great meadow, and on the other side was a forest of white walnuts (hickories) of nigh fifty acres, covered with grass knee deep. All this piece of ground was in general good and contained about four hundred acres of a measure greater than that of Paris: the soil is black and light. I took up on the border of the little river of the Natchez, half a league from the great village of that nation, and a league from the fort; and my plantation stood between these two and the fort.

"As soon as I was put in possession of my habitation, I went with an interpreter to see the other fields, which the Indians had cleared upon my land, and bought them all, except one, which an Indian would never sell to me: it was situated very convenient for me, I had a mind for it, and would have given him a good price; but I could never make him agree to my proposals. He gave me to understand, that without selling it, he would give it up to me, as soon as I should clear my ground to his; and that while he stayed on his own ground near me, I should always find him ready to serve me, and that he would go a-hunting and fishing for me. This answer satisfied me, because I must

> have had twenty negroes, before I could have been able to have reached him; they assured me likewise, that he was an honest man; and far from having any occasion to complain of him as a neighbor, his stay there was extremely serviceable to me."

> Du Pratz, M. Le Page. *The History of Louisiana ; Translated From the French of M. Le Page Du Pratz*. Baton Rouge: Published for the Louisiana American Revolution Bicentennial Commission by the Louisiana State University Press, c1975.

> (Note: Fort Rosalie, in the country of the Natchez, was at first pitched upon for the metropolis [i.e., capital] of this colony.)

Yet another French traveler speaks highly of the Natchez landscape:

> "But though it be necessary to begin by a settlement near the sea; yet if ever Louisiana comes to be in a flourishing condition, as it may very well be, it appears to me, that the capital of it cannot be better situated than in this place. It is not subject to inundations of the river; the air is pure; the country very extensive; the land fit for everything, and well-watered; it is not at too great a distance from the sea, and nothing hinders vessels to go up to it. In fine, it is within reach of every place intended to be settled."
>
> (Charlevoix, Hist. de la N. France, III. 415.)

During those 30 years of friendship, the French built a fort and a small settlement (1716) near the mounds of the Natchez where St. Catherine's Creek empties into the Mississippi. Later, in 1728, Sieur de Chepart (or Detcheparre in some accounts), a notoriously brash individual and close friend of Governor Perrier, took command of the post and fort at Natchez.

The records of the time generally hold the viewpoint that the new Commandant was, to put it mildly, hard to get along with. He represented what historians today understand as the typical European outlook toward the Native Americans. He summarily ordered the Indians off some of their land - which were their most sacred districts - so he could farm it himself and reap the benefits of this rich and fertile area of the country.

The Natchez leadership split among themselves as to how to deal with this situation. The more aggressive group decided to basically ambush the new Commandant in his own fort.

Two of the old Chiefs who had been friends of the French since Iberville's day had recently passed away, so rather than try the diplomatic solution as the old Chiefs would have, the new young leaders decided to teach Chepart a lesson. They told him that they were coming to pick up some supplies from the fort because they were going on a hunting party and would share the catch when they returned. Not only did Chepart not realize how dumb he was to accept such a ridiculous demand in the first place, but he actually gave the Indians the run of the fort.

They appeared one morning to pick up the muskets and ammunition and then, (surprise, surprise) they turned on the French. Having stationed war parties around the French houses and military posts earlier, they quickly slaughtered almost the entire French male population. Most of the women and children were held as hostages. The Natchez freed the African slaves to make their own way out of the area.

The ambush was successful. Chepart was disposed of and unfortunately many were killed. Some of the French women were able to escape and as they spread the news, panic began to spread down the river. New Orleans trembled in anticipation of an Indian attack, which never came. The French retaliated and began a war that lasted until 1730 when the Natchez as a tribe were essentially eliminated from the face of the earth.

"The Natchez Indians ultimately lost the war and were forced to abandon their homeland. Following their defeat at the hands of the French, the few remaining Natchez refugees joined other tribes, including the Chickasaws, Creeks, and Cherokees. Today, Natchez Indian descendants live in the southern Appalachian Mountains area and in Oklahoma."

(http://mshistory.k12.ms.us/index.php?id=4)

12
LATE 1720's – MAKING SAUSAGE ON THE COTE DES ALLEMANDES

A few months before we arrived, several ships carrying Germans from Alsace and Lorraine had made port on Louisiana's coast near Biloxi. The company settled them a bit upriver of the new capital. We could claim a bit of kinship, as it were, with these German people who were really under the rule of France at home, because we were both sent over by the Company of the Indies.

As I write this, over a decade later, it is very fortunate that our German comrades from the Rhine arrived when they did. Most of the Canadians and the Frenchman who had been in the colony prior to 1720 were not doing very well. Truth be told, they had fallen under the spell, probably spread by the Spanish, that the hills and rivers of the New World were literally flowing over with gold. What they neglected to realize was that you can't search for gold unless you can eat first.

Luckily, our Rhenish friends did realize this. About 30 miles upriver from the capital, they planted the rich lands along the river and was soon producing more food than they knew what to do with. Their hard work paid them many dividends. The first year they produced good crops of tobacco, corn, rice, beans, peas, and other vegetables. The same hurricane that greeted us when we arrived in 1722 did much damage to their farms and harvest that year. However, within the next two seasons, they were supplying New Orleans regularly with produce. They had cultivated 115 arpents* of land and harvested 612 barrels of rice as well as a wide variety of vegetables. According to one Company census, they had 51 hogs and 12 cows.

One of their number, Monsieur, or should I say Herr, Lothar Bayer, had become a good friend of mine through our market transactions over the years. This week, now that the weather had turned cooler again, I had been invited to go upcountry to join Lothar and his family in their annual boucherie**. Pere Raphaël, had graciously allowed me time to take part of this annual fall festival. Leaving my seconds in charge of the kitchen and the garden I begin to pack for the trip upriver planning to spend a week or so.

The following morning, I went to the river market very early and met with some of Lothar's neighbors to arrange for passage back upriver to Le Côte D'Allemandes. It was a simple matter, and soon arranged. The next morning, we would leave early for the trip which should only take the greater part of the day. Lothar and his Frau were expecting me. When we arrived that evening, I was warmly greeted and fed a filling autumn farm supper. We all retired early, because we knew we had a big day tomorrow.

The morrow dawned bright and cool, a perfect day for a gathering. As usual, some of Lothar's and Marguerite's neighbors showed up, and a fine fat boar and sow had been picked to grace our tables this winter. I was not a stranger to boucherie, we had them in the old country on my parent's farm by the lake in the forest for as long as I can remember. This day, I did not take part in the slaughter, but was there to help with the blood gathering and butchering of the animals. My main goal this particular day was to learn how the Germans made their fine sausages.

Now making sausage is not such a hard thing to do, the hardest work is the cleaning and the preparing of the intestines to hold the sausages. This work fell to Lothar's two sons, Hans and Wilhelm, now mostly known by their French names, Jean and Guillaume. In the old country, these Germans had come up with an ingenious device, a tube made out of leather that they attached to their water pump and on the other end of the tube was a very narrow nozzle. With this device which they called a hoose, they were able to flush out the intestines and cleaned them unlike anything I had ever seen. They also use this hoose to force the intestines inside out.

Doing this allowed us easy access to scrape the fat off the inside of the intestines. Once this was done the only thing that remained was stuffing the intestines with the sausage mixture.

This was a tedious job as it had to be handled one spoonful or handful at a time.

As to the preparation of the actual sausage stuffing, I do not know where to begin. There are literally thousands of recipes one can follow to create this fine meat dish.

Symbols and images of a boucherie

One can start with the poorest cuts of meat from the animal, such as the ears, the nose, the feet, the tail. One can add as much or as little fillers such as breadcrumbs, or grains, or cheese as you wish. There also are ancient recipes, from almost every culture, that includes adding the blood of the animal to the sausage mixture. Variously called the black pudding, boudin, or blood sausage, these recipes are either loved or hated according to the taste of the individual. For my contribution to the boucherie, I decided to make a sausage recipe that I discovered in M. Massailot's cookbook, my treasure from France, called Royal Saucissons.

* An arpent is an old French land measurement, about 40 feet of footage along a stream or river.

** Boucherie: a community event or party held in early fall. The local people get together to celebrate the fall harvest, picnic, and share the bounty of the land.

RECIPES

ROYAL SAUCISSONS

<u>Translation:</u>

This translation was found on a colleague's website at http://18thcuisine.blogspot.com/2013/12/royal-saucissons-or-thick-sausages.html
Here you may also purchase a translation of M. Massialot's entire work.

Having provided Flesh of Partridges and of a fat Pullet or Capon, a little Gammon and other Bacon, and a piece of a Leg of Veal, all raw, with parsley and celery, let them be well chopt with Mushrooms and Truffles, and season'd with Pepper, Salt, beaten Spice, and a Clove of Garlick; adding also two whole Eggs, three or four Yolks and a little Milk-cream. Then roll up this Farce into thick pieces, according to the quantity that you have of it, and to the end that it may be dressed, without breaking it, let it be wrapt up in very thin Slices cut out of a Fillet of Veal, and beaten flat upon the Dresser, for that purpose; so as the Sausages may be made at least as thick as a Man's Arm, and of a convenient length.

When they are thus order'd, they must be put into an oval Stew-pan, with a great many Bards or thin Slices of Bacon at the bottom, and stopt up close; covering them with Beef-stakes, and other Bacon-Bards. Afterwards, the Pan must be set between two Fires, taking care that they be not too quick, and the Sausages must be bak'd or stew'd in this manner about eight or ten Hours. As soon as they are ready, let them be remov'd from the Fire, and left to cool in the same Pan: Then they must be carefully taken out so as none be broken, and all the Meat round about must be taken away, with the Fat.

At last, you may cut the Sausages into Slices with a sharp Knife and set them in good order in a Dish or Plate, to be serv'd up cold to Table. If there be occasion to make a Galantine at the same time, with the Royal Sausages, it may be dress'd in the same Stew-pan."

YOUR TRICENTENNIAL MEMO

LA COTE DES ALLEMANDS
(or The Saga of Alsace-Lorraine)

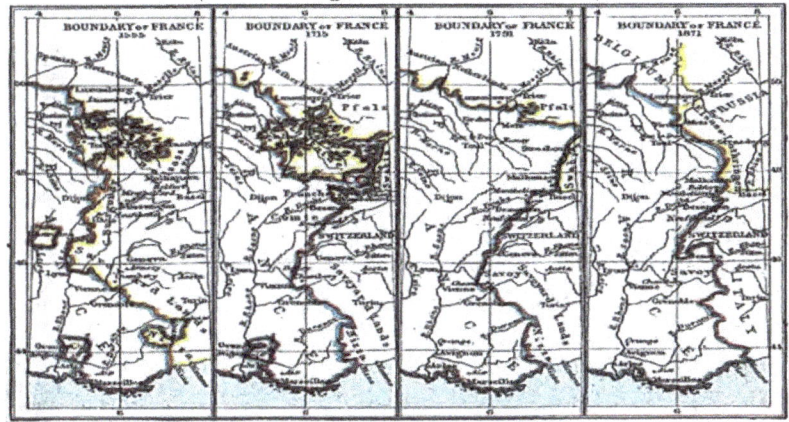

The ever-changing borders of Alsace-Lorraine

One of Louis XIV's diplomatic goals was the extension of France's boundaries to its "natural" frontiers. In the east, those natural boundaries were the Rhine and the Alps. For most of the Sun King's reign, the Rhine was, indeed, France's northeastern boundary, at least until it entered the Low Countries.

The achievement of this boundary line was to have an important effect on the development of the Louisiana colony. Born of seventeenth century European geopolitics, a phenomenon that cchocs down through Louisiana genealogies is "The Saga of Alsace-Lorraine." Perhaps the best way to capture the *je ne c'est quois* or ambience of Alsace-Lorraine is through a quotation from a book about wine that attempts to characterize the region.

"A traveler at the time of the French Revolution found it incredible that this land, so clearly intended by nature to be part of Germany, was actually annexed to France."

As with wine, the culture of the region can be understood as a blend of German Weltanschauung and French sensibilities. These people were far enough away from either the French or German seats of power that they were able to live out their lives in relative peace and security. When John Law, in the midst of his infamous Mississippi Bubble, transported a "great number of Germans" to settle in the Louisiana country, it was these people from which he drew the hardworking farmers that would become crucial to the survival of new capital at New Orleans. We probably will never know how many shipped out, how many died in French ports, or on the trip over.

Once landed on the Gulf Coast, the German mortalities continued. For the purposes of this study precise numbers really do not matter. Germans and Swiss immigrants DID arrive and, what is more important, stay in Louisiana and eventually settle along the Mississippi. In 1717 John Law's Mississippi Company, (later called the Company of the West, still later renamed the Company of the Indies) took over the management of the Louisiana colony. It then proceeded to perform several actions which directly or indirectly affected the development of Louisiana's Creole Cuisine.

It ordered Bienville to build New Orleans. Then, under Company direction, a group of Capuchins was sent to the colony to build the church and function as the religious leaders of the new city. To continue to populate the country the Company recruited a few thousand Germans from the Rhineland to transport to New Orleans and build farming communities. Those that survived the trip were sent upriver a few miles to what later became called the German Coast.

Later, again under the Company direction, the Ursuline nuns were sent to take care the hospital and the educational needs of the new capital. Also, the Company arranged for many thousands of Africans to be brought from its holdings in West Africa to New Orleans to be sold throughout the colony. All of these factors taken together provided the population, the demography, and the means to begin feeding itself.

Without these actions by the Company of the Indies, the Creole Cuisine that we know today would never have come into existence. It is in this context, our fictional friend, Frère Gerard prepares to make his sausage to bring back to the Presbytère.

From Baton Rouge to the Gulf, the Mississippi snakes its way down past New Orleans. Striving ever south, a 1000 years ago, the mighty river punched a hole in its natural levee (at modern-day Donaldsonville) to create a more direct route to the Gulf which we now call Bayou Lafourche. From this point the Mississippi flattens out a bit and flows almost west-to-east until turning south once more just past New Orleans.

During the French century of the 1700's, a stretch of river, centered on today's Donaldsonville, was populated by the German immigrants as they arrived in Louisiana. At that time there was literally nothing between the Tchoupitoulas plantation immediately to the west of New Orleans and the settlement at Pointe Coupèe, right above modern-day Baton Rouge. Nothing, that is, except the rich alluvial lands on either side of the mighty river. Here is some of the richest farmland in the Louisiana.

Unlike the French colonists, of uncertain repute, sent from the homeland in the early years of settlement, the Germans were industrious farmers and soon began producing large amounts of good food for the colony. Called the Côte des Allemandes (German Coast) it was a haven for the German and Alsatian immigrants who arrived in Louisiana during the 18th-century. Under the command of D'Arensbourg in late 1721 and early 1722, the German farmers established three villages along the riverbanks and began their work of feeding the colony.

To this day, those contributions are remembered in the geographical names of Bayou des Allemandes and Lac des Allemandes which commemorates their settlement in today's River Parishes.

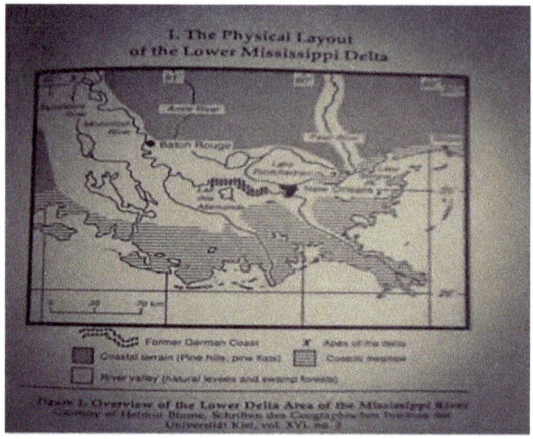

Figure 1: Overview of the Lower Delta Area of the Mississippi River (Courtesy of Helmut Blume, Schriften des Geographischen Instituts der Universität Kiel, vol. XVI, no. 2

John Folse, a famous Creole chef in SE Louisiana - himself descended from these Alsatian settlers - speaks of the number and types of foodstuffs the German Coast provided to the new capital throughout and beyond the French colonial period.

> *"The immigrants originated essentially from the south and west of the so-called Holy Roman Empire, essentially along the Rhine, where they had since Roman times served as the "garden spot" of the empire." Those regions "were known for cattle and dairy farms; wheat, grain, and white wine fields; and barley grown for breweries to make beer." On their farms in the Rhineland, "chestnuts, peaches, apricots, figs, almonds, and lemons flourished. The {German} settlers cultivated vegetables they had known in Germany but grew new ones as well.*
> *The . . . gardens LIKELY (my emphasis) included leaf lettuce, onions, radishes, cabbage, beans, ?tomatoes?, corn, peppers, celery, endive and a variety of root vegetables. . . . they quickly adapted to rice and sweet potato crops in Louisiana. Mint and herbs grew in the kitchen gardens and were used fresh {or dried}. Important herbs MAY HAVE INCLUDED garlic, horseradish, thyme, sweet marjoram, coriander, caraway, fennel, and rosemary."*
> (Folse, 2005, pp. 85 - 86)

Providing more evidence in refutation of the popular starvation and woe reputation of the Louisiana colony, Chef Folse continues to catalogue the foods sent to New Orleans during this era. Food lists continue and include:

---Mustard greens, collards, turnip tops, beet tops, parsley, spinach, and purslane
---Venison, sausage, beef, and hams; rabbit pie, roasted duck or squab
---Red boudin, pork cuts, and bacon, pork cracklings, fat rendered into lard
---Butter, cream, cheese, and eggs
---Pies made from cherries, apples, plums, peaches, strawberry, blackberry, raspberry, elderberry, custard, cheese, crookneck squash, and mincemeat
---The Mardi Gras Fassnachts – doughnuts sprinkled with sugar (beignet-like;

> *"Only at Christmas were precious items such as almonds, raisins, currants, citron, and orange peel used in baking."*
>
> *Coming from the Rhenish regions famous for wine and beer, the German Coast also produced, "cherry bounce, beer, fruit wines made from persimmons, Muscadines, black cherries, blackberries, strawberries, and peaches."*
>
> *"Additionally, coffee was a popular beverage and is still served in many German homes with every meal."*
>
> (John Folse, 2005; pp. 85 ff)

From the time of their arrival, the German immigrants began speaking French and intermarried with the early French settlers. Over the subsequent decades they intermarried with the descendants of the latter as well as the later Acadian arrivals. Together they helped create Cajun culture. For example, German settlers introduced the diatonic accordion to the region, now a major instrument in Cajun music.

13
EARLY 1730's – MARKETS, MARSHES AND MEAT

Another week, another market day. Today I was not going to the market alone. It was time to introduce my apprentice, Etienne, to the wild frontier town that was his outside world.

New Orleans had seen steady growth since the hurricane of 1722. Enough folk had finally arrived from the old country to make regular markets viable. Viable that is, but not very organized. The markets, scattered all over town, challenged even the most experienced cook when it came to locating foodstuffs.

From the levee to the edge of the swamp at the back of town, and almost everywhere in between, one could find food and goods of a bewildering variety. By far the safest market - and I use the term loosely - was at the levee. But that was not our destination today.

On virtually every street between the river and the cypress marsh, chants, calls and songs filled the air as Natives, townsfolk, and even some slaves from the nearby farms and settlements wandered about calling all to purchase their goods. Again, Etienne and I were not looking here. We were heading to the "black" market (pun intended) on the back, swampy, edge of town.

I say black market for two reasons. During the last few years, the Company had shipped quite a few Africans to Louisiana, and unfortunately, their fate was not a happy one. Those who did not die in the passage over, chained in the horrendously steamy and disease-ridden holds of the slave ships were doomed to live out the rest of their lives in bondage.

Once here, in addition to their regular servitude, slaves were encouraged to plant their own gardens to help feed themselves. They are also allowed to sell their surplus for their own or their masters' benefit. According to our law, slaves also have Sundays free to learn about our Lord Jesus and to attend to their own affairs. It has now become their custom to gather at the open space in the rear of town to buy and sell, to congregate, and even to worship, in their somewhat heathen fashion.

Not all of what they sell here are the products of their own industry but are acquired through trade with other merchants and suppliers - both legal and illicit - hence the double meaning of "black market". So now, as we approached what even now some locals are calling, Congo Square, I instructed Etienne to stay close, to attend to the business dealings, and pay attention to our surroundings. Well, things did not go exactly as I had hoped.

Oh, the impatience of youth! As we wandered around the market, assessing the foodstuffs and other wares for sale, Etienne kept wandering to the edge of the swamp, and I had to keep calling him back. Finally, his persistence paid off. I got tired of chasing him around, and as we had not made any purchases yet, I decided to go with him a few steps into the cypress swamp.

We humans are a curious lot, if something is not of immediate use to us or our interests, we tend not to see it. Having lived in New Orleans over 10 years now, the swamp, not being of any use to me, had become invisible. For about 15 minutes, we picked our way around stinging vines and thick brush, finally emerging into the swamp.

I looked up and sucked in a deep breath of humid air at the magnificence that surrounded me. Just a short distance away from the market, the Cypriere had closed behind us. The city had disappeared, and we stood in another world.

A palmetto swamp

Above loomed ancient cypress trees, towering hundreds of feet high, their "knees" sticking out of the mud and water for yards around their base their branches filtering out the sun and shading the swamp in a faded light. Scattered about were huge deep-rooted palmetto, whose broad fan-like leaves had sheltered the early huts of New Orleans settlers, from the poorest Native to the colonial governor. My imagination ran wild with what might be sheltering under them now… snakes, bears, wild pigs?

Etienne suddenly froze in place, his sharp, youthful eyes intently focused on a subtle movement in the green gloom. Disregarding my whispered questions, he darted forward, plunged into the knee-high waters, and grabbed onto what appeared to be a long log. My heart pounded frantically when I recognized his prey… a 4-foot-long alligator, with at least 1 foot of him all teeth! He had the beast by the tail, and despite its violent thrashing and angry hissing, he managed to drag the alligator onto the muddy bank.

I dived into the battle, thinking of nothing except those snapping jaws that threatened to rip off Etienne's leg, and between the two of us, we managed to pin the creature to the mushy ground and dispatch it with the large knife I carried with me every time I went to market.

Fear turned into fury, and I harshly berated him for such a foolish adventure, and while he pretended to be sorry, he insisted that the opportunity for so much free meat, along with a valuable hide to use in trading, had been too good to pass by. However, I believe he may have reconsidered his actions as we struggled to drag the creature back to the Presbytère!

Young Louisiana alligator

The alligator, now reduced from a vicious reptile to a future meal, caused a small scene in the marketplace. We were regaled with methods of skinning it and cooking it by the Natives, the slaves, and almost everyone who witnessed us trudging home with the gator in tow. I had my own ideas, however. For the past few months, I have been experimenting with different sauces. Harking back to my training in France and taking full advantage of the copy of Massailot's cookbook which I had acquired, I had mastered the three Sausses Meres, the basic sauces for all of French cooking.

Our potager had begun to produce a wide variety of vegetables and herbs. I wanted to take full advantage of them. While alligators were quite common in the Cypriere, they nevertheless were unusual in our diet. My idea was, at our next Sunday dinner, I would add some alligator in sauce to our usual herb rice and bread.

As Etienne and I returned from the black market with our catch and a few little purchases from some - let's say - unknown sources, I began to reflect on how different life was here in Louisiana as compared to home in France. When we had returned to the Presbytère, I set Etienne to cleaning the kitchen, storing our purchases, and preparing his kill, skinning and butchering it to use in our dish for Sunday's meal.

As Etienne set about his chores, I sat down at my desk to make some notes, anxious to test my sauces. Sometimes we do things we shouldn't, for instance, my nutmegs and my saffron may be evidence of this. Sometimes we must do things whether we want to or not, such as eating a joint of wild beef on Friday because that's all there is. Such lapses in diet and fashion, due to our sometimes-extreme circumstances, would probably merit an excuse in heaven.

I had no worries this Friday, however, and I had a large quantity of alligator to dine on!

RECIPES

GERARD'S ALLIGATOR SAUSSE ESPAGNOLE

- 1 small onion
- 1 small bell pepper
- 1 celery stick
- 3 toes of garlic
- Cooking fat to cover bottom of pan 1/2 inch
- 1 pound alligator meat
- Seasoned flour
- 1/2 cup bacon grease
- 1/2 cup flour
- 1 quart of chicken stock
- 3 bay leaves
- Salt, cayenne pepper, and sugar to taste

Fry off the meat you will be using, in this case alligator. Remove the meat and set aside. In the same pan, add half a cup bacon grease. Now make the brown roux (see Chapter 4) for roux instructions). Be sure to chop and make ready the onion, green pepper, celery, and garlic beforehand.

Slowly add the half cup of flour slowly, stirring constantly, until the sauce is well blended. Continue to stir as the sauce browns to the desired color, a dark brown like coffee with just a little milk in it. You are stirring to keep the flour and the sauce from sticking to the bottom of the pan.

When the color is as you desire, remove immediately from the heat and stir in the chopped vegetables. This stops the cooking. Stir everything together well, then return to a low heat, add the stock and keep stirring. Add the sugar, salt, bay leaves, and cayenne pepper. Stir well and cook on low for ten minutes, stirring occasionally. Taste the sauce and adjust the seasoning. Add the alligator back into the pan, cover and cook through. Serve over rice, garnish with chopped green onions and parsley

YOUR TRICENTENNIAL MEMO

The capital city, while growing, was still an isolated pocket set at the top of a curve in the river in the middle of a vast wilderness. Bounded by the river on one side and surrounded on the other three by a vast cypress and palmetto swamp, there were only two ways in and out of the city.

The river was the primary connection with the rest of the world, but the second route - the old Indian portage back to Bayou St. John which leads to Lake Pontchartrain and the Mexican Gulf - was also well traveled.

While most certainly beautiful, the swamps were extremely dangerous, ever-changing and treacherous, so once in the city, people tended to stay put, venturing forth only on the most urgent business. Nevertheless, since the city's whole purpose was to be a trade center, there was a constant flow of goods and people in and out of town. This transience led to an increased sense of isolation among the permanent inhabitants. These factors all combine to create a peculiar outlook on life. This peculiar outlook became known as Creole.

The geography of the settlers' isolation and the French attitudes towards living in close quarters with the Natives and the African slaves, the necessity to survive by their own wits, all combined to produce this Creole culture. Furthermore, the settlers were no longer constrained by the traditions or officialdom of the old country. The inhabitants now saw and did things differently.

In France, a priest such as Gerard would never have dared to include so much meat and certainly no sauces into a daily monastic diet. Fish, on the other hand, had been eaten in their cloisters since time immemorial. In New Orleans, however, the surrounding waters were so abundant with useful and delicious seafood and fish, it would hardly have been a sacrifice to include these into a daily diet, especially since supplies from France arrive only sporadically.

Life was beyond different in the young city. Tailors, seamstresses and materials were in such short supply that clothing was made from whatever came in on the ships. Even priests and brothers could be seen wearing lace cuffs and slippers. This was received with scandal among some citizens, but most of them found themselves in the same situation.

Dealing with all of these freedoms was a mixed bag for the colony, but it also contributed to the rise of the Creoles, as life in the colonies offered such rich and varied opportunities to do learn new ways and experience such an air of unbridled freedom.

14
1730's – A VISIT TO THE URSULINE POTAGER

    Spending many Christmases with the Ursulines feeding the poor at our holiday feasts in the Square was still on my mind as winter melted into spring. One morning I was taking stock at the Presbytère's potager. For twelve years I have been working in the garden, working hard in all kinds of weather. My efforts were rewarded with a great deal of produce and herbs for the kitchen. After twelve years, however, it was time to reorganize the garden. Of course, most of the actual plants would remain the same. The years have shown me that the various vegetables and herbs grow well in certain locations but did poorly in others. So much was obvious.

    This, though, will not be an easy task. Much has changed in the past twelve years. More and varied produce is arriving every year, brought here by the different people that were coming to this new land. They bring with them the seeds of their countries, and as those seeds grow and adapt to our climate, our food selections bloom along with them. The Natives have also taught us much about what is naturally found on the land and how to collect and prepare it. However, there is still much I do not know.

    To begin, I decided to seek more information and advice from others in the city as to what they plant and when, and how they arrive at the maximum yield from the limited space they have. I am about as familiar with Tante Suzanne's potager as my own, but there is another potager nearby with which I have only a passing familiarity.

    When the Ursuline sisters moved into their permanent convent a couple of blocks away, their potager took on a different tilt, as it were, from mine and Tante Suzanne's. Their convent is adjacent to the city's hospital and the sisters are officially in charge of it, so the Ursuline potager has a much larger planting of medicinal herbs and flowers along with fruit and vegetables.

Not only will I get a different viewpoint on garden planning and organization, but I may very well learn a few new things as well.

So resolved, I set off on the next market day to inquire into the Ursuline convent garden. My first contact, as always, is Sister Stanislaus. As a young sister, she had been among the first 12 who had arrived in Louisiana in 1727 to care for the sick and establish the Ursuline mission in the new colony, and over the years we had become friends.

She was delighted with my request to tour her garden. "Now a medicinal garden is somewhat different than your potager, Brother Gerard," she began, "and although many of the plants are the same, we use different parts of the plant for different reasons than you would in the kitchen. For instance, we make much more use of the flowers than you would. But did you know that many flowers are edible? They add color and flavor to a dish and have as much nutrition as many vegetables and fruit. You will need to speak to Sister Francis Xavier, as it is she who plants and maintains the garden. It is her domain as part of the operations of the hospital. I will see when she may be available to meet with you."

As luck would have it, Sister Francis was just coming in from the hospital and was planning to harvest some herbs for her regular afternoon of medicinal preparations. I had always thought of Sister Francis as a very quiet and reserved woman by nature, but she surprised me by how eager she was to talk about her potager.

We walked out into the garden situated in the rear of the convent grounds and convenient to the hospital across the street. Several young women, all dressed in somber gray, tended the garden. These were the girls I had heard of, those that came from France and were cared for by the sisters until appropriate husbands could be found for them. Until then, one of their duties seemed to be gardening, and given the size of Sister Francis' potager, the more hands the better.

Sister bent down and picked a flat green leaf from a plant that I know well and grows in my own garden. "Take that old weed, the dandelion, as an example," the nun continued, "in the kitchen I am sure you have used it in your salads and soups."

"Indeed," I responded, "not only that, but one can grind the roots to make a respectable substitute or addition to coffee. It can also produce a fair wine or beer for lack of grapes. Dandelion tea is also very good for the settling the stomach."

Sister Francis continued to guide me through the garden, clearly warming to the role of tour guide and obviously proud of her potager. Her face brightened as she expounded the medicinal virtues of various varieties of native peppers, along with many more herbs such as rosemary and tansy. Local species of peppers, she explained, commonly called cayenne or guinea peppers are usually thought of as a seasoning, also served a purpose in the medicine cabinet.

As gently as possible, I steered the conversation away from the use of herbs as medicines and talked about their culinary uses. I was very interested in the herbs I was not too familiar with, herbs that I may be able to use in my kitchen. I recognized many wild native plants scattered among the herbs and flowers. In a wet corner of the garden grew a large patch of cat tails, which, she explained, were excellent to eat if harvested when the shoots were young, and one uses only the tender center of the plant. A lovely patch of purslane grew near the edge of the garden, used, she said, to add a wonderful lemony flavor to cooked greens.

Wild nettle grew along the back wall. "If harvested when the shoots are young and boiled to remove the thorns, it makes a nutritious side dish, "she said, "and it is easy to grow. This land is blessed with many natural plants to feed us and keep us well, if we only take the time to learn about them. No one needs to go hungry in New Orleans!"

I must admit, though, that I was surprised to see a large tree in the corner of the garden, one that I had seen in the swamps and wooded areas. A weed, I thought, yet here, in her garden, it flourished with the other plants.

"Elderberry," she said when she saw me scrutinizing it. "The berries are very nutritious as well as being a good medicine, and I'm told it even makes a passable wine. You can dig up a young tree at the edge of the woods, or I can give you some seeds to start a tree of your own," she said, then waved her finger under my nose, "but not for making wine!"

Her patch of wild strawberries also intrigued me. "But you have to keep a close eye on them, for just about every wild creature will try to get to them before you do! We use the leaves and roots as medicine, but the berries go on our morning table, and they are quite a treat."

The convent garden's air was particularly sweet this day as the orange trees were in full bloom, promising a yield of sweet oranges in the fall. Sister shared her recipe for orange bread, which she insisted was a perfect complement to Trout Margery with crab meat dressing, and I promised I would try it with the first oranges I picked from the trees around the Presbytère.

What impressed me the most was the garden's layout, with plants situated in locations based on how much sun they liked or disliked, seasonal plants that grew tall and shaded those that did not care for full sun, and so much more. I learned a great deal from the good Sister. I left with many good ideas on how I would arrange my own potager, and a few new recipes as well.

In turn, and to thank her for her time and wisdom, I shared with her my recipe for riz au lait, and even brought her a pound of rice, some raw brown sugar and a large nutmeg to go with the recipe. She smiled and thanked me, but when I promised I would return another day to learn more about medicinal plants, and maybe even begin planting a few "medicine" plants in my own potager, she absolutely beamed!

RECIPES

CATTAIL SIDE DISH

Cattails have been used a food source for hundreds of years. They are on par with cucumbers and asparagus, with 1 1/2 cups of cattail shoots providing 16 calories, 1 grams of protein and 5 grams of carbohydrates. Combined with seasonings, they make a nutritious and refreshing salad.

IMPORTANT NOTE ON HARVESTING PLANTS!
Make sure you are taking plants from a clean environment. Roadside cattails are not a good source as they will probably have been exposed to road run-off and oil. Always wash cattails *thoroughly* before bringing them into your kitchen.

- 2 cups young cattail greens
- 3 strips of bacon
- 1-2 tsp bacon fat
- Salt
- Pepper
- 1 toe garlic, chopped fine
- 1 tablespoon chives, chopped fine
- 1 cup chopped mushrooms

Harvest the cattails when they are young shoots. The older the plant, the tougher the shoots will be. Peel away the outer layers and use only the soft inside shoots at the heart of the plant.

Heat the oil in a pan and fry the bacon. Crumble bacon into small pieces. In the hot pan, sauté all the ingredients until they are tender.

Serve hot as a side dish for chicken or fish, with hot bread.

YOUR TRICENTENNIAL MEMO

The colony of Louisiana, and especially the settlement at New Orleans, needed nurses to run its hospital and care for the sick. In France, this mission belonged to the Daughters of Charity, and Commissioner Jacques Delachaise wanted some of these "gray sisters" to come to Louisiana to solve his hospital situation.

The Daughters of Charity had their hands full in the homeland and could not spare anyone to answer the call of the Commissioner, but the Council of the Navy which ran Louisiana's affairs was able to find some Ursulines who were willing to take on the mission. The problem, however, was that the Ursulines, closely allied with the Jesuit order, were not that interested in nursing. Their primary mission, both at home and in the far-off colonies, was to save souls through female education.

In their philosophy, the best way to encourage the growth of the Catholic faith at home, as well as gain new converts in the colonies, was to educate the women. These women would in turn return to their hearths and homes and use their considerable influence on "the home front" to increase and expand the practice of Christianity among their families. Ursulines were teachers first, and everything else - including nursing - was a secondary consideration.

While they did take care of the hospital, their main focus was always the school they established for the girls and women of the colonies. Of exceptional note, the school served more than the French colonists. Since conversion was a prime motive in emigrating to the New World, an important part of their mission was to convert the Indian women and girls as well as the African slaves brought in by the company. This educational mission of the sisters also extended to providing New Orleans with an orphanage.

These missions and the far-flung nature of an economy based on plantations up and down the river as far north as Baton Rouge (and beyond) gave rise to a "boarding school" facility at the convent as well. Along with day students from the city and immediate surroundings, the Ursuline school for girls became a foundational part of the city and colony that still exists to this very day.

One of the more charming legends that emerged from the French settlement of New Orleans and the educational activities of Ursulines was that of the "casket girls." This legend originated as part of the European Creole culture which came to define New Orleans during the antebellum and reconstruction periods in Louisiana history. The forced emigration of the lower classes of Parisian society in the early days of Louisiana is well documented, but there was a lesser emigration of officials, military officers, and craftspeople as well. As the Creoles (descendants of these emigres) coalesced into the bourgeois and semi-aristocratic classes of New Orleans society, no one wished to trace their heritage to the common women of light virtue who populated New Orleans during these first decades.

Among that female population arriving during those first years were several shiploads of young ladies from various schools and orphanages around Paris. These young women, both of high and low virtue, became the foundation of the casket girl legend. Supposedly provided with small boxes for their trousseau by the crown (the caskets), they arrived in New Orleans and were taken in by the nuns until husbands could be provided.

Apart from the notions of the 'caskets' and the Ursuline sponsorship, such ladies did arrive and were quickly married off. These marriages led to the birth of many first-generation Creoles (defined as persons born in the colony of parents who had come from the Old World, including both Africa and Europe).

AN EARLY FEMALE EMIGRÉ TO LOUISIANA

Whether the girls had caskets or were provided for by the Ursulines is wide open to question. The Ursuline Order in New Orleans today is on record as saying such a series of events or personages did not exist during the 18th century. Although, from the sisters' point of view, their main mission was the education of the colonial female population, the authorities in France and Louisiana had hired and paid them to run the Royal Hospital.

When the twelve Ursuline nuns arrived at New Orleans in 1727, their convent was not yet a reality. They were housed in temporary quarters across town from the hospital which they were supposed to manage, maintain, and staff. For seven long years the "nurses" had to trudge from one corner of the new settlement to the other corner where the patients were located (near what is today the Old Mint). Finally, in 1734, the convent was completed across from the hospital.

For centuries, Catholicism has been noted for many things, some good, some not so much. But one thing no one quibbles about is that the Catholic church is past master at ritual and ceremony. Neither were the Ursulines too shabby at putting on a show. As they prepared to move to their new convent, they wanted to officially announce their mission to and show New Orleans why they had come to the New World. On July 17, 1734, in the heat and humidity of a Gulf Coast summer the ceremonial procession from their old quarters to the new convent took place. Incidentally, this is the first recorded parade in New Orleans history.

> *"The streets were a quagmire after three days of unremitting rain. Dozens of little girls, pent up all day waiting for the skies to clear, were restless. They broke into spirited song when the procession finally marched forth.*
>
> *"In the muddy streets of the frontier town, rank and class still mattered to the nuns. Messieurs Bienville, governor, and Solomon, intendant, honored us with their presence. The nine women constituting the little religious community 'went out in order,' the Mother Superior and her assistants took pride of place behind the canopy sheltering the revered sacrament.*
>
> *"At first glance this processional display of social order gives an impression of traditional hierarchies, but a closer look reveals some surprises. Marching in the parade in places of honor were women who belong to a ladies' fraternity, a devotional organization that saw plantation mistresses falling into step with carpenters' wives and women of color."*
>
> *Emily Clark, Masterless Mistresses; The New Orleans Ursulines and the Development of a New World*

*Society, 1727 – 1834 Chapel Hill N.C.:
University of North Carolina Press, 2007)*

Paraphrase: After moving to the new convent in July, 1734: "It had been planned originally make this building a combination Hospital, convent and school, but the place was far too small for this and through the intervention of Father de Beauvoir, a special building was erected for the housing of the sick. Sr. St. Xavier Hebert took charge of the sick on September 1, 1734. It was not long before the hospital was transformed, and the nuns elicited the highest praise from officials for their faithfulness and efficiency." [p. 137]

Paraphrase: In the 40's and 50's the nuns experienced much trouble dealing with the hospital. Between perennial underfunding, and squabbles between physicians and surgeons, and patients, the Ursulines were forever between the arguing factions. The whole matter was submitted to the new governor, Kerlerec, ... and eventually matters were straightened out. [p. 138]

Paraphrase: ... January 1770, the Sisters decided to give up the care of the hospital. A search of the convent archives has failed to disclose any Papal Bull releasing the Ursulines from this task, as has been stated by Gayarre and other writers. Thus, the Ursulines were now able to devote their entire time to ... education.
[p. 183]

*Roger Baudier, The Catholic Church in Louisiana.
(New Orleans: A.W. Hyatt Stationery Mfg. Co. Ltd.,1939):*

After their Grand Procession, the Ursulines operated the Royal Hospital in New Orleans from their arrival in 1727 until 1770. Sister Francis Xavier Hebert came to the city in 1734. She immediately set to work to create an herb garden.

> *"Sister Xavier compounded the medicines for the Royal Hospital and became the first woman pharmacist in the New World. The teas, infusions, and distillates which she brewed from the herbs in her garden*

> *represented the greater part of what was available for the treatment of the sick. In colonial times...the herb garden was vital in providing medicines..."*
>
> The Old Ursuline Convent Cookbook

> *Sister Xavier's herb garden became critically important to the lives of the people of New Orleans."*
> http://old-new-orleans.com/NO_Women.html

Sister Xavier Hebert was in charge until 1763. She managed to keep the Royal Hospital functioning throughout this trying period.

The Ursuline Order in New Orleans fulfilled their nursing obligations into the Spanish colonial era. Passing the nursing baton to other organizations, the nuns went on to become famous not only for their prayers but also for their medical support during the 1814-15 British invasion and Battle of New Orleans. Even until the present time they continue to be a cultural force in the city which - in no small part - they brought into reality.

15
EARLY 1730's – SOME CALAS IN THE FRENCH MARKET

Nobody knows exactly when the market started. It was the first thing we saw as our boats pulled up to the new river town. This was no surprise to our small group of clerics, nor especially to me. As "Brother Kitchen" it was quite natural to me to land in a marketplace. After all, one of the main functions of a town is to be a market center.

One of the first things Monsieur Bienville did was to order that the new streets of New Orleans be protected by a levee. Built on the already slightly higher ground here at the river's bend, the workers and slaves had heaped up a long pile of earth along the bank in front of what was to become the square, the church, and its attendant structures. Between levee and river, some crude piers and docking areas were built.

The German farmers who had settled up the river had managed to get most of their first harvest in before the hurricane. The King's plantation across the river - jokingly nicknamed Algiers, because all the Africans brought to the colony were landed there first - was producing a steady supply of garden vegetables. At some point between 1719 and our arrival, a marketplace had sprung up on the levee in front of the square to exchange these goods and more.

It was primitive, informal, and a somewhat wild place at first. Fights and thievery were common. Hunters, fishermen, oystermen, German Coast farmers, the Tchoupitoulas Natives, Algiers, and the surrounding concessions (aka plantations), all congregated there once a week or so to peddle their goods. I soon learned that it is every man (or woman) for themselves.

Admittedly, things have become somewhat more settled as time has gone by and the town has grown. The market is a vibrant place, alive with chatter, exchange, some occasional music, and lots of noise and high spirits. One of the most common cries to be heard thereabouts is that of "Belle cala! Tout chaud!" (Lovely calas! Good and hot!) which can be heard around the market and the square. It is the morning cry of the Indian and African women beckoning the hungry (and not so hungry) to come and sample their delicious calas or rice cakes.

On that memorable day, as we arrived, not only was I introduced to the New Orleans market, but as my Capuchin brothers and I ate these wonderful rice cakes, I learned a valuable lesson of life in the new colony. In France, our daily bread was always made from wheat flour. In New Orleans we had three different kinds of flour. Wheat being a somewhat rare commodity, we would make great use of flour ground from maize or rice.

These wonderful cakes thereby taught me an essential lesson in preparing meals in this New World. I eagerly absorbed this lesson from the old cala women as they took the calas piping hot from the boiling fat, wrapped them in a clean towel, put them in a basket or bowl, and rushed through the streets with their welcome cry ringing on the morning air.

Soon after, in our primitive Presbytère kitchen, I could simply take the calas out of the frying pan and drain off the lard by laying them in a colander or on heated pieces of brown paper. Then I would serve them in a hot dish, sprinkled over with sugar and eaten hot with café au lait.

RECIPES

CALAS (RICE CAKES)

This is a simple recipe, passed down through the centuries. The old cala women who walked the streets of the Vieux Carré for over two centuries had as many variations on the recipe as their number. The following Creole recipe is a splendid example.

- 1/2 cup of rice

- 3 cups boiling water
- 3 eggs
- 1/2 cup of sugar
- 1/2 cake of yeast
- 1/2 teaspoon of grated nutmeg
- Sugar
- Boiling lard

Put 3 cups of water in a saucepan and let it boil hard. Wash half a cup of rice thoroughly, drain and put in the boiling water. Let it boil until very soft and mushy. Take it out and set it to cool. When cold, mash well and mix with the yeast, which you will have dissolved in a half cup of hot water. Set the rice to rise overnight. In the morning, heat three eggs thoroughly and add to the rice, mixing and beating well. Add a half cup of sugar and three tablespoons of flour, to make the rice adhere. Mix well and heat thoroughly, bringing it to a thick batter.

Hot calas served with two syrups

Set to rise for fifteen minutes longer. Then add about a half teaspoonful of grated nutmeg and mix well. Have ready a frying pan in which there is boiling lard sufficient for the rice cakes to swim in. Test by dropping in a small piece of bread. If it becomes a golden brown, the lard is ready, but if it burns or browns instantly, it is too hot. The golden-brown color is the true test. Take a large deep spoon and drop a spoonful at a time of the preparation into the boiling lard, remembering always that the cake must not touch the bottom of the pan. Let fry to a nice brown.

Drain on brown paper. Sprinkle with sugar. Enjoy.

<u>Modern Adaption:</u>

Here is a more modern recipe from La Bouche Creole (Pelican Press, 1981):

- 6 tablespoons flour
- 3 heaping tablespoons sugar
- 2 teaspoons baking powder
- 1/4 teaspoon salt
- 1/4 teaspoon vanilla
- 2 cups cooked rice
- 2 eggs
- Pinch of nutmeg
- Cooking oil
- Powdered Sugar

Mix together the flour, sugar, baking powder, salt, and vanilla. Thoroughly mix the rice and eggs together in a separate bowl. Add the dry ingredients to the rice and egg mixture. When thoroughly mixed, drop by spoonful into the hot deep fat (about 360 degrees F) and fry until brown.

Drain on paper towel. Sprinkle with powdered sugar and serve while hot.

Other variations are to serve with honey or (my favorite) Steen's Cane Syrup instead of the powdered sugar.

YOUR TRICENTENNIAL MEMO

As you may have noticed from Frère Gerard's tale of the early New Orleans market as well as the importance of rice as a staple in the colonial kitchen, the Creole use of rice in the New Orleans diet is as old as New Orleans itself. Creole recipes for rice and rice cakes and pretty much everything else, however, would have to wait over 150 years before anyone would write them down. Here presented are stories and recipes about rice cakes from very early cookbooks, which also give us an insight into the creole culture from which these wonderful treats emerged.

Made from the simple and abundant (at least by the 1730's) ingredients, eggs, rice, flour, and sugar, these cakes were a morning staple in Creole New Orleans at least until WW II.

> *"Belle cala! Tout chaud!" Under this cry, the cakes were sold by the ancient Creole Negro women in the French Quarter of New Orleans. These delicious rice cakes were eaten with the morning cup of coffee.*
>
> *The cala woman was always seen upon the streets, until the last few years. She made her rounds in a quaint bandana tignon, guinea blue dress and white apron, and carried on her head a covered bowl, in which were the dainty and hot calas. Her cry, "Belle cala! Tout chaud!" would penetrate the morning air, and the Creole cooks would rush to the doors to get the first fresh, hot calas.*
>
> *The cala women have passed away, but the custom of making calas still remains. In many homes of old Creole lineage, the good housewife tells her daughter just how "Tante Zizi" made the calas in her day, and so are preserved these ancient traditional recipes."*
>
> *From the book, Picayune Creole Cookbook, first published by the Times-Picayune, New Orleans, in 1901.*

16
1730's - A BOUCAN FOR PENTECOST

All good things come to an end. So goes the old adage. And so it happens every year here in New Orleans. Lent and Easter have come and gone, Pentecost approaches. Take note, here I am talking about the weather, not the Holy Days. April and May are the months of change in Louisiana.

The fine weather, the cool, dry air that comes in October and lasts through the holidays finally begins to move out during Easter Tide. Soon, it will be miserably hot again, the mosquitoes return with the thunder showers, and the air is often so damp that clothes and bodies rarely dry out completely. But another October will come, and we pray and hope and count the months, and try to stay cool as best we can.

My kitchen routine also begins to change with seasons. My apprentices and I begin to plant the potager for the summer harvest, we begin to move the cooking fires outside and away from the stuffy indoor hearths. We have managed well enough for the past dozen or so years.

The community has made great progress growing our parish, both spiritually and physically. Church and Presbytère, as well as new homes and shops, have filled some of the empty spaces first laid out by Messieurs La Tour and Pauger. The Levee Market is now a group of semi-permanent stalls and open spaces for farmers and artisans to sell their products.

New Orleans has actually begun to resemble the French villages and bourgs of our homeland. Behind the Presbytère, the brother's kitchen and potager have taken shape. There is even some extra space wherein we can expand the cooking and garden domains.

This year, Père Raphael has given me a mission as well. As well as organizing my demesne for the summer ahead, I am to plan and execute a Pentecost feast for our Convent and the

Ursulines, (and even the few Jesuits around) to begin the hot season.

My first decision was to use one of the earliest cooking methods Europeans learned from the Natives, as we stumbled into this new world, the technique of buccaning. The New World "Indians"- as the Spanish called them - used this method to prepare the abundant game available on the islands and the continent.

Now you may well object that cooking meat outside on an open flame is nothing new. We have been roasting meat on a spit since Abel slowly "burned" the best of his flocks to God Almighty and made Cain jealous. But it was the method of the wood frame and the smoking which the islanders taught first the Spanish and then we French settlers in the West Indies.

Native American cooking method (not *bouccane*)

Here on the continent and in the forests of Louisiana, especially the Florida Lands across the great Pontchartrain Lake, is found an abundance of wild turkey. Hunters from the capital, often traverse these lands and even much further to provide our market with an abundance of fresh game. So I prepared a buccane to cook some turkey birds outside for our Pentecost feast.

To buccane a bird or any other piece of meat is a fairly simple process. Beginning with a lot of twigs about a half-inch in diameter, the first thing to do is to build a frame consisting of several squares. A good size is to make each section about 1 pied (Old French for approx. an English foot) square. The twigs or branches are lashed together with twine or bits of string or even stripped bark.

Next attach the meat to the frame and hang it over an outside fire pit about 5 *pieds* above the flames so it cooks very slowly and use the heat of the smoke rather than the heat of the flame. Now, in buccaning turkey birds, the best method I have found is to prepare a marinade and soak the turkey birds - after plucking and cleaning them - for a day or so. Split the birds and half attach them to the frame using the same materials and just let him smoke from early in the morning until supper time.

RECIPES

TURKEY BOUCANNIER

To prepare a citrus marinade: blend together the juice of 5 oranges, a small spoon of cayenne pepper (whole or ground), the juice of 2 lemons, and a blend of spices on hand -- Frère Gerard probably used salt, garlic, paprika, and a bell pepper. Cook the garlic and pepper down to very soft. Blend the whole mixture together with olive or bear oil and mix with about 2 gallons of water. This is for one bird. Adjust the quantities for the number of birds to be smoked. Soak the bird(s) for at least a day in the marinade, and then buccane as described above.

Our 21st Century version

We used a fresh turkey, about 15 pounds and soaked it for 2 days in the marinade below. Prepared for a Fourth of July family dinner, we roasted the bird for 2 hours in 325° oven early in the morning before sunrise. The turkey was then smoked over mesquite coals for 2 to 3 hours as we prepared the rest of the dinner later in the day.

Modern Adaptation:

- 5 oranges
- Cayenne pepper (whole or ground)
- 2 lemons
- Salt, garlic, paprika, blend to make about 15 tsp.
- 1 bell pepper
- 1 1/4 cup cooking oil
- 5 tablespoons honey marinade OR a modern cheat = McCormick's Baja Citrus

First bake turkey in the oven, then placed on the BBQ grill to smoke. Prior to baking/smoking prepare a citrus marinade. Since a turkey tends to be rather large, we prepared 10 liters of marinade.

Use the modern cheat or blend together the above spices, chopping or pureeing the bell peppers to add to the marinade base. Using five empty two-liter soda bottles, begin by squeezing a whole orange into a measuring cup. This normally produces about a quarter cup of juice.

Add a quarter cup of cooking oil, a tablespoon of honey and one ounce of the spice powder (about 1 tablespoon). Mix well. Fill the cup with water and pour into the two-liter bottle. Rinse the cup and pour the water into the bottle as well. Repeat the process until you have five bottles of marinade base (one third of the bottle).

Place the marinated turkey in the oven and roast for two hours. Transfer to a grill or smoker and let it cook for a few hours until it's done and ready to eat.

Serve with Roasted Herb Indian Corn.

YOUR TRICENTENNIAL MEMO

The term buccaneer derives from the Arawak word buccan, a wooden frame for smoking meat, hence the French word buccane and the name boucannier for French hunters who used such frames to smoke meat from feral cattle and pigs on Hispaniola (now Haiti and the Dominican Republic). English colonists anglicized the word boucannier to buccaneer.

About 1630, some Frenchmen who were driven away from the island of Hispaniola fled to nearby Tortuga. The Spaniards tried to drive them out of Tortuga, but the buccaneers were joined by many other French, Dutch and English and turned to piracy against Spanish shipping, generally using small craft to attack galleons in the vicinity of the Windward Passage. Finally, they became so strong that they even sailed to the mainland of Spanish America and sacked cities.

Buccaneer." Wikipedia: The Free Encyclopedia. Wikimedia Foundation, Inc. Last modified on 16 December 2014 at 16:02. Web. Accessed 13 January 2015.
http://en.wikipedia.org/wiki/Buccaneer

It is appropriate to the theme of this culinary history that the various roasted and smoked meats found within are suffixed "boucannier." Since its founding, New Orleans has always been associated with pirates and smugglers (see Chapter 18). Indeed, much of the local economy of Louisiana during the French period (1699 – 1762) and extending into the famous encounter between Jean Lafitte and General Jackson in the Battle of New Orleans (1815) was based on consumer activity dependent upon the fruits of piracy.

17
1730's – THE HOUMA VISIT

When the d'Iberville expedition first arrived in Louisiana, many villages of our Native brethren lined the rivers and streams between La Balize and the Arkansas Post. Over the next three decades, as we learned more about les petits nations, we Europeans realized that here in the New World, the native people do not stay in one place very long.

Entire villages and towns move about quite freely and quite often. For instance, my current mission to the Houmas nation will take me upriver to the Pointe Coupèe settlement, then back downriver a few leagues below Baton Rouge to where the Mississippi forks. At that point, we will travel down La Fourche (the Fork) into the swamps, streams, and lakes that is the marsh to the south and west of New Orleans. In all of these places we hope to meet with the Houma people and bring them the Good News and learn from them the ways of catching and cooking the abundant seafood and fishes that inhabit our rich new land.

I am traveling to these settlements with Father Anselm. Pere Raphael has sent him to minister to the Houmas and to the Frenchmen at Pointe Coupèe and beyond. I am tagging along to help him in his work, and not incidentally, to learn as much as I can from our 'little brothers' about local food production.

Travelling north past Baton Rouge, the land begins to rise. To the east, the terrain rolls away in hills and gullies, with bluffs very much like cliffs along the river. To the west stretches a vast flatness of grasslands and meadows, which we call prairie in French. The settlement at Pointe Coupèe lay on the western side of the St. Louis (the official French name of the Mississippi). More specifically, it is situated on a loop in the river that has been cut off from the mainstream and now forms a lake. Folks moving up from Baton Rouge and even the local Indians often call the place False River. Pere Anselm and our party stayed there a couple of months, while Father preached the Word, and made arrangements to start building a permanent chapel.

Since the locals were Frenchmen like ourselves, and - more to the point - cooked with the same ingredients as I do, following the same methods, cooking on a hearth, there wasn't much done here in the kitchen that I did not already know. I spent most of my time, helping with the chapel and exploring the surrounding country.

The land on this western bank is the rich alluvial prairie, which is perfect for the plow. Large farms were already established. On the eastern side of the river, the land was much more broken up and vast forests covered the hills and bluffs along the bayous and streams running down into the St. Louis. It was a rich hunting ground for Natives and settlers alike, and the forest trees were filled with nuts, berries, and fruits of all kinds. This indeed is a wondrous land. The Lord has blessed our countrymen in being able to come and partake in its bounty.

Monsieur d'Iberville first found the Houmas on the hills and bluffs of the eastern side of the great river. But, as I wrote earlier, these New World folk do not stay in one place for long periods of time. Pere Anselm and I did, indeed, find some of the Houma nation at Pointe Coupèe, but by the time we arrived, most of their people had moved south to the big fork in the river below Baton Rouge.

As I had been looking forward to learning about the watery food resources that abound in Louisiana, I was excited when Pere Anselm finally decided to visit the scattered Houma nation down La Fourche. So, after some pleasant months, we left the rich farmlands around the False River and headed down the St. Louis toward La Fourche.

Our first stop was at the town which had been a Native community long before we Frenchmen stumbled into the mouths of the great river. Since the first explorers arrived some thirty years ago, it had been occupied by the Bayougoulas, the Chitimacha, and now the Houmas.

Here at the river fork, we stayed for a few days to get some sense of where we were headed. Pere Anselm sought information about their beliefs and spiritual culture. I befriended the hunters, the women, and the fishermen to see what they fed their people and, more importantly, how they acquired and prepared their food.

In this quest for information about the acquisition, preparation, and consumption of the local *fruites de mer*, the very first thing I learned from the Houmas is that - most interestingly - the Native nations do not eat their symbolic or sacred animals. The Houmas' "totem" is the red crawfish, and they would never think of consuming it. It was the same for the other petits nations as well. Each Native tribe had such a sacred animal, never to be consumed.

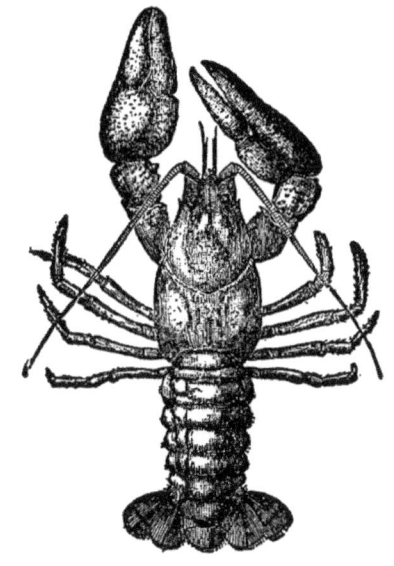

As to the crawfish itself, in French, l'ecrevisse, this water dweller is very like a miniature lobster. Most of the other nations find it very tasty, specifically the tail or claw meat. Despite being small and rather difficult to extract, the meat is also used in a variety of delicious dishes. After peeling enough crawfish, one can produce many fine meals.

Anyway, since the Houmas do not prepare or consume them, for now I considered the other fishes and their kin. La Fourche itself as well as the numerous streams, bayous, lakes, and ponds that are the Houma homelands provide a wealth of tasty species. It took me a while, but I was finally able to distinguish among the gar, choupique, catfish, paddlefish, sunfish, bass, eel, sac-a-lait, sturgeon, gizzard shad, and buffalo fish.

Traveling down the La Fourche closer to the Mexican Gulf, the types of fish multiplied to include drum, croaker, speckled trout, redfish, flounder, and mullet from the coasts and bays. Along with the various finfish, during our extended visit we caught and consumed oysters found abundantly in the lakes and coastal waters. Everywhere from the St. Louis down to the Gulf, there were huge amounts of mussels, shrimp and crabs.

From the marsh itself, I learned to prepare - and surprisingly, really enjoy - frogs of extraordinary size along with turtles, terrapins, and alligators. Finally, even though my Houma friends and guides showed me how, I couldn't bring myself to consume the snakes.

THE COMMON BUFFALO
Megastomatobus cyprinella (Cuvier and Valenciennes)

One of our three Louisiana Buffaloes, this species contributes to the very important Buffalo fishery of the Mississippi Valley, which may attain in a single year a total catch of 17,000,000 pounds, with a value of over a million dollars. The Common Buffalo was first made known to science when described by two French zoologists from specimens taken in Lake Pontchartrain. Like the other Buffaloes, it has received very many confusing popular names. It may be distinguished by the characters indicated in the key, and by the head characteristics illustrated elsewhere. Buffalofishes are well equipped to strain out from muddy river bottoms the food which they eat. [...]

Along the Bayou La Fourche the Natives gathered the harvests of the waters in many methods. The Houmas harvested the catch with hooks, lines, hoop nets made of rabbit-vines, cone-shaped traps made with wooden slats, trotlines (a local creation where many hooks are dangled from one strong line stretched over the entire stream) and weirs (sort of a fence or corral set into the stream). Sometimes, fish were speared in shallow water by night and sometimes poisoned. This technique was usually employed in summer when the small streams were low. Poison was obtained from the horse chestnut, or buckeye, the root of the devil's shoestring, or catgut as well as green hickory nuts or walnut hulls. The Natives would crush these materials and stir them into a pool, where the fish, with their gills paralyzed, floated to the surface.

Once the seafood is gathered, there is virtually no difference between our civilized way of cooking and preparing the meal, and the cooking ways of Houmas and other nations in the region back then. Well, maybe one difference, all of their cooking is normally done outdoors over a fire pit, whereas ours is usually done over the fire of an indoor hearth. Nevertheless, boiling, baking, broiling, roasting, frying, and parching are all accomplished on the bayous and marshes surrounding La Fourche just as in the royal kitchens of Paris. Separate pots are used for each type of food prepared. Meat, vegetable, grains, or fish are usually cooked separately, except when combined in common soups, porridges, stews, and mush. Whereas we use olive oil, lard and butter for cooking, and here in the New World bear oil is mainly used. Now it's time to take or catch and enjoy the results of our labors.

RECIPES

BASIC FRIED FISH OR SHELLFISH

Frying means cooking something in hot oil. In colonial Louisiana that meant either bear oil, olive oil, lard, or butter. Seasoning the seafood with some salt and placing it into the heated oil is the simplest method. One can fry in deep fat (about an inch or two in a home kitchen) or simply in a pan coated with the fat or perhaps a quarter to a half inch in depth. Seafood generally cooks through very quickly. Depending on the size and thickness of the food being cooked, anywhere from a minute on each side to no more than five minutes a side should do. If deep fat is used the fish, oysters, shrimp, etc. will be done when it floats. That's it!

The art of turning cooking into cuisine is what makes a culture like the Creole famous and sought after. Knowledge, experience, openness to new ingredients and methods, a sense of simplicity, and even some playfulness all combines to make a process as simple as frying into a work of art. A first step may be adding more spices and herbs to the seafood before the frying. A common second step is to "bread" the seafood in flour, breadcrumbs, or a combination of both. After these have been done and tested to your taste, the addition of sauces or the combination of other meats or fish with the fried morsels is a final step in the potential endless line of variations on the frying theme.

To get started, try these dishes to explore the basics of fried, breaded and sauced seafood.

FRIED SHRIMP

Remove the heads and peel the shrimp; reserve the heads and peels for making a seafood stock. Season the shrimp with salt and pepper, fennel and/or ground coriander to add that "Louisiana" taste. In a pan heat up your fat of choice until a small ball of meat or some bread sizzles when it is dropped in. Keeping temperature in mind, add one or two shrimp until they began to sizzle, then add the rest of the shrimp one at a time until they all are happily sizzling away. Let them fry until pinkish brown in color and they begin to float in the fat, no longer than five minutes. Remove with a slotted spoon or spatula and drain on paper towels until cool enough to eat. Enjoy!

BREADING (SIMPLE)

Mix a cup of flour and a cup of cornmeal together, add some salt and cayenne pepper. Begin with this simple mixture, then add other herbs and seasoning to taste. Vary the type and grind of the flour and cornmeal as well.

Place the mix in a clean, empty plastic tub. Get the deep fryer or a heavy pan ready, place the pan on the heat and add about one half inch of oil (of your choice). Have the fish soaking in water or beer.

Place a fillet or some "nuggets" in the flour, close the lid and shake the tub until the fish is coated. Using the same test for temperature (as above) place one small piece in the oil, when it begins to sizzle, add the fillet or the nuggets. Bread the rest of the fish in the same manner, and fry for about five minutes. Judge the time by the thickness of the fish and turn over at least once in the hot oil. Remove with a slotted spoon or spatula and drain on paper towels until cool enough to eat. Enjoy!

BREADING (COMPLEX)

Use two types of breading, a flour mixture as above and some breadcrumbs in separate plates. Soak the fish as above, but also prepare and egg/milk wash (seasoned as you like). Prepare your hot oil and proceed.

Shake the wet fish in the flour mixture, then remove fish from the flour and quickly dip into the seasoned wash. Remove from the wash and roll in the breadcrumbs. Repeat until you have enough to fill the pan. Place all the fish into the pan and let fry for five to eight minutes (depending on size). Turn over at least once in the frying process, remove with a slotted spoon or spatula and drain on paper towels until cool enough to eat. Enjoy!

These same breading techniques work well with shrimp, oysters, chicken, pork chops, and small, thin cuts of beef.

YOUR TRICENTENNIAL MEMO

About fifty miles upriver from New Orleans, the Mississippi opens one of its largest distributaries in SE Louisiana. On the river's western bank, a large bayou drains some of its mighty waters through a rich and fertile plain down into the Gulf. So large, in fact, that its name defines it, not as a bayou, but as a fork in the great river. Later usage has demoted it to a bayou, but Bayou La Fourche still remains the fork in the river at present day Donaldsonville. Even in the earliest French records, this river fork and the land around it was occupied.

Figuring out which Native group lived where in Lower Louisiana is an on-going puzzle. Between 1699 and 1803, the Louisiana Indians grew and shrank in numbers, they moved around, merged together, broke apart, fought with each other, lived with each other in the same villages and towns, battled the French settlers, traded with them, intermarried (or interbred) with Frenchmen, Spaniards, each other, and even some British wanderers. It is safe to say that basically they were rovers of the swamps and rivers of SE Louisiana.

Comparing and analyzing the colonial sources along with modern studies of archaeology, tribal histories, and Native Louisiana folklore, a picture emerges of nomadic groups who survived along the edges of the marsh and the various rivers and bayous that is the Gulf Coast of south Louisiana. In many ways the wanderings of the Gulf Coast natives mirror the semi-nomadic lifestyle of the buffalo hunters of the same era on the North American Plains.

In simple terms, all of these family groups and clan/tribes followed the game migrations. Seasonal villages were built along the group's migratory cycle. People came and went with the seasons or with the flux in population. Different groups merged together and broke apart as climate conditions, landscapes, game populations, and human politics demanded.

Unlike our neat Euro-American farmsteads, settlements, ranges, and ranches, which we claim and call our private property, Native Louisianans lived in the best places they could find. For over a millennium before the French arrived Natives had lived at the fork, definitely one of the "best places" in the area.

The French called the site Lafourche-des-Chitimachas, after the regional indigenous people. Here in 1699, Iberville smoked the peace pipe with the Chitimachas. Traveling upstream he met the Bayougoulas and the Houmas. Further on were the Tunica.

Later the Tunica joined the Houmas, then fought with them. The Tunicas eventually moved north to the Red River confluence and the Houmas south to Bayou La Fourche. By then, the Chitimachas and Bayougoulas had merged, and had been absorbed by the Houmas. In any event, the now consolidated Houmas spread out down La Fourche and over the marshlands on either bank. It was here that Frère Gerard found them in the 1730's.

Today, Native Houma Indians may be found all over Louisiana. Our readers need to be aware that although the evidence is overwhelming, the Federal government still does not recognize the Houmas as a Native nation! Typical of the injustice caused by the silly action or non-action of the US bureaucracy, we should do all we can to right this wrong. To learn more about Louisiana's largest Indian nation and their battle for recognition and against this blatant injustice, please visit: https://unitedhoumanation.org

‡ The descriptions of the local aquatic species and methods of harvesting them have been paraphrased from Kniffin, et. al., pp. 204 ff.

18
1730's – A SMUGGLER'S PARADISE

I love market day, especially in the spring. The market was busier than usual today. The freshness in the air drew us out of our homes. There are plenty of the usual staples available - rice, Indian corn, and vegetables - and crawfish will be plentiful, as well as alligator meat. Definitely some crawfish to bake in a nice pie, but me… I was on the lookout for the latest shipments from the spice and herb merchants, and of course, those we called the "traders."

They bring us goods of all kinds through the southern swamps of Barataria, Des Allemandes, Segnette, Lafourche, and through the harbors at Mobile and La Balize. If law-abiding citizens want to eat, we need these traders that frequent the bayous and the river levee. The authorities call them smugglers, but for the most part, they turn a blind eye to the smugglers' presence in the colony. No doubt because many of the goods they supply grace the authorities' own tables and homes as well and clothe their wives in nice laces and linens.

Without the smugglers, those in authority would suffer the lack of goods just as much as the rest of us. Nor do the traders consider themselves to be smugglers. They see themselves as a business supplying the colony with much needed goods - for a healthy profit, of course - despite the hefty restrictions of the government. True, some are villains and thieves, and many are rough and reckless, but most seem like normal men, and even a few are as debonair as the wealthiest citizens of colony.

Several know me by name, and as I passed by, I could hear calls of "Ho, Tante Suzanne, come see what I have today, just for you!" I smiled and promised to stop back on my way home to see their wares and chat a moment, but for now, I had just one thing on my mind… spices!

The food offerings this morning were many, and their aromas wafted toward me on the cool morning air. The scene on the levee offered food for the eyes as well. Colorful peppers from New Spain, mounds of salt from the local Natives, cloves, nutmegs, mace shipped from the exotic East Indies through Mexico, allspice from the Caribbean islands, just to name a few. Of course, I could now produce most of these herbs and spices in my own potager, but as always, space and time do set limitations. Besides, it is always nice to get out of one's daily routine, see people, and do something a bit different.

Like any good chef de cuisine, I try to think ahead as to what spices or vegetables would be useful in the upcoming months, and though my spice cabinet already held quite a few jars and packets of spices, I could always use more, not to mention a goodly store of salt and sugar.

Keeping in mind the luscious fruits and vegetables that would soon be coming into season, I am always searching for a new spice as well as to replenish the ones I was sure to use, and to my delight, today I discovered turmeric, a rich red-gold spice that would be excellent on fish and poultry, or even on vegetables. I purchased an ample sack full, enough for my kitchen and a good bit to share with Frère Gerard. It will be interesting to see what kind of recipe he will devise to use this spice!

I could not resist stopping by a mound of fragrant, spicy peppers. I remember Maman's stories of her birthplace in Africa and how peppers were a favorite there. In an odd way, I felt my ancestors with me on the levee. They, too, must have strolled through their village marketplace, enjoying the sights and smells, thinking of how to best feed their families.

Tomorrow, I will be cooking fresh chickens with a new combination of herbs… a savory mixture of thyme, celery, black pepper, sage, cayenne, and bay leaf blended with chopped garlic, bell peppers, chives, parsley, and green onions that I will sauté in rich bear fat. To this, I will add the exotic turmeric, and a bit a lemon zest for some zing. And green beans, fresh from the garden, with a loaf fresh bread.

As the day was drawing to a close, I met Frère Gerard and we sat down on the levee with cans of steaming coffee. I opened my apron to show my companion the treasures hidden therein. Inside were five elongated fruits of red and green color, a half-dozen precious brown nuts, and a handful of little dried out black pods. "Where did those come from!?" exclaimed Gerard. "Shush", I said, "you want the whole levee to hear you?"

His feigned innocence reminded of when we first met a few years earlier. We discovered that we shared the responsibilities for running the kitchen and the potager for a large family and were almost neighbors. As I settled into the new city and workplace, I often noticed this interesting looking fellow at the markets in town. He always seemed to be to be a bit out of place. Over the next few seasons, we became fast friends, sharing cups of coffee on the levee along with recipes, gardening ideas, and methods of running kitchens.

Earlier today I had come across one of my acquaintances from the bayous and swamps west of the city. This is why the spices were hidden in my apron. Now to be shared with my close friend were some wonderful chili peppers, nutmegs, and cloves. He gratefully accepted a few of the chili peppers, two of the nutmegs, but left the cloves this time around. On my part, I was already thinking of the wonderful puddings and desserts I was planning to make for the household's next Sunday dinner.

RECIPES

HERB/SPICE CHICKEN

As a preface to the following recipes, it may prove useful to see a list of the herbs and spices actually used by French chefs in the seventeenth century. The following are herbs, spices, and other seasonings were listed throughout the recipes of <u>Le Cuisine Royal et Bourgeois,</u> by François Massialot, Paris *by Chez Charles de Sercy, au Palais, Seconde Edition. M DC XCIII. AVEC PRIVILEDGE DU ROI.*

…parsley, green onions, cloves, salt, pepper, nutmeg, capers, truffles, mushrooms, garlic, limes, coriander, fines herbs, shallots, white pepper, sauces/gravy - anchovies, egg yolks, stock (ham, veal, etc.) oil, vinegar

Modern Adaptation:

- 1 large chicken, cut into quarters
- 1/2 cup chopped green onion
- 1/2 cup chopped celery
- 1/2 cup chopped bell pepper
- 1/4 cup chopped parsley
- 1 tablespoon chopped garlic
- 1/4 cup corn oil (unless you can get bear fat oil!)
- 1/2 teaspoon thyme
- 1/2 teaspoon dried sage
- 1/4 teaspoon cayenne
- 1/2 teaspoon black pepper
- 3 large bay leaves
- 1/2 teaspoon turmeric
- 1/2 teaspoon salt
- 1 tablespoon lemon zest
- 1/2 cup corn meal
- 1/2 cup corn flour
- 1 well beaten egg
- 1/2cup milk
- 1 cup melted butter

Preheat oven to 450 degrees. Heat the corn oil in a large saucepan, and fry the green onions, celery, bell pepper, parsley, and garlic until tender. Stir frequently.

Add the salt, turmeric, thyme, sage, cayenne, black pepper, oregano, and bay leaf. Mix well. Simmer over a low fire for 2 minutes, then remove from heat.

Spread half the mixture on the bottom of a 9 by 12 pan, then add 1/2 cup of the melted butter to cover the bottom of the pan. Place in the oven until the butter is sizzling.

Rinse the chicken and lightly pat dry. Add the milk to the egg and beat until well mixed. Put the flour, beaten egg, and corn meal in three separate bowls. Dip a chicken quarter into the flour until covered, then dip into the egg mixture, then roll in the corn meal. Repeat for each quarter chicken.

Lay the quarters on top the mixture in the pan, then use the rest of the mixture to spread over the quarters. Sprinkle the lemon zest over the quarters then dribble on the butter. Bake for 30 minutes, until the skin is golden and crispy.

Serve immediately, with a slice of lemon and a sprig of parsley on top.

BAKED GREEN BEANS IN CITRUS

- 1 pound of fresh green beans, washed and with tips removed
- 1/2 cup chopped chives
- 1/4 teaspoon salt
- 1/2 cup melted butter
- 1/2 cup orange juice
- 1/2 teaspoon lemon juice
- 1/2 teaspoon lemon zest

Place beans in a shallow baking pan. Add the butter, half of the orange juice, the lemon zest, salt and pepper. Toss well.

Cover the pan and bake for 10 minutes at 250 degrees. Toss and turn the beans, then bake for another 10 minutes.

Remove from the oven, then add the chives and the rest of the orange juice. Toss well and serve.

SIMPLE CHICKEN MARINADE

(From an English translation of original French 1752 recipe from the 18th century Les Dons de Comus)

When a chicken fricassee has not been eaten, to disguise it, one soaks each limb in beaten eggs, then you coat them with fine bread, and you fry them well blond (light golden brown). It only takes a moment, as long as the frying is very hot. We serve this marinade garnished with *perrsil* (parsley). Once you dip your chickens in a batter, and you will serve them the same.

- Leftover baked chicken
- 2 eggs in a shallow bowl, well beaten
- 1 cup fine breadcrumbs in a shallow bowl
- 1 cup flour in a shallow bowl
- 1/4 tablespoon each of dried parsley, cayenne, thyme, and rosemary

Cut the chicken into uniform and manageable pieces.

Add the herbs and spices to the flour and mix well until blended. Dip a piece of chicken into the flour and coat it well, then dip into the eggs, and finally coat with breadcrumbs.

Repeat for each piece of chicken. Deep-fry until golden brown. Remove from oil, drain, then lightly sprinkle with parsley and salt.

CHICKEN LE BALIZE WITH A CARIBBEAN KICK

- 1 small onion or half a large one
- 1/2 a green pepper
- 1 stalk of celery
- 5 toes of garlic
- 1/3 of a bunch of parsley
- 1 jalapeño or to taste
- 2 teaspoons allspice
- 1 teaspoon ginger
- 1/4 teaspoons cayenne or to taste

- Salt to taste
- Corn flour/or meal
- 2 large chicken breasts and 3 leg quarters
- 1 large, sweet potato, sliced in circles (like chips) or sticks - your choice

Chop the veggies into a traditional Louisiana mirepoix (onions, green peppers, celery and carrots). Make a rub with some cornmeal and the spices. In the bottom half of a broiler pan (the kind that used to come with new stoves - maybe still do???) sauté the mirepoix for about 10 minutes, add some chicken stock, if it dries out too much.

Rub the chicken pieces with the spiced cornmeal. Place some sliced sweet potatoes in the bottom of the pan. Grease the top sheet of the pan, arrange the chicken on the top with the remaining potato slices. Bake at 350° for 2 hours.

CRAWFISH PIE

(English translation from *Tourte l'ecre*visses - Massialot Cookbook)

Cook the crawfish with a glass of white wine after washing them well. Take the paws and tails, and pile everything else in a mortar, to pass it through the challis (? an early blender?) with a little bouillon & hot butter. Then rearrange the whole in your *tourtiere* (a pie pan or pie shell), with salt, pepper, nutmeg, chives, mushrooms in pieces; (join or put together) the other pie shell on top, seal it around the edges and cook.

Serve with lemon juice. You can also chop your crawfish, & make a paste of them with carp milt, mushrooms, pike, morels, truffles, butter & other seasonings. Serve with lemon or orange juice.

<u>Modern Adaptation:</u>

- 1 pound crawfish tails
- 2 pie shells

- 1/2 cup bell pepper
- 1 tablespoon chopped turnip
- 3 toes garlic
- 1 stalk celery
- 1 cup sliced mushrooms
- 1/2 teaspoon salt
- 1/4 teaspoon cayenne pepper
- 1/4 cup basil leaves
- 1/4 teaspoon thyme
- 2 tablespoons butter
- 1/4 cup dry white wine
- 1/4 cup heavy cream
- 1 cup vegetable oil
- 1 cup all-purpose flour

Bake one pie shell first about 10 minutes in a hot oven (450) or until brown, cool.

First you make a roux. For this recipe we want to make a blond - or light golden brown - roux. In a heavy pan or skillet, heat the oil until it just barely begins to smoke. Using a whisk, sprinkle in a little of the flour and whisk to blend. Repeat this until all the flour has been mixed in. Roux can easily burn, so don't stop stirring! (See Chapter 4 for roux instructions.) When it is blond, remove it from the heat and pour it into another bowl so it will not burn in the hot pan.

Finely chop all the vegetables and add to the pan. Sauté the mushrooms and all the vegetables until tender. Add the rest of the ingredients, and 1/4 cup of the roux, then reduce heat and cook for 10 minutes until much of the liquid is gone. Set mixture aside for 30 minutes to cool and thicken.

Pour mixture into baked pie shell, then cover with second pie shell. Bake until golden brown.

YOUR TRICENTENNIAL MEMO

As Suzanne's story shows, many of the ingredients in French Louisiana are no different from those elsewhere in the world… a fish is a fish, and lemon is a lemon, and beef in one part of the world is the same as beef in another part of the world. It was the variation of ingredients from so many different cultures that sparked the Creole cooking style.

Alligator, turtle, and crawfish are probably the most exotic protein sources in use along the Gulf Coast, and along with shrimp, fish, oysters, and crabs (fairly "normal" along any seashore), Louisiana game, beef, pork, and poultry are the same as any found in the American colonies. Grains, fruits and vegetables found here are also pretty universal.

It is the use of herbs and spices in Creole cuisine that set it apart in the culinary world. It was the imaginative use of these herbs and spices that cooks like Suzanne and Frère Gerard infused into their "normal" recipes that began the Creole cooking traditions that we have inherited.

Many cooks like Suzanne had been born into a world where the chili, in its myriad varieties, was a common kitchen item. Allspice, native to the Caribbean, was also common by the 1700's. Nutmeg, mace, and cloves were under the monopoly of the Dutch controlled East Indies. They were expensive, but not too uncommon.

As for herbs to be found in a New Orleans kitchen like Suzanne's, the ancient herbs of the Old World included tarragon, chervil, thyme, sage, rosemary, parsley, green onions, basil, savory, capers, mushrooms, garlic, limes, coriander, shallots, and bay leaf. Virtually all of these herbs could be found growing in the backyard potagers of the Louisiana capital. By the time Governor Bienville retired (c. 1740), cooks could look out at their potagers and see even the most exotic vegetables, fruits, herbs, and spices from almost every continent on Earth.

Legitimate mercantile trade between the great maritime empires as well as resources which came up from the bayous north and west of the Balize and Barataria supplied New Orleans with just about anything that could be grown in a garden. Added to the Old World produce, cooks early on included many herbs and vegetables from the New World, including file' (sassafras), pecans, and cayennes. Cocoa and vanilla beans, however, still had to be brought in from New Spain.

Given these copious collections of spices, vegetables, and herbs that could be had in and around New Orleans in the mid-eighteenth century, it remained for the cooks and chefs to explore tastes, experiment with various flavor combinations, and create dishes for their respective families. Those first Creole cooks were able to apply the age-old cooking techniques and uses of seasonings from Africa and Europe to a New World palette of foodstuffs. Louisiana and the nearby coast and streams expanded availability of seafood and the forests to the north added American wild game to the Louisiana diet.

Along with their traditional seasonings and garnishments, New Orleans' location at the apex of the Mexican Gulf's trade network added allspice, pecans, beans, squash, and maize. The genius and culinary heritage of those early Creole chefs and their kitchen apprentices succeeded in creating an entirely new, unique, and American culinary tradition.

AN ESSAY

smuggle | 'sməgəl | verb [with obj.] move (goods) illegally into or out of a country: *smuggling cigarettes from Gibraltar* | (as noun, *smuggling*): *cocaine smuggling has increased.*

In the Western Hemisphere, the newly christened "Atlantic World", during the 17th and 18th centuries, smuggling was a way of life. The following essay proposes that, for all intents and purposes, smuggling was normal in New World marketplaces, including New Orleans. Furthermore, the market at New Orleans included the spices, vegetables, and herbs that were commonly found in the gardens and marketplaces of Mexico, Europe, the Mediterranean, Africa, and South America. These (usually illicit) foodstuffs, combined with the victuals available in Louisiana through normal food channels, i.e., meats, grains, oils, fruits and vegetables, etc., became blended together to create the foundation of Louisiana Creole Cuisine.

New Orleans sits at the geographical apex of the colonial trade networks of the Caribbean and Gulf of Mexico. Throughout the 18th and 19th Centuries, it was the link between these networks and the North American continent. It served as the exchange depot between the continent and the Atlantic empires of Spain, France, and the Netherlands (and to a limited extent, the British, as well). When combined with the history, legends and stories of the piratical activity of the Lafitte brothers at the turn of the nineteenth century, these facts would seem to indicate that the New Orleans market was a smuggling capital of the Gulf/Caribbean region throughout the 1700's. Central to this "culinary history" is whether or not there is a case for such smuggling, specifically of foodstuffs, into the New Orleans market. Our time frame is limited to the French colonial period, officially 1718 to 1763 in New Orleans itself, but extended to 1699 to 1770 for the lower Louisiana colony. The verifiable and the probable contents of a typical Creole pantry in French New Orleans rests on the outcome of this question.

There are numerous foodstuffs and ingredients that can be verified in the kitchens of the colonial capital. Available historical records are replete with reference to various protein sources (meats, fish, eggs, nuts, cheese), and grains (maize, rice, wheat flour, etc.), and fruit (oranges, pineapple, grapes, plums). They are less helpful in referring to vegetables which tend not to specify. Sources usually refer to them as generic "vegetables". And even less so to herbs and spices, which are perhaps the defining flavors of New Orleans' cuisine. Items of specific interest in this study are tomatoes, pepper varieties, clarification of garden vegetables, and spices available through world trade.

Without question, the most famous smugglers/pirates in Louisiana history were the Lafitte brothers, Pierre and Jean. While certainly part of the history of French Louisiana, their activity in Barataria, Lafourche, Baton Rouge, and New Orleans post-dates the time frame of this work. Nevertheless, while the brothers Lafitte brought notoriety, a certain acceptance, economic and organizational refinement, and great profitability to Gulf Coast piracy and smuggling, they did not invent it. They inherited it. A brief excerpt from Lyle Saxon's Lafitte, the Pirate best sums up this legacy.

"For 50 years before Lafitte saw it {in 1810} men and women had been living on Grand Isle and there were a cluster of houses half buried in the rank undergrowth.

Smuggling was only a part of the Islanders lives, for they were also trappers and fishermen, their luggers made the long journey to the New Orleans market over and over again, carrying loads of fish and shrimp and oysters. They knew these curving bayous as the average city dweller knows the streets between his home and his office. The reedy labyrinths of Barataria held no mysteries for them.

They had learned 100 hiding places for themselves and their boats in the vicinity of the city and when their luggers were loaded with contraband goods rather than with fish, they felt safe from pursuit or attack.

For nearly 50 years they had pursued their dual interests {smuggling and fishing}... it was an accepted thing..." (pp. 40-41)

"The pirate's vessels' brought in shipload after shipload of captured slaves to the harbor at Barataria; and the terrified savages ladened with chains, were dragged into the barracoon.

Prior to 1810, ... the smugglers had bought their slaves from Cuban slave traders. But under Lafitte's regime a simpler and more direct method of supply was arranged. Nowadays the ships from Barataria went well armed and well manned. They lay in wait off the Cuban coasts and intercepted the slave ships as they came from Africa. Instead of buying the cargoes they stole them, and frequently burnt or scuttled the ships. Or sometimes the vessel with its cargo, but oddly empty of crew, was brought back to Grande Terre. And all of this in the name of Spanish prizes.

This kind of "purchase"- as the corsairs called it - had double advantage: the slaves cost nothing, and the long voyage to Africa was eliminated. Then to, with Lafitte's powerful connections in New Orleans, the slaves were easily sold.

Other richly laden prize vessels were brought into port: merchantmen, their holds filled with silks and spices from India ... At one time Lafitte's storehouse was filled with goods of English manufacture. All this of course from Spanish vessels ... or so it was said." (p. 46)

Saxon, Lyle. Lafitte the Pirate.

Two items of note may be drawn from this description. First, the dating of organized smuggling in the New Orleans region goes back to at least 1760 and probably earlier. Second, the mention of specific merchandise, other than slaves, which were the primary stock of the smugglers, namely "holds filled with silks and spices from India."

The Lafitte brothers not only assumed control over most of SE Louisiana's smuggling activities, but more importantly, they came into the acquired knowledge of decades of exploration and exploitation of the watery pathways and passes between New Orleans and the Gulf. Legitimate trade and travel passed up the Mississippi from the government post at the Balize to the city and beyond as well as the established passage through Lake Pontchartrain and Bayou St. John.

By the beginning of the nineteenth century, the Carondelet Canal allowed water passage for trade and travel up to the walls of the city. The Lafitte's' predecessors, meanwhile, during the eighteenth century, established trade ways beyond the ken of the French or Spanish authorities from the islands of Barataria Bay and the mouths of Bayou Lafourche. Traveling up Lafourche from the Gulf to its Mississippi source at Lafourche-des-Chitimachas (now Donaldsonville, La.) was a relatively straight shot. There had been a settlement there since before the arrival of the French in 1699. The other passage, up through the swamps from Barataria Bay to the riverbank opposite today's Audubon Park was somewhat trickier.

This map shows the route through Barataria Bay to Bay Dogris, then up Bayou Perot into Lake Salvador. At the northern end of this lake is the outlet to Bayou Segnette which takes one to the river and the modern town of Marrero.

Prior to the Lafitte's activity in the early 1800's, there is evidence that these routes had been well established by the 1750's. While there are no records of this trade - smugglers rarely keep books - there is no reason not to suppose that as soon as New Orleans was able to receive travelers and trade, someone from the coast was willing to supply the markets. The following remarks by two later scholars would seem to settle this question of the existence of a thriving smuggling economy in French Colonial Louisiana.

"During the 16th and 17th centuries, especially among the Spanish and French colonies (less so with the British and Dutch) "... the American colonies were chronically short of hard currency. Existing for the benefit of the mother countries, they were ... not supposed to develop their own commerce with each other. The colonists would have starved if they had followed the Empires' rules. Almost everything they needed had to imported. But they were only allowed to buy their supplies from vendors (approved by the mother state) at a high price ..."

"With the Caribbean "a Spanish lake", ... The only ways for the other nations of Europe to participate in New World commerce were through contraband, which became a way of life for the colonists early on, and through piracy. The colonists developed methods of conducting local business by barter and traded with forbidden ships that were floating bazaars."

"Santo Domingo withered from inattention ... as Havana rose in importance. Contrabandists of various flags came to La Española's north coast (Hispaniola), firing their cannons to alert the locals to come and trade. Buying up salted meat and hides, they drove up the price of beef in Santo Domingo. Worse, a cargo was intercepted of three hundred Bibles. Lutheran Bibles. The archbishop was alarmed; no Protestants were permitted in the New World."

"Madrid's response to loss of control over La Española was a spectacularly ill-advised order in 1605 to depopulate much of it, withdrawing the population to an area around the {capital} ... The entire northern coast of the island, and all of the west, was left unoccupied. ——"The pirates moved in."

From Sublette, pp. 26-27.

"In September 1714, it seems, a vessel bearing a permit from the governor of St. Domingue came to Mobile for "repairs" after

> *encountering a storm. There is no record of any trading transactions, but "disabled by a storm" was so common a pretext for illicit traffic that the statement at once makes one suspicious."*
>
> *The Crozat regime tried to prevent unauthorized trade with the colony but this only "increased the popular ill-will because of the great need at the time of foodstuffs. Early in 1716 a request for {food} was sent to St. Domingue." Some supplies were sent including rice, brandy, and wine, but at exorbitant prices. The regime then tried to establish St. Domingue as a "general depot of food supplies for the province {of Louisiana}. Nothing was done with the suggestion and smuggling seems to have become more common than ever.... In September 1716, {even} Bienville on his own account sold 800 deerskins at four reaux each and a considerable amount of lumber ... {the regime}* refused to alter the conditions that had caused the development of an illicit traffic; therefore, they were unable to suppress it."*
>
> * { } = my inclusions
>
> *From Miller-Surrey, pp. 370-371*

Shannon Dawdy, an anthropologist from the University of Chicago, does archaeological digs in New Orleans and goes well beyond these two academics. In her comprehensive work on French Colonial Louisiana, Building the Devils Empire, she establishes - as fact - smuggling in the colony during the 1700's. Her essay within, "Smuggling Empire", (pp. 115-134) provides ample documentation that the Louisiana economy was based largely, if not mostly, on the trade of illicit goods throughout the Gulf of Mexico and the Caribbean with Spanish, British, Dutch, and other French colonies. Her archaeological digs in New Orleans as well as her research as documented in her various books and essays all confirm that New Orleans was a significant part of a greater Gulf/Caribbean commercial world.

Through this network came the vegetables, herbs, and spices carried by the larger international trade of European colonialism. The 18th century can be viewed as the height of the much-touted Columbian Exchange through which flowed a delicious mix of spices from India and Africa, vegetable and herb seeds and plantings from the Mediterranean, Northern Europe, Africa, Mexico and the Caribbean islands.

Now what remains to be established is the nature of the goods traded, specifically food, beverages, spices, and vegetable plants that found their place in the potagers and kitchens of Creole French New Orleans.

Looking at the following scholarship regarding the foodstuffs issue, we find a good sense of just what sort of vegetables, herbs, grains, meats, were to be found in French colonial Louisiana.

> "New Orleans served as the central agricultural market where small farmers sold or bartered rice, greens, figs, sweet potatoes, eggs, and hams in exchange for imports such a sugar, coffee, wine, cloth, and furnishings. ... Plantation slaves came to New Orleans on Sundays to sell the surplus of their provision plots... Records show that they came on other days as well... to peddle produce and street food. ... Native Americans frequented town, peddling fresh fish and game, bear oil, corn, herbs, and Persimmon bread, in addition to deerskins." pp. 104.
>
> Building the Devils Empire, "Mercantilism and Alternative Economies"

While this food list gives us a good solid ground for what could be found in a typical Creole pantry, the task still remains to specify the "greens", "provision plots," "produce and street food" grown in the cities potagers, and the spices that were to be acquired through this "alternative economy." Throughout the various sources supporting this essay, there are many mentions of such particulars as ...

> "Indian trade items", "Household sundries", "Fine goods", "foodstuffs considered contraband", "French imports stocked in city shops, or browse for delicacies in the bustling open-air market."
>
> Dawdy, p.106.

> "France treated Louisiana as an importer of flour, alcohol, and a few more luxurious foodstuffs, but supply lines were too tenuous and shipments always too small or spoiled for colonists to rely on..."
>
> Usner. p. 198

{Author's Note: Could the "luxurious foodstuffs" mentioned possibly be the spices, herbs, and other luxury ingredients from France?}

Finally, as a finishing touch, we have this note from a newly discovered, translated, and published journal from 1720's Louisiana. Marc-Antoine Caillot came to Louisiana in 1727, as an employee of the Company of the Indies. In his luggage was a trunk, common among virtually all travelers from Europe to its colonial territories, containing…

> "Mercantile policies embodied by the Company's right to complete control over imports and exports rendered any alternative trading systems illegal but actual enforcement of those policies proved difficult. Not all the goods loaded onto the Durance (or other trading ship) could be considered legitimate. Before setting foot in the colony, Louisiana bound passengers (not to mention ships' officers) ranging from high-level administrators to soldiers destined for the lowest ranks of the outpost workforce took every opportunity to fill their trunks with contraband trade items that might help them sustain or further themselves once they traversed the Atlantic. Demand for metropolitan fashion accessories was high in the colonies…"

A Company Man, p. 60 n. 98.

M. Caillot also tells of stewing some birds with bell peppers upon his arrival in Louisiana.

A Company Man (p.72)

The documents examined so far, mostly based on government records and memoirs, are useful for setting the context of this culinary history. But they become inadequate resources for identification of the actual food and recipes that are being prepared. References to actual food, especially vegetables, herbs, and spices, are sporadic and very general in nature.

The 17th and 18th centuries saw very little in the way of cookbooks or recipes that were written down. Thankfully, though, a few were prepared in those years and do give us insight into these foodstuffs. For instance, François Massialot, did write a cookbook that was published in 1699 and revised

178 · JON G. LAICHE

throughout the 1700's. Simply leafing through his work, one can extract the following vegetables, herbs and spices by just reading through the recipes.

> ...*truffles, mushrooms, morrells, garlic, onion, St. George's mushroom, cucumbers, shallots, artichokes (hearts), asparagus, hearts of lettuce, beets, leeks, peppers (green & hot), carrots, celery: also, Lemon, oranges, orange flower water, limes, parsley, bay leaf, sorrel, chervil, thyme, fines herbs? Flowers? bouillon, anchovies, vinegar, oil (olive?), butter, fat rendered into lard, parmesan, wine red or white, macaroons, flour (wheat?), almonds, pistachios, pecans (native), quartre épices*, capers, salt, pepper, nutmeg, cloves, cinnamon, mustard, Filé, allspice...*

*quartre épices= pepper, cloves, nutmeg, ginger.

† *provided by Louisiana's Native Americans*

To this we can add the following food items that were provided by the Germans who settled upriver from New Orleans on the German Coast in 1721. By the middle of this decade, they were providing...

> "The gardens {of the German Coast} LIKELY (my emphasis) included leaf, lettuce, onions, radishes, cabbage, beans ..., corn, peppers, celery, endive and a variety of root vegetables. ... they quickly adapted to rice and sweet potato crops in Louisiana. Mustard greens, collards, turnip tops, beet tops, spinach, and purslane were also provided from here.
> As well as "chestnuts, peaches, apricots, figs, ... flourished."
> Mint and herbs grew in the kitchen gardens. Other important herbs MAY HAVE INCLUDED horseradish, sweet marjoram, coriander, caraway, fennel, and rosemary." ...(the German coast also provided) cream, cheese, and eggs; as the century progressed, this area was also providing pies made from cherries, apples, plums, peaches, strawberry, blackberry, raspberry, elderberry, custard, cheese, crookneck squash, and mincemeat."

Folse, John. The Encyclopedia of Creole and Cajun Cuisine. Gonzales, LA: Publishing Division, Chef John Folse & Co., 2004.

These above listings give us a much clearer picture of the ingredients and items that may have found their way into Frère

Gerard's and Tante Suzanne's pantry. Virtually all of these items were available to French cooks in the old country. This is not to say that some were not rarer than others. Even so, I feel it is not unreasonable to hold that, between international trade routes, the Columbian exchange, the Caribbean-Mexico-North Gulf coastal trade route, as well as the gardens of old New Orleans; many if not all of these ingredients were available to the cooks of French Colonial New Orleans.

Therefore, by the end of his first decade in New Orleans, Frère Gerard potentially had a pantry and a garden as well supplied as any in the old world. The only remaining item in question is the tomato. While this staple of modern Creole cuisine was certainly grown in Mexico and probably in the Caribbean during the 18th century, it was unpopular among the French who thought it was poison.

There is no documentation either way as to whether Gerard or Suzanne ever ate a tomato. Turning again to the work of Dr. Dawdy, we are only left with a tantalizing mystery as to the presence of tomatoes and their introduction into the gardens of French Louisiana and into Creole cuisine.

Some of the sources suggest that possibly the Acadians used them in their "country cooking" after the 1750's. Tomatoes definitely entered the creole equation during the Spanish period, roughly 1770 to 1803. However, beginning in the late 1800's, historians have used both documentary evidence and archaeological evidence to do their work.

We close this essay on ingredients with some evidence from Dr. Dawdy's digs.

> *"Archaeologically, seed types of the nightshade family are well represented, probably from peppers or tomatoes. Although native to South America and the Caribbean, these savory fruits had become key elements of many West African cuisines by the middle of the seventeenth century. The most likely route for their entry into the Louisiana repertoire was via enslaved cooks. In the French colonial period, however, this was not a transmission that fit with the French recipe for colonization, which, according to those scripting the colonial story, centered on the exchange of knowledge and resources between Native Americans and Europeans, including recipes and foodstuffs.*

It is remarkable that not one of our writers mentions these fruits or other ways in which Africans contributed to local foodways, despite the fact that Africans and their descendants comprised one half of the nonnative population and undoubtedly dominated the kitchen in slave-owning households. While we know that gumbo derives from the Bantu word ngombo, for okra, an ingredient itself imported from Africa, our writers do not mention either food."

*A Wild Taste of Food and Colonialism in Eighteenth Century Louisiana."
Shannon Lee Dawdy, University of Chicago*
http://www.academia.edu/1450883/

19
1733– HUNTING IN COLONIAL LOUISIANA

Now, once again the Holy Season of Lent was on the doorstep, and while beans and fish would be our main source of protein for the approaching six weeks, it was always necessary for a cook to have some meats available for the sick and travelers. Many of the hunting expeditions were already coming back downriver with the catch from winter hunt. Word came to the potager one morning while I was setting out some young sprouts of spring vegetables.

"Frère Gerard! The hunters are coming downriver!" a young passerby called. "They left Cannes-Brûlées this morning."

I notified Father Superior that I would be absent from the Presbytère this afternoon and probably most of the day tomorrow. It was one of my small joys to sit and talk with these wild and free chasseurs and even more to listen to the tales of bears, wild cattle, and even wilder Indians, as well as other adventures in the Arkansas woodlands.

Etienne and I went across the square to the levee, and I began teaching him how to assess the quality of the meat being sold. All in all, we picked up several nice large cuts of fresh wild beef. We brought these back to our kitchen where we hung a few cuts up to dry and began preparing the rest to be either salted or cooked.

As we shopped, I kept a lookout for three of my fondest friends who should be arriving among this company of hunters. As I impatiently scanned the flotilla of large dugout pirogues coming around the crescent bend just south of the city, the wind brought the unmistakable baritone of Robert singing his canoeing song. As the boats closed in on the docks, we began to hear Diane's lilting treble. I jumped for joy, began yelling their names and waving my welcome, soon catching their notice. Their third companion, Jacques, guided the lead pirogue into the soft mud at the bottom of the levee, and the others soon joined it.

The American Bison, often called 'wild cattle' by French settlers.

"Frère Gerard!" they hollered back, waving to me with smiles on their faces. Robert (row-bear), Jacques, and Diane were professional hunters who travelled the valleys west of the great river every fall and winter to hunt down, dress, and preserve their collective, cumulative kills to take down to New Orleans every spring.

These days the region stretching from the Mississippi up into the Ozark mountains was a hunter's paradise in every imaginable way. Clean air, clean water, a dense forest bursting with fruits, nuts, and wild game of every description, all there for the taking. Such country was the dream of every yeoman and farmer from Western Europe. In the old country such forests were reserved for the nobility. Resourceful and intelligent young peasants like Robert, Jacques, and Diane would have been forbidden to ply their trade - a trade based on the love and respect for nature and her ways - usually under pain of death.

But here in this New World they found that their hopes and dreams were only bound by their imagination and efforts. This was doubly so for Diane, for in the Old World, she would not have had the remotest freedom to follow a man's career as a hunter. She and Jacques were once a couple several years back but had come to an understanding that they were not destined to be a love match. Still friends, Jacques had encouraged her natural abilities with all things wild and to be honest had taken advantage of her God-given nature talents to find game and food out in the wild.

    I had come to know them at the levee market over the past few years and respected their love for and understanding of the wilderness, especially the notion that they only took what Nature would provide and never killed for sport or fun. I also admit, if pressed, that their stories were sometimes worth more than the meat and forest foods they brought to market.

    On this occasion, the three hunters had come downriver bringing a cargo of bear oil, buffalo, deer meat and skins, small game, turkey, and waterfowl. I was sure as well that they would have many stories of their adventures in wilds of Arkansas and their travels on the river. I particularly liked the stories about the Indians, and the different Native traditions for greeting and trading with visitors. Many such encounters involved much singing, dancing, smoking, storytelling, and feasting, all which must be done before bartering could begin. Sometimes, there were new herbs or spices brought from the Indians, and ideas of how to cook with them.

    I hurried down to the bank to greet the travelers and to assist them as they began to unload their cargo. This year, they also brought back a load of dried mushrooms and fruits, including delicious figs, sweet and thick with flavor. My mouth watered as I thought of how I would bake them into a loaf to be served with dinner this coming Sunday and make some into a jam to spread on our fresh baked bread in the mornings.

    It was all I could do to keep from tying them down and demanding that they regale me at once with tales of their winter's adventures. Having been closed up in the Presbytère and kitchen since the Christmas feasts and festivities, I was all too eager to hear some news of the world beyond New Orleans. The first order of business, though, was unpacking and setting out their wares for sale to the gathered crowds, all eager for news and something different to eat.

Finally, after offloading their winter's catch to first come, first served townsfolk and the rest to local middlemen and merchants, I sent my young assistant back to the Presbytère to begin the salting, drying, and smoking of my hoard. Someone touched my arm, and I spun around to see the smiling face of Tante Suzanne, who had also completed her shopping, and it took no convincing at all to get her to join us. She, too, will enjoy the stories and could offer a few of her own.

We soon had filled out our larder with enough meat, pork, beef, and alligator to last many weeks. This store would complement the fresh fish and poultry available almost on a daily basis either at the market or out of our own backyard. Now in the Presbytère we do not eat such rich meals, especially meals containing meat, very often. Nevertheless, I keep a lot on hand for the poor, for our friends in the city, and for special occasions as well. As the sun began to set, we all trooped back to the Presbytère for a hardy dinner and, of course, a long conversation.

In my kitchen, places had been set for us to relax and eat of some of my "famous" viands. Even the kitchen staff ceased their work and joined us for the reunion. As we ate a hefty pot roast with a rich cream and garlic sauce, I was mesmerized by tales of the friendly Arkansas Natives and the adventures that occurred while stalking their prey.

Their stories of battling with the Osage enemies for hunting lands and streams sent shivers up my spine. Diane could not resist scandalizing me and kitchen staff with stories of Jacques' spectacular amatory failures with the native maidens of the Arkansas Post, much to the young hunter's embarrassment and the general amusement of the entire company.

Meanwhile, Robert just shook his head at the silliness of their antics and smiled an avuncular smile at their somewhat tall tales. He himself could not resist embarrassing Diane about an incident wherein she actually caught herself in one of her own beaver traps, luckily with no serious injury. The staff and I returned to our work and the frivolous banter lasted long into the night. Finally, in the wee hours, the entire company - hunters, clerics, and apprentices - drifted off to sleep one by one, and I walked Suzanne home.

The following day, after a Mass of thanksgiving for the bountiful season and safe return of the hunting parties, the last of the meats were put away, Robert, Diane, and Jacques took their leave. We would see each other many times over the next several weeks. But for now, they went off to renew contacts with other friends and business associates, to visit some distinctly non-clerical haunts and establishments, and to make preparations for their next voyage up the Arkansas & St. Francis River Valleys.

RECIPES

COLONIAL BUFFALO STEW

On high feast days and special occasions, a stew of wild cattle and vegetables from the potager would not have been unusual. This "Colonial Beef Stew" uses a mix of ingredients common to French (and European) gardens of the eighteenth century, while adding some American Native flavor with a variety of peppers. Striving for more authenticity to foods of SE Louisiana in the 1700's, one can substitute beef for buffalo.

- 4 pounds stew meat (beef or buffalo), cut into one-inch cubes
- The Trinity: 1 medium onion, 1 large green pepper, 2-3 stalks celery), plus 4 toes garlic
- 1 medium or 1/2 half a large turnip
- 4 small carrots
- 2 medium parsnips
- 1 large sweet potato
- 2 small banana peppers
- 1 small hot pepper
- 1 pint of beer
- Oil and flour to make a roux, water

First, you make a roux! (see Chapter 4)

Chop fine the Trinity and the chili peppers, set aside to stop the roux. In a large stew pot, heat a half cup of olive oil (any other fat will do, except butter), add a half cup of flour and begin stirring to "fry" the flour, add another quarter cup of flour, continue stirring and watch the color of the roux. When it reaches the desired brown color, immediately add the chopped vegetables to halt the cooking process. Leave the heat on, and begin to sauté the vegetables, about 5 to 10 minutes until tender. Add the beer and enough water to fill the stew pot about three quarters full.

Bring to a simmering boil and then add the cubed meat. Bring back to a full boil. While waiting for the meat mixture to boil, peel and cut the turnip and parsnips; add to the stew. Return to a full boil, cover and move to a low flame. Let this mixture cook for about a half or three quarters of an hour. Meanwhile peel the sweet potato, cut or slice into small chunks or slices. Slice the carrots into disks about one quarter inch thick. Add to the pot and continue cooking until the meat and the vegetables are tender. You may need to add some more water about halfway through the process.

Serve over rice.

Author's Note:

Earlier this season Frère Gerard and his student Etienne stumbled upon an alligator in the Cypriere. Accidental as this episode was, it does illustrate the place of hunting in the Louisiana economy. The alligator also represents a cross-over between fishing and hunting.

Either way, it is acquisition of food from the local wilderness. Frère Gerard, working out of his convent kitchen, would probably never have had occasion to do much hunting. But he would have procured many of the products of the hunt from the marketplaces both on the levee and in the back of town.

One distinct difference between hunting in Louisiana today and hunting in Louisiana in the 1700's would have been the availability of the American Bison, or the buffalo. Well attested in the sources, beef from the wild "cattle" of the prairies west of

Baton Rouge and Pointe Coupèe was common on the tables of French Louisiana. The wild beef (or buffalo) came from animals that are very numerous on the prairies west of the great river.

As the hunters travel even further north and west these animals are very easy to harvest and not only does their meat taste good, but the Natives taught the settlers to use every tiny bit of the buffalo. The skull, the bones, and the horns are all used for the manufacture of various tools and implements. The tongue and the heart are delicacies of the finest flavor, the skins and fur make excellent materials for clothing, blankets, and coverings.

YOUR TRICENTENNIAL MEMO

Marquette and Joliet first came upon the Quapaw Indians at the mouth of the Arkansas in March of 1674. The Quapaw (whom the French called the Arkansas) welcomed them with open arms. After a few days of dancing and feasting among these beaux hommes who were "civil, liberal, and happy", the French expedition returned upriver to report their discoveries. The next French expedition arrived among the Quapaw in March of 1681.

After a short visit, they continued down the Mississippi to its mouth into the Gulf of Mexico. There, La Salle formally claimed the entire Mississippi Valley as a French colony named Louisiana. Upon the return trip, he left Henri de Tonti a huge tract of land along the mouths of the Arkansas (don't you just love how these Europeans went around giving land away which didn't belong to them ?!?!) and the Arkansas Post was established. La Salle, unfortunately, would never see the Arkansas again. Having found the mouth of the great river from the north, the Crown sent him back, this time to approach from the Mexican Gulf. As the story goes, he overshot the mark, got stranded in present day Matagorda Bay on the SW Texas coast, and was eventually murdered by his crew.

The Arkansas Post was the only European settlement west of the Mississippi at the time, and even though the post was sparsely settled and even abandoned occasionally during the colonial period. Even so, it continued to serve La Salle's vision as a waystation between the Illinois Country (Upper) and Lower Louisiana.

Excerpts from a section of the Arkansas History website, "European Exploration and Settlement, 1541 through 1803", continue the story:

The settlers, occasional and permanent, began hunting and trading hides and other animal products. Throughout the eighteenth century, the vast majority of the population of Arkansas was engaged in hunting for the fur and skin trade as bourgeois (trading post managers), engages (hired hands), and hunters. By 1712, the French had learned of the abundance of bears in Arkansas and the value of bear oil, which was used for cooking, as a protection against mosquitoes, or (when applied to the body) as a cure for rheumatism. The French and the Quapaw hunted and traded for bear oil, tallow, buffalo meat, and skins and shipped them to New Orleans.

In this economy, these traders were joining the Quapaw who were already hunting and processing animal products not only for subsistence but for trade with the French. The complementary economy of the two peoples in Arkansas was the beginning of a middle ground, a mixing of culture between French and Indians. In contributing to this middle ground, the French in Arkansas followed a familiar pattern. In the early eighteenth century, many of the French men in the Mississippi River Valley had come from Canada, and they helped determine the cultural and gender relations in the region. They were the coureurs de bois, Frenchmen who traded and lived among the Indian peoples in New France.

Within the frontier environment of New France, the coureurs de bois were able to assert independence from colonial authority and create relationships with the Indians of New France. By the late seventeenth century, those relations extended as far as the Great Lakes and the Ohio and Mississippi valleys. The Canadian coureurs de bois who made their way down the Mississippi found it much easier to make a living by hunting and fur trading than by farming in the cold climate and short growing season of Canada.

French hunters were first drawn to the St. Francis River. The river's mouth at the Mississippi River made it easily accessible to the hunters. Moreover, the bottomland forests and canebrakes at the mouth of and along the St. Francis River provided excellent habitat for a number of wild game, especially bison and bears. These hunters were the principal suppliers of buffalo tallow, bear oil, and buffalo meat to New Orleans and the lower Mississippi Valley. Acquiring the meat of wild game was necessary in early colonial days because of the lack of cattle and enough cleared land to raise them. At the end of every summer, hunters from Canada and the lower Mississippi River traveled on the great river to rendezvous at the St. Francis River, where they remained through the winter.

Once the hunting season was over, the hunters collected their products and began the process of making bear's oil, a skill they learned from the Indians and preserving the meat. One technique of meat preservation was to cut the meat from bison flanks into strips and dry it in the sun. The other was to salt the meat. The area around the St. Francis River proved valuable in the latter process because salt was easily available in the area. Throughout Arkansas, salt springs had long supported an Indian trade in salt. Besides being used to preserve the meat, salt was also sold in New Orleans. The success of the hunters was evident yearly. On one occasion in 1726, two Canadians supplied 480 tongues of bison to New Orleans."

Excerpted from: "European Exploration and Settlement, 1541-1803"

http://www.encyclopediaofarkansas.net/encyclopedia/entry-detail.aspx?entryID=2916 Accessed 2/27/17.

Since those early days at the Arkansas Post, Louisiana's very existence has always been intimately tied to its food. The above quoted discussion on hunting provides some documentary evidence of the birth of Louisiana cuisine. As promising and delicious as these foods indicate, Creole cuisine and the colony itself got off to a less than stellar beginning.

For the first thirty years, at least, it was often a toss-up as to whether or not Louisiana would - in the most literal sense - even survive. Nevertheless, by the middle of the eighteenth century, enough people had arrived, and enough land had been put under cultivation to insure a relatively steady supply of foodstuffs. During that first half century, the colonists, the generally friendly Louisiana Natives, and (after 1719) even the African slaves also provided a significant stream of protein sources through the ancient practice of hunting.

As the colony slowly evolved into reality, New Orleans (and Lower Louisiana) acquired its food in three ways. The first and legal way to acquire it was buying it from the company stores or the government warehouses that were supplied from France. The second way was to grow or catch it. All houses in

New Orleans and certainly all the farms and plantations around New Orleans had their own gardens. The third way was to faire la Marché, which is French for making or doing the market or making or doing groceries, which is the origin of New Orleans slang "making groceries," which is still used today.

The French Market in the Vieux Carré, that we know today, did not exist during the French colonial period. It was a creation of the Spanish administration in New Orleans after 1770. However, during the French era, there was a market on the levee and there were a few markets in and around the city. Most notably, the market at Congo Square at the rear the city was a place where the slaves were allowed to assemble and sell their wares among themselves and to the general public.

Then as now there were also the street vendors, people who came from the surrounding areas to sell whatever they had by walking up and down the street calling out their wares. Farmers from the German Coast and slaves from the surrounding farms and plantations sold their surplus produce to the colonists. Fishermen and hunters came to the marketplaces to sell the catches acquired through their industry.

The hunting economy in French Louisiana provides an interesting insight into the mixing of cultures that created the Creole society and Creole cuisine. Since the arrival of the French in 1699, local Natives had provided the colonists with game and seafood. This protein supply channel continued to flow through the entire colonial period into the American period, and, to a lesser extent, into modern times.

As is often noted, the very existence of the colony, at least during those first 30 years, was often due to the Indians feeding the colonists. Another protein channel, surprisingly, flowed through the African slaves who were imported into the colony. French attitudes toward the Natives and toward the Africans they imported as slaves was markedly different than the other Europeans who came to America. The Code Noir - the Black Code - gave French masters the leeway to arm their slaves in order that they might provide not only their masters but themselves and the marketplace with meat from hunting activities.

Finally, a segment of the French colonial population were professional hunters. By the time of New Orleans' founding, virtually all of the men and probably a goodly number of women in the Louisiana colony were hunters by choice or necessity. A few miles beyond the coastline of the first French settlements on the Gulf, vast game-filled forests and prairies stretched all the way to the Arctic. In the case of New Orleans itself, the first clearing on the river, in the 1720's, did not even fill what is today the Vieux Carré. Beyond and surrounding the primitive homes and emerging street plan was a cypress and palmetto swamp filling the space between the Mississippi and the Lake Pontchartrain.

Natives burning out the 'dugout' of a new pirogue

Native Americans had, of course, harvested these vast areas and waterways for meat and seafood as well as the region's natural nuts and fruits. It was only natural that as the European population continued to grow (about 500 or 600 in 1718 to over 2000 by 1730), there would emerge a professional class of hunters who would travel into the swamps, forests, and prairies to acquire a steady stream of meats and fish that were easily sold to the more settled public.

These hunters used the dozens of rivers, bayous, and lakes to travel to where the game was to be found. Up the Mississippi and its more southern tributaries was the most popular route into the hinterlands, and from the coast, the Pearl, the Pascagoula, and the Mobile/Alabama river corridors were well travelled. Leaving the Mississippi at Pointe Coupee or along the Red River and further north, the Arkansas, would bring the hunters to the vast bison covered prairies. Indeed, any direction into the interior would lead the adventurers into a land literally overflowing with game animals.

Among the first of the Ursulines to arrive in Louisiana, Sister Stanislaus {Madeleine Hachard} writes of large quantities of game being supplied to the Ursuline convent by hunters, including deer, rabbit, bear, squirrels, wild fowl, and wild cattle or buffalo. Domestic beef, pork, and poultry were supplied to the colonists by the farms of the German Coast as well as their own backyards and the plantations surrounding the city.

While professional hunters ranged far and wide through the Mississippi Valley to supply Louisiana and New Orleans with meat and skins, there was, as well, plenty of game (and seafood) to be had a short walk from the capital city. Surrounding New Orleans, and all the way upriver to Baton Rouge, was La Cypriere, the cypress/palmetto swamp which continues, to this day, to permeate the landscape.

The dominant flora was the ancient cypress, towering hundreds of feet high, their "knees" (roots) sticking out of the mud and water for yards around their base. These were interspersed with the deep-rooted palmetto, whose broad fans provided shelter from the rain, either under the palm itself or as roofs on everyone's first shelters from the meanest Native to the colonial governor.

Over the years as the city grew, lots were cleared, and houses, barracks, and warehouses were built, and the Cypriere was pushed back. Up and down the river, farms and later plantations, were established. Fields were cultivated and planted in rice, tobacco, and indigo, along with vegetable gardens, all of which made similar inroads into the swamp. But even today, the Cypriere stays, and if the land is not maintained, it returns.

Scene typical of Louisiana swamps

Even so, as a food resource the Cypriere was filled with game and waterfowl, with seafood, crawfish, and crabs. Along with streams and lakes to facilitate travel, the cypress swamp provided food and shelter to any pioneering spirit. It was a regular haven for runaway slaves, vagabonds, and other free spirits. Yet even these became regular food suppliers to the colony.

Daniel Unser, in what has become the standard treatise on the economy of the Louisiana colony, provides some interesting insights into the place of hunting activities within the French Louisiana food chain.

> *"But food is never simply an object of exchange; is also a means of exchange. By trading in particular food items, Indians, Africans, and Europeans interacted closely and influenced each other culturally. Colonies were 'dietary frontiers', as Ferdinand Braudel has observed, where 'eating other people's bread' involved both profound change and stubborn conflict. Production and peddling of foodstuffs in small quantities constituted a sphere of social interaction that generated a unique creole diet in North America while serving as a source of economic autonomy for Indian settlers and slaves in the 18th-century lower Mississippi Valley." p. 192.*

> "By 1708, when the colony of Louisiana numbered fewer than 300 people, Indians in the vicinity of Mobile regularly exchanged game meat and grain for firearms and gunpowder. For fourteen deer carried to Fort St. Louis in 1710, an Indian hunter could acquire his first musket." p. 193.
>
> "The Superior Council assumed responsibility for fixing the price of basic food items, forwarding on September 27, 1721, "That no venison shall be sold in the future priced above 16 livres for an entire deer, eight livres for a half and four livres for a quarter. "...according to a fuller tariff issued the following year, buffalo beef was set at eight sous per pound..." p. 193.
>
> "France treated Louisiana as an importer of flour, alcohol, and a few more luxurious foodstuffs, but supply lines were too tenuous and shipments always too small or spoiled for colonists to rely on... " p.198
> Usner, Daniel H. Jr. Indians, Settlers, & Slaves in a Frontier Exchange Economy. Chapel Hill and London: University of North Carolina Press, 1992.

As outlined above, residents of French New Orleans and lower Louisiana in the eighteenth century had ample food resources available to them. Native foodstuffs from the hunt, the bounty of Louisiana forests and waters, produce from dozens (if not hundreds) of kitchen gardens, both in and out of the city, imported items from France, from the Illinois country, and especially the Mexican/Caribbean (legal and illegal) trade routes supplied the colony and capital with lots of food. Nonetheless, there were occasional shortages of certain items (most mentioned are wheat flour, salt, and wine), but even these could be overcome with Native resources.

> See also the blog entry of August 7, 2012,
> Hypothesis: They Had to Eat" http://wp.me/p2luJc-1T

It has often been said in local cookbooks and culinary discussions that the essence of Creole cuisine is the ingenious blending of French techniques and styles to local ingredients. Here can be seen that this is exactly what the early citizens of this city on the crescent have been doing from the very beginnings of New Orleans.

SOMETHING TO THINK ABOUT...

Next time you are buying groceries, as you survey the meat case, skip the meats from long domesticated animals such as chickens or pigs and consider the more exotic choices. Turkeys, ducks, pigeons (doves), and quail were only found in the wild until very late in the history of animal husbandry, and while domestically raised in plenty today to supply the supermarkets, even now these fowl are still hunted by sportsmen.

As for the non-winged consumable meats, beef cattle by far dominate the American diet. Consider then, other meats such as rabbit, squirrel, deer, and buffalo (bison). Rabbit and buffalo are now raised domestically for meat, while deer and squirrel remain as one of the last vestiges of pure products of the hunt.

It is also wise to remember that even chickens, pigs, goats and sheep have been domesticated for only a few thousand years in the long stretch of humanity's search for "tonight's dinner." So, as you pick up that one pound of ground beef or, feeling adventurous, a package of dressed and cleaned rabbit, reflect on what those first Louisiana colonists had to do to get protein on the dinner table. It may remind you of that old joke about the recipe for rabbit stew:

"First, you catch a rabbit.

20
1738 – A VISIT FROM NATCHITOCHES

My nose tingled with the aroma of fresh coriander as I cut some leaves for tomorrow's grand breakfast. When Frère Gerard first gave them to me, I was not sure they would sprout, but to my surprise, they did, into a luscious riot of aromatic greenery. I tasted a few leaves, letting the mellow yet spicy flavor cover my tongue. I moved to the shallots, picking two from the ground.

On the way into the house, I chose a bright red pepper from the bush next to the kitchen. It would add a bit of heat to the dish. Stale bread rendered into crumbs and the fresh wedges of farm cheese I had just acquired yesterday from the German traders on the levee would be an excellent topping to the dish.

I knew Louis St. Denis and his lovely lady, Manuella, would be pleased with my creations. Having come from New Spain, Manuella will no doubt be familiar with cilantro. Most of the other herbs and vegetables I plan to use while they are visiting with us from Natchitoches will no doubt be just as familiar. But I would be willing to wager my box of recipes that she has never had them in the way I cook with them!

Still, I know Manuella to be a good cook as well, and when I found her waiting for me in the kitchen, I was not surprised. We sat together at the table by the window, sipping my special blend of cinnamon-spiced coffee and sharing our love of cooking.

I met Manuella some time back when she and Louis visited the city on their annual shopping trip here. Exchanging pleasantries soon revealed a shared passion for good food. Having come from a well-to-do family, she had been trained early on how to run a household and a kitchen, but her real pleasure was cooking. On that very first trip so long ago, I gave her several sacks of herbs and spices to add to her spice cabinet, which delighted her to no end. We parted as friends, and through the years, she and Louis never fail to visit when they come to New Orleans.

As we talked, she told me about their life on the plantation in Natchitoches, many miles upriver from New Orleans. Although she had her own chef, she insisted on planning the kitchen garden and even the daily meals, and she loves exploring new recipes, new spices, new ways of cooking.

When I told her of my plans for the cilantro, how it would be infused into beaten eggs along with many other ingredients, then covered and baked to a fluffy golden-brown omelet and topped with melted cheese, her eyes twinkled.

"I must have that recipe, Tante Suzanne" she said, "and I will share some of mine. Perhaps you'd like the spicy meat pies I make for Louis."

"And the day before you leave for home, I will take you to the levee to see the traders, where you will be able to fill your spice cabinet with all sorts of things."

Manuella smiled. "Traders? Do you not mean smugglers?"

I nodded my head in agreement and returned her smile. She had told me many of Louis's exploits of the past, and we both knew that some of his activities were the very definition of smuggling. She told the tale of how in 1714, when trading with New Spain had been strictly forbidden that it had not stopped Louis. Armed with his passport and a few trunks of merchandise, Louis, his three French lieutenants, and a few Indian stragglers walked boldly into the fortress of St. Juan on the Rio Grande in a manner befitting the emissary and trade ambassador of His Most Catholic Majesty of New France and Louisiana.

"Perhaps," I said, "but without them, we would not have the blend of seasonings or fruits and vegetables that we enjoy. And do not think for a moment that the wives of the city fathers are not down at the levee, trading just as I am. How else would they get the silks and laces and feathers that grace their dresses and hats?"

When the conversation turned to politics, as it often did in New Orleans, she told me how her Louis had resigned his command in Natchitoches and retired, and how his petition to the Crown to return to New Spain had been denied.

"It has saddened him greatly," she said," and I know he is not well because of it. He has never told me of the problems that led to this, but the Crown assured him that he will remain in royal service. It did not please him, though. While we love our plantation in Natchitoches, we did so want to return to New Spain."

Bust of St. Denis

I thought for a moment of asking her what maladies he suffered, and if he should perhaps visit the good Ursuline sisters at the hospital before returning home but thought better of it. I would, however, package several potent healing herbs for her to take back with her in the hopes of improving his health.

Our somber thoughts disappeared when I took a pan of fresh baked herb bread from the oven, and as we shared a slice with our coffee, our talk turned back to cooking, ending the day with a pleasant chat on the best way to cook a buffalo roast.

RECIPES

NATCHITOCHES BUFFALO ROAST

Acquire a buffalo roast of your choice (we chose an eye of round roast), about 2 or 3 pounds will feed a family of four. Prep for roasting as you would any beef or pork roast.

<u>Original (Tricentennial) Recipe:</u>

Prepare a traditional Louisiana mirepoix (or Holy Trinity plus Pope):

- 1 medium bell pepper
- 1 medium onion
- 1 or 2 stalks of celery
- 3 or 4 toes of garlic (i.e., The Pope)

Finely chop the vegetables. In a large iron pot (with cover), coat the bottom with olive oil, and sauté the Trinity until soft, add some beef stock and stir until hot.

Rub the buffalo roast with an herbal rub of your choice. Place the roast fat side up into the pot, cover, and put it into an extremely slow oven (280° to 300°) OR an electric slow cooker for several (4 or 5) hours.

When the roast it done, remove the roast and set aside to rest. The remaining sauce is now essentially a beefy vegetable stew. Add some more stock and cooking flour, bring to a boil, season to taste (salt, pepper, Creole seasoning, etc.) and let boil for 15 to 30 minutes. If desired, slice the roast and add the meat to the gravy.

Serve with potatoes or rice, green beans, and hot bread.

Colonial Recipe:

Much stays the same, except the cooking. In place of an oven or slow cooker, the Native or colonial would cook the roast over a fire, either enclosed in a large fireplace or outdoors in a fire pit. The iron pot containing the meat and vegetables would be placed among the hot coals at first for a half-hour to an hour, then moved to a cooler area at the edge of the coals for the remaining several hours. If the inside fireplace had the luxury of a built-in brick oven, the pot would have been placed there much like in our modern ovens.

BUFFALO MEAT PIES

- 1 tablespoon + 1 teaspoon lard
- 1 bunch of green onions (about 8)
- 1 stalk of celery
- 1 bell pepper
- 1 medium head of garlic
- 1 large onion
- 1 pound finely ground buffalo meat (ground beef may be substituted
- 1 pound finely ground pork
- 1 tablespoon flour
- 1/2 cup beef stock
- Salt, cayenne, red pepper to taste

Chop all the vegetables as finely as possible. Sauté in the tablespoon of lard. Push the veggies to the edge of your pan, add the teaspoon of lard, and fry-off the buffalo until it browns. Push the buffalo to the pan edges and repeat the fry-off with the pork. No need to add more lard.

After the pork browns, mix everything together in the pan, season with the salt and peppers, and cook for several minutes until well mixed and browned nicely. There should be no chunks of meat left. Remove from heat and let the meat mixture cool a bit. Add the flour and the 1/2 cup of beef stock. Use a potato masher or a dough cutter tool to thoroughly mix and grind the mixture. When done, the mixture should be moist and hold together in a ball.

If you are experienced at making pie dough from scratch, prepare enough dough for a large pie. If not, purchase pre-made pie dough that comes in a roll.

Roll out the pie dough and cut into discs about 5 inches in diameter. Fill each disc to about 1/2 inch from the edge and stopping in the center. Do not overfill or stack the meat mixture too high. Fold the dough over forming a half-moon shape, then crimp the edges together with a fork.

Deep fry for 4 to 5 minutes until golden brown.

YOUR TRICENTENNIAL MEMO

A FEW WORDS ABOUT THE HERITAGE OF NATCHITOCHES CUISINE

From the Trinity River in Texas northwards to the Arkansas River, Native American speakers of the Caddoan language inhabited a vast region where forest, hill, and prairie come together. When the French arrived to establish the Louisiana colony, two of the first explorers, Jean Baptiste de Bienville and Louis Juchereau de St. Denis, found three confederacies of these Natives living in well-ordered villages and towns along the Red River and in the surrounding territory.

For many decades prior to the Europeans' arrival, these Natives of the Eastern Woodlands had been very successful in answering what is perhaps humanity's oldest question, "What's for dinner tonight?" Consideration of Louisiana Creole cooking should begin in this region, for here along the Red River, the meeting of Native American, French, and Spanish cultures combined to produce foodways that have become unique in the world and are even sometimes called the first truly American cuisine.

The vast forests of North America - mostly east of the Mississippi* - were exploited by the Natives to provide a major source of protein to their diets. Along with the venison and the meat of small game and birds, the forests also offered pelts such as beaver, mink, and rabbit, as well as deer skins to be made into clothing and outerwear. Beyond the Mississippi Valley lay the great prairies where could be found the most prized of all resources for meat and skins...the American Bison.

> *"This forest environment enabled the Natives as a group to become the most productive farmers in the region. Just prior to the European colonial period (16th and 17th centuries), their economy was organized along the same lines as most of the Southeastern Native groups. In the spring, "men and women planted corn, beans, squash (the three sisters), and watermelon** together, and during the summer the men hunted for deer, bear, and small game in the surrounding forest, while women collected wild fruits and nuts. Following the fall harvest, the men went on extensive winter hunts, sometimes heading west to stalk buffalo." (p. 1)*
>
> Colonial Natchitoches. Burton, H. Sophie and Smith, F. Todd. Texas A&M Univ. Press, College Station, TX: 20082

* Note: In the Louisiana territory, the forests extended beyond the Mississippi through its western tributary valleys, into what is now East Texas, most of Arkansas, and the Ozark range of Arkansas and Missouri.

** Note: Watermelon actually came to America as part of the Columbian exchange. It originated in Africa in ancient times and spread throughout Southern Europe during the Middle Ages. Colonists and slaves brought the melon to America in the sixteenth and seventeenth centuries when it was adapted by Native Americans.

As Bienville and St. Denis explored the Red River valley, they encountered the Natchitoches Indians who were a Caddoan speaking confederacy made up of three tribes. They comprised the eastern-most group of three Caddo confederacies which occupied the western edge of the Eastern Woodlands.

This first contact was only a quick reconnaissance mission. In the years to follow, as the French settlers pushed beyond the coastal swamps and beaches of the northern Gulf Coast in the early 1700's, that adaptation and mingling of the Native, French, and African foodways would begin to take shape.

The early pioneers really had little choice as the political situation in France did not, or would not, provide much support to the fledgling Louisiana colony. Indeed, it is one of the major themes of this work to show that Louisiana, as neglected as it was by France, was able to survive and grow, and by the time of Spanish rule in the 1760's, it had become a reasonably healthy colony.

In both north and south Louisiana, the Native Americans introduced Europeans and Africans to grains such as maize used for bread, and grits; crops like sweet potatoes, squash, and beans, and local game including deer, turkey, and fish, along with many other newly accessible foods. The Red River Indians added agricultural tips and techniques to this emerging food culture.

Their native cooking methods were not that much different than those of the new European settlers, with the only major difference being that the Natives cooked outdoors, while the settlers preferred to cook indoors. However, in the early decades in Louisiana there were not many "indoors" to be had, so the colonists had to deal with outdoor cooking as well. As the colonial era progressed, the Natives would also be instrumental in helping the Europeans adapt to the inland and coastal fishing techniques of the New World. This resource would evolve into a central feature of the food culture the Gulf South.

The newcomers added foods of importance to these Native resources. Europeans brought carrots, turnips, beets, cabbage, and lettuce. In the ensuing decades, Africans contributed okra, yams, peanuts (although originally from South America), watermelon, collards, hot peppers, and pepper sauce. Pork was central to the early settler's diet, so many pigs were brought to the new world, and pork was soon adopted by the Natives.

Germans from the Rhineland, who arrived in Louisiana before the Acadians, contributed sausages such as andouille and boudin, and Creole or brown mustard. The Caribbean influence was later incorporated through the bean and rice dishes like red beans and rice or *congri* (crowder peas and rice). Native Americans also more specifically contributed filé and a fondness for corn bread.

When the French established a trading post on the Red River among the Natchitoches group, the interests of New Spain were aroused and a Spanish post was created fifteen miles to the west at Los Adaes, further streamlining this basic food production economy. These settlements created the Louisiana/Texas border which has existed up to the present day. Because of this border connection, Natchitoches became one of the success stories of French Louisiana, as the triple connection between Native Americans, the French, and the Spanish produced an active and vibrant trading system.

Such is the story of steady growth throughout both the French and Spanish colonial periods that constitutes the history of Colonial Natchitoches. The sequence of Indian trade, plantations, and ranches as means of production gave rise to a settlement that was one of the most important imperial frontier posts of the eighteenth century.

In early 1714, St. Denis, twenty-four Frenchmen, and some Natchitoches Indians began building a fort and two warehouses on an island in the Red River near the villages of the three Natchitoches tribes - the Yatasi, Dousitioni, and Natchitoches. The fort was named St. Jean Baptiste de Natchitoches, and the two warehouses became the core of the future town. St. Denis had been ordered there by LaMothe de Cadillac, Governor of Louisiana, to open trade with the Natives, and, possibly, the Spanish. Indeed, for the first few decades, the new settlement's economy was based on this Native and interimperial (illegal) trade.

The mercantile economics that dominated the European colonial activity during these centuries established that colonies only existed to serve the Mother Country. As such, trade between the Spanish, French, and British territories in the New World was forbidden. The reality for the colonists of these three empires was that such trade was required sheerly for survival.

Smuggling was a way of life for most Americans of the seventeenth and eighteenth centuries. St. Denis, on his mission to Natchitoches and beyond, was officially there to search for and assist a Spanish priest in East Texas. His REAL mission was to open trade between New Spain and Louisiana.

A caballero of New Spain

His many adventures in New Spain (Mexico), his successful marriage to a high-born Spanish Señorita, as well as his leadership of the Spanish entrada into the Texas province were all a result of his trade negotiations with the Spanish authorities. Official trade was never established, but the provinces of New Mexico and Texas supplied western Louisiana with cattle, horses, and sometimes hard coinage through most of the French colonial period and, of course, officially during the Spanish regime in Louisiana.

Three phases of settlement at Natchitoches can be seen as a cornerstone in the development of the Louisiana colony and the foundation of the Creole culinary tradition.

Phase 1 - Trade

As a general rule, the opening phases of French colonization in America entailed establishing relationships with the local Natives. St. Denis had proved especially adept at this task. His earlier travels and explorations with Bienville and others around the Louisiana territory had shown him to be a natural diplomat with the locals and, further along, with the Spanish authorities in New Spain and Texas. The Louisiana governor, Cadillac, who sent St. Denis up the Red River, was seeking to capitalize on his diplomatic talents to further build-up the colony's trade revenues.

The Red River Indians, like most Native Americans, were eager for European goods. Iron tools, weapons, cook pots, etc. were in great demand along with textiles and such embellishments as beads and medallions. In exchange, the Natives offered foodstuffs (along with agricultural and hunting tips and techniques), pelts such as beaver, mink, and rabbit, deer skins for the textile industry and, most prized of all, buffalo skins.

For the first few decades of Natchitoches' existence, this trade became foundational to its economy. The official Indian trade along with the unofficial trade with Spanish East Texas enabled the solid foundations for the colonial presence in western Louisiana. After settling in, the colonists soon found the need for a more reliable economic cash flow. This gave rise to the plantation stage.

Phase 2 - The Plantation Stage

The plantation stage had little or nothing to contribute to food history other than the general increase in money and wealth, which allowed for more supply and experimentation with foodstuffs. Plantations were established as tobacco farms first, and then evolved into cotton plantations as politics and the economy evolved as well. The creation of plantation gardens and plantation kitchens adds a culinary element to the gradual evolution of foodways but doesn't come into flower until the nineteenth century.

Phase 3 - Ranches

Another unintended effect of the plantation economy was to provide an impetus to the ranching phase. Ranching evolved by mid-century as a foundational part of the food culture of Natchitoches and became an ever-increasing part of the food supply chain of the Louisiana colony as the century progressed.

By the middle of the century, the economic sequence described above included flourishing cattle ranches and horse farms beyond the river's bottom lands. In the uplands and forests surrounding Natchitoches, this ranching activity also provided a living for the middle-class people, those between the planter elite of the plantations and the poor of the city who were relegated to remnants of the ever-shrinking Indian trade.

Another important aspect of the ranching economy was the supply of beef cattle; pork and mutton were also raised extensively.

Cattle along the Red River

The National Park Service provides an excellent summary of the end result of those Creole traditions discussed above:

CREOLE FOODWAYS

Homegrown vegetables and fruits, wild game, fish, breads and "extension foods" like gumbo and étouffée, combined with spices like red cayenne pepper and filé (dried, ground sassafras leaves), provide the basics of Creole cuisine. Other traditional dishes include smoked bacon, ham and sausage in various forms: boudin (rice and sausage stuffed casings), andouille (smoked sausage) and plain smoked sausage used as seasoning in other dishes. Tasso (smoked and dried strips of meat) reflects the American Indian practice of drying foods to preserve them.

> *Revealing a strong Spanish influence, meat pies (crusts stuffed with ground beef, ground sausage and spices, reminiscent of empanadas) and tamales are also staple foods in a Creole home. Other fundamentals of a Creole diet are dirty rice (flavored with savory meats and spices), cornbread dressings, stuffed mirlitons (chayote squash), gratons (cracklings or fried pork skins), and boulets (meatballs made of seasoned ground beef served in a roux or tomato gravy). With the abundance of pecans in the area, popular Creole desserts include pralines, pecan pies and pecan cakes. Café has long been a traditional drink in Creole households, as have lemonade and iced tea.*
>
> *http://www.nps.gov/nr/travel/caneriver/creoleculture.htm*

AN AMUSING HISTORICAL ANECDOTE

The War of the Quadruple Alliance
(aka in Louisiana as The Chicken War)

Philippe d'Orleans, Regent of France for his great grand-nephew, sold Louisiana to John Law's Mississippi Company. A new administration, led once again by Bienville, moved back into power, and incidentally began to build a new town at a crescent in the river. Louis St. Denis was left in command of Natchitoches. A new conflict in Europe - The War of the Quadruple Alliance - reached the Gulf Coast in April of 1719. Sandwiched between the company's new trading partners in Spanish East Texas at Los Adaes, and the harbor and fort at Pensacola, Bienville decided to act at once.

Bienville sent word to his friend on the Red River to prepare for war, and from Mobile, launched an attack on Pensacola. The battle for Pensacola has been likened to a modern football game by more than one source. The French kicked off by taking Pensacola almost at once. However, neither Mobile nor Pensacola were well supplied in those early days, so the victors had to send the Spanish prisoners to Havana because they could not feed them.

The Spanish moved into the Red Zone on their possession (to continue the football metaphor) by capturing the French officers and sailors who transported the prisoners and sent a small fleet to recapture the harbor and attack Mobile. They scored by driving the French out of Pensacola, but still holding the ball, they plodded on too long and failed in their attack to capture Mobile.

By this time, St. Denis and his Indian army had arrived from the West, and a French fleet had also shown up. The French got the ball back and scored again when St. Denis and the other French forces recaptured Pensacola. Once again, they had to ship the prisoners back to Havana, but his time they held the officers hostage against the return of the French ships and crews.

Meanwhile, St. Denis had left Natchitoches under the command of one Philippe Blondel. To ensure that this Western Front did not miss any of the glory to be had in this latest great war, Commander Blondel mobilized the Grande Armée de la Natchitoches - all seven of them - and led the attack on the Spanish colonial powers of Texas - all two of them - at Texas' easternmost post, San Miguel de Los Adaes. After scattering the few dogs that formed the first line of defense, the presidio at Los Adaes was sacked immediately. One lay brother and one ragged soldier who made up the whole garrison there were captured without a fight.

The battle was not over yet though. Among the French prizes taken at the mission was a flock of chickens, who resisting capture, put up such a squawking and fluttering about that the French cavalry was thrown into route, as Blondel was thrown from his horse. Blondel quickly reformed his cavalry (that is, the horse he was riding). The chickens were quickly subdued, and the French expedition returned to Natchitoches in triumph.

All hilarity aside, this action did give French colonialism a huge psychological boost. They had, after all, defeated the main "threat" to the existence of French Louisiana.

Finally, after all was said and done, the referees in Europe negated the whole affair with the Treaty of the Hague by giving everything back to the Spanish and returning the Gulf Coast to the status quo that existed prior to the war...but not before the French forces at Pensacola destroyed the town.

Oh... and they didn't return the chickens, either.

21
1740 – COFFEE, CHOCOLATE AND WINE

It was going to be a good day! The smell of freshly roasted coffee beans was drifting from the levee market into my kitchen on Ursuline St. behind the family home on Chartres. One nice thing about the central location of Louisiana is that coffee is usually not too hard to obtain.

Officially, while shipments from France are the primary source of this delightful beverage, they do not arrive with any regularity, if they arrive at all! But supplies from the Caribbean are copious and arrive with regularity though contacts in Spanish Pensacola as well as up the western waterways of Lafourche and Barataria. As such, I always have plenty for my kitchen and to share with my good friend, Frère Gerard, and his Presbytère.

I first met Gerard over a mess of shrimp and fish, fresh caught from the river. Dressed in his splotched and stained kitchen habit partly covered by his apron, he hardly looked like a monk. Over the next few seasons, our shared vocation, profession, and passion for cooking and kitchen management had fused us in a remarkable friendship. He loved to interrogate me about the fancy and special dishes and desserts that I would prepare for the Famille Marigny. On my part, hearing about his stews, bouillabaisse, sagamite, and breads he made for his brothers at the church taught me many ways to stretch my resources in the kitchen.

We spent many market days and pleasant sunsets over several pots of coffee discussing herbs, gardens, spices, recipes, local gossip, politics, import/export, and food supplies. Of course, we never solved anything, but we came up with all sorts of variations on the recipes we shared. We both engaged in many experiments both separately and apart as to the best way to brew a pot of coffee. While Frère Gerard's goal was to keep available a rather large pot for most of the day without letting it go stale, I did not have to create such a large amount of coffee for my family. I chuckled as Frère Gerard added more sugar to his coffee, breaking my reverie about brewing the dark elixir.

"I see your sweet tooth is no longer satisfied with just a bit of sweets, no?" I teased.

"No," he said, then smiled. "Well perhaps… but what is coffee without sugar? Speaking of sugar, have you met the new sugar merchant from Martinique?"

Over the past few seasons, we had gotten to be regulars in the marketplace where we were now able to trade freely with the merchants, and the smugglers often kept for us the rare items like the spices and other Caribbean and Spanish American imports.

Our conversation continued on yet another day. After one busy morning of bartering in the marketplace, we sat with steaming cups of coffee, discussing how we occasionally used the various spices in our cooking. One of the great challenges of being a cook here in this remote colony and, to my mind, one of the most enjoyable aspects of running a kitchen, is taking the plainest of our everyday stores of flours, fats, grains, and meats, and combining them with a little of this and a little of that to arrive at new textures and new flavors.

Soon our conversation turned to brewing coffee. For years, both Frère Gerard and I had often added things to coffee just to stretch our sometimes-meager supplies, but this was usually confined to roasting some grain or roots that would have little noticeable effect on the coffee's flavor.

"But what about other things," he said, "something that will add flavor, maybe some spices? We could try adding different things to the brew and see what happens."

I agreed that it would be a fun task. As we rummaged through my spice cabinet for possible additions to the brew, I told him that as a young child, I had heard rumors about the Ethiopians adding such spices as ginger, nutmeg, or cinnamon to their coffee.

"Of course, these spices were usually beyond the reach of our poor kitchens back then," I told him, "at least until we moved to Mobile and were running the prosperous ranch there. Even so, the master of the house usually didn't want his coffee to be an object of experimentation and I never really considered using those few expensive spices that I hoarded so jealously. Not to mention that coffee, itself, was not so easy to come by in those days."

But that was many years ago, and Frère Gerard and I were able to share coffee on an almost daily basis, especially now since Monsieur de Clieu had started his coffee plantations in the French islands of the Caribbean. Also, now that New Orleans has become more settled, British, Spanish, and Dutch ships regularly trade with Pensacola and Barataria, which makes access to various spices much more available.

We immediately took out the cinnamon, cloves, nutmeg, ginger, allspice, and vanilla beans, which certainly offered some interesting possibilities, and on a whim, I plucked several mint leaves from the branches tied to the drying rack.

"Cinnamon first?" I suggested. Frère Gerard grinned and nodded. "Then the nutmeg, vanilla and ginger... and maybe some cocoa?"

Like children with a new toy, we added cinnamon to our cups and reveled in its delightful flavor. It was a wonderful discovery, a particularly good fit for the winter holidays. Cups laced with vanilla, nutmeg and cocoa also added wonderful flavors, while ginger added a bite that would be useful when a person had a cold or a chill.

Nor was our experimenting limited to just coffee. We took down the tin of cocoa and played with it as well. It was delicious with a bit of vanilla or nutmeg added, but the addition of crushed mint leaves was absolutely delightful!

Cocoa is as available in New Orleans as coffee, and its use among the colonies around the Gulf and Caribbean goes back as far as anybody can remember. As long as there was a New Spain there was the trading of chocolate. If not as popular as coffee, chocolate is certainly second place among the special drinks that we enjoy here in Louisiana. One of our friends, Sister Stanislaus at the Ursuline Convent, wrote home - perhaps with a bit of exaggeration – that "...we drink it every day."

Our use of chocolate can be compared to our consumption of wine. Sometimes consumed on a daily basis, wine nevertheless is a distant second to the water we drink as we go through our everyday activities. We decided to experiment by creating a mulled wine, spiced with nutmeg and ginger, to be served warm. That brew was also a success.

As often happened, our conversation turned to wine, since Frère Gerard was concerned about laying in a supply of wine - both culinary and sacramental - for the Presbytère.

"Of course," I said with a wink," what is a Catholic Church without wine for the Holy Sacrament?"

He shook his head. "More so, what is a "French" Catholic Church without a good French wine, eh? You know as well as I that the erratic schedule of supply ships from the Mother Country makes the wine supply chancy at best. Also, the wine itself is inconsistent in quality. Sometimes the wine is of good quality," Gerard mused, "but just as often the wine is a very poor vin ordinaire. We have planted some grapes on the backside of the potager, but it will be a few more years before any meaningful number of clusters can be harvested."

"So," I said," soon you will be teaching me the art of wine making!"

He shrugged. "Until then, wine may be in short supply. Lucky for us, some traders are arriving from Barataria in the morning, with a variety of merchandise from Pensacola and

Havana, including some good Spanish American wine. Not French, but Spanish wines are almost as good. Still, we will need to be on the levee very early to make a good buy."

"So," I asked, "should we try to add spices to the wine?"

Gerard smiled. "As long as it is table wine and not church wine!"

Like children, we played long into the afternoon, and by the time I waved goodbye to Frère Gerard the crickets were chanting their evening song. So, this evening, as Frère Gerard made his way back to the Presbytère, we are resolved to become even more adventurous upon our next meeting.

RECIPES

COFFEE

There are no set recipes for flavored coffee, cocoa or wine, as everyone will like some spices and dislike others. Like Suzanne and Gerard, be daring, experiment, and have fun!

The Perfect Pot of Coffee

At its most basic level, brewing is simply gathering coffee beans, roasting them, grinding them, and placing them in boiling water. From this point on, all it takes is imagination and a variety of cooking techniques. Pouring boiling water over ground coffee beans is probably the most popular way of doing it, and this was certainly the method used in most colonial households. In 1710, a Frenchman invented the coffee bag, a linen bag filled with ground coffee which would be steeped in a pot of boiling water.

Boiling coffee is as simple as it gets. Put a pot of water on the fire to boil. Grind as much coffee as you plan to use. When the pot is bubbling merrily, spoon in as much coffee as you desire. The most common ratio is about one cooking spoon per quart of water.

The major objection to boiling coffee is that the method itself leaves the coffee grounds suspended in the finished coffee.

This leaves three options; (1) let the grounds settle, (eggshells help) (2) strain the coffee through a sieve or cloth, or (3) consume the grounds with the beverage.

The French method is to place the ground coffee in a cloth of some sort in a sieve and then place the sieve over an empty pot, then slowly pour the boiling water through the coffee and let it drain through the sieve into the pot.

This method requires a little more patience and skill, you want to let the grounds and the water steep as long as possible before draining into the pot as a finished beverage. Both of these methods are refined with experience, as you figure out the particular grind of the coffee between fine and course as well as the amount of the grounds to use in relation to the amount of the water to produce your perfect cup.

Adding spices to the brew is simple but will require a bit of experimentation on your part to get the right mix that brews the desired flavor you prefer. For cinnamon, cloves, nutmeg, ginger, allspice, and vanilla, begin by adding 1/2 teaspoon of the selected spice to the grounds, then brew as normal. For cocoa, start with 3/4 teaspoon or the coffee may overpower the chocolate flavor. Serve the with a dollop of whipped cream and enjoy!

SPICED COCOA

Hot cocoa is remarkable with spices added to it. You can follow the directions on the back of the cocoa can for making it into a hot drink, but if you use milk instead of water, or better yet, cream instead of milk, you will get a much richer drink. Vanilla and nutmeg go well with the cocoa, and cinnamon and ginger give it a bit of an enjoyable bite, but the mint is truly a delightful addition. Use fresh mint for the best flavor. Place several leaves into a cup of boiling water, and let steep for at least 10 minutes, then add the water to the cocoa mix. Add a peppermint stick to the cup and serve.

SPICED WINE

People have been making spiced and mulled wine for hundreds - if not thousands - of years, and it is a great way to improve an inexpensive vintage and the colonies received a lot of "inexpensive vintages" from the mother country. Wine does well when spiced with savory as well as sweet spices. Try a red wine with rosemary, or a white wine with sage. Of course, nutmeg, cinnamon, cloves, ginger, and allspice work quite well, and anise is a particularly good.

Boil a half cup of water and add the desired spices to the water. Allow to steep for 10 minutes. Add 1 teaspoon of the spiced water to a glass of wine and taste, then continue to add the spiced water slowly until you have the flavor you desire.

Beyond the wines received from Europe, the colonists were adept at making wines from local fruits. Muscadine vines were native to the Louisiana colony, as well as cherries, peaches, and oranges. All of these were used in colonial times to produce wines and brandies.

YOUR TRICENTENNIAL MEMO

The Columbian Exchange reached full flower during the 18th century. Because of the expansion of trade by the Atlantic powers and the increase of wealth provided by the new colonies of America and the East, the European upper classes had the means to explore and experiment with the new foods and drinks coming from these exotic locales. Also, the leveling effect on class and economic opportunity provided by the vast lands of the

New World allowed the expansion (in very general terms) of the European middle classes into the "good life."

The courts at Versailles, Madrid, Berlin, Vienna, and in Augustan England set the tone for fashion, frolic, and feasting. Imitated in the capitals and in the backwoods throughout the New World, culinary as well as other fashions became motivating goals among the frontier societies.

> *Discussions among culinary and other historians go far in illuminating these ideas:*
>
> *"But the great revolution at the end of the 17th century, so far as desserts were concerned, was, first of all, the increasingly widespread consumption of ices and sherbets, which had originated in Spain and Sicily, and second, the accompanying amount of dessert with tea from China, coffee from Arabia, and chocolate from America. There would be no point in recalling the countless debates regarding the properties of coffee and chocolate..."*
>
> *Culture and Cuisine by Revel, Pages 165-66:*
>
> *"In England, the coffeehouse was to develop into the gentleman's club, but in the rest of Europe it became a café. Marseilles appears to have had the first coffee house on the continent, in 1671. Paris followed a year later with a series of not-very-successful enterprises, and it was 1686 before the Café Procope - welcoming, clean and luxurious - opened, the first true Paris Café. Three years earlier (1683), coffee had come to Vienna, when the Turks - retreating from the siege - obligingly left some sacks of green coffee beans behind."*
>
> *Food in History by Tannahill, p. 275:*

Miller-Surrey's Commerce of Louisiana adds:

> *"... the settlers of Louisiana had been accustomed to exchange peltry and a little lumber for sugar, tobacco, cocoa, molasses and other island products as well as for European goods, which were often long-delayed if brought directly from France (this trade with the French West Indies abruptly stopped with the establishment of a Crozat regime)."*
> *p. 369*

With regard to trade with Mexico:

> "The Company (of the Indies) continued to attract Spaniards to this province. In 1722 the statement was made that during the four years preceding, many from Mexico had come to Mobile and... numerous commodities from that area were in use. The latter included... cocoa that sold at 18 and 20 livres a quintal." pp. 392.

In the 1740's under Vaudreuil:

> "... New Orleans became somewhat of a center for Spanish trade. To it came merchants from Cuba, St. Augustine, Pensacola, St. Bernard Bay, St. Joseph Bay, Portobello, Santa Maria del Darien, and Cartagena... it was proposed to send special boats up the river to carry their wares to New Orleans. This will enhance the value of their share in the piasters, smoking tobacco, cocoa, and logwood brought by the Spaniards." p. 404.

Miller-Surrey, The Commerce of Louisiana
during the French Regime, 1699-1763.

Similar to the documentary evidence above, original records such as ship's manifests, official records of trade and exchange, as well as explorer's journals and governmental communications abound, leave no doubt that coffee and wine were commonly available in coastal Louisiana. Virtually from the beginning of the colony in 1699, chocolate (cocoa), was always available, but it became more popular later in the 18th century after the accession of Louis XV.

This documentary evidence goes far in showing the existence and use of these beverages in French Louisiana. The Letters of Marie Magdeleine Hachard (Sr. Stanislaus in 1728) mention "...(the sisters) make much use of chocolate with milk and coffee. A lady of the country has given good provision of it." (Letter II)

Of course, none of these official sources include the well-established smuggling economy that provided Louisiana with well over half of its economy. Given the availability of these commodities there is no reason to doubt that during the French regime, New Orleans cooks of the first and second Creole generations (1730 to 1803) had access to these foods as they fed New Orleans, Biloxi, and Mobile as well as points north to the Arkansas River delta.

These eighteenth-century developments in the European (and colonial) diet set the tone for much of the modern use and misuse of our food resources.

APOLOGIA PRO CHICORY

The thing that makes New Orleans coffee unique is the chicory. There is little firm documentation that this blend was used in the early days of New Orleans, but the circumstantial evidence for this is overwhelming. Chicory (endive) was grown in French gardens as early as 1650, but exactly when the root became a staple in New Orleans coffee is an open question.

We know that the French used it to stretch coffee during the 18th century. Even Napoleon's quartermasters used it. We know the French in Louisiana drank coffee from the beginning, as it is listed in all the ships' food and trade records as a regular import. We also know that French Louisiana was chronically short of food supplies. So it should come as little surprise that putting these facts together and say they probably had coffee and chicory in Louisiana by the 1730's. It was certainly known and used by 1800. The inhabitants of Southeast Louisiana were drinking coffee 154 years before Seattle was even founded!

The Cafe' du Monde began serving its world-famous coffee and beignets (fried doughnuts dusted with powdered sugar) when Seattle was only 9 years old and hadn't even become a town. In 2006 (the year after Katrina) the Port of New Orleans handled 206,000 tons of coffee giving it 20% of the US market share. The Port of Seattle doesn't even come close. People travel from all of the world to drink New Orleans coffee. While Seattle may claim to be the "Coffee Capital of the Country" and have a lot of coffee houses, the coffee culture of New Orleans far outshines it in antiquity and ubiquity. Not only does New Orleans have its fair share of coffee houses, but virtually EVERY house in the city and region is a coffee house (certainly every house inhabited by someone of Creole or Cajun descent!).

Today, New Orleans is THE largest coffee port in the USA. And I quote:

> "As the country's major coffee-handling port, the Port of New Orleans has 14 warehouses covering over 51 hectares of storage space and six roasting facilities."
>
> http://www.worldportsource.com

So why the big secret? I honestly do not know, maybe we just want to keep it all for ourselves. It is also an ancient and time-honored tradition in New Orleans that coffee is NOT just reserved for breakfast or coffee breaks. Creoles and Cajuns drink coffee all day long.

New Orleans tradition also poses another question, when did coffee become an adult beverage? Mama used to fix us a glass of coffee-milk with a splash of coffee and some sugar in it on any given morning. In any event, there is nothing so sublime as sitting out on the veranda on a cool spring morning with a hot cup of café au lait (coffee blended with steaming-hot milk) and your favorite pastry.

The Port of New Orleans' first citizens were a diverse mix of backwoodsmen from Canada, craftsmen and troops from John Law's Company, convicts, prostitutes, slaves, and wanderers. In 1721, a census revealed a population of 470 people that included 277 whites, 172 blacks, and 21 Indian slaves. In 1722, the Port of New Orleans became the Louisiana colony's capital. After 1731, more reputable colonists started coming to the Port of New Orleans. By 1740, even though the city still suffered many difficulties, this population mélange was blending into the unique Creole culture that is New Orleans to this day. It is pleasant to note that our unique blended beverage was one of the levelers.

The following is not an inaccurate description of the coffee we drink in New Orleans!

Noir comme le Diable
Fort comme la Mort
Doux comme l'Amour
Et chaud comme l'Enfer

Or, en anglais ...

Black as the Devil
Strong as Death
Sweet as Love
And hot as Hell!"

http://www.gumbopages.com/food/breakfast/ca

22
1740's SUZANNE COOKS FOR CHRISTMAS

The wheel of the year turned once more, and Noël is fast approaching. This is easily my most favorite time of the year. Here in Louisiana, the weather is perfect almost all of the time during this season. It isn't as warm as when I was a little girl in the islands, nor as cold as the people from France often describe the Noël season in their homeland. Cold enough to brace the blood but not so cold as to slow down business and commerce in the city, the weather only serves to create a prosperous and vibrant holiday season.

By now, I have been here long enough to establish the Marigny's household kitchen and garden as a well-run operation, so it's only with a glad heart that I sit down at the beginning of December to plan this Christmas season. The first step, of course, is to set the menu. Not just the menu for the main meal, but also all the accompaniments for before and after, as well as foods and treats to keep around the house throughout the festive season. This plan structures the shopping and food gathering for the next several weeks.

Once the menu is decided, and the necessary shopping done, it is time to begin decorating the house for the Yuletide gatherings and festivities. Since time immemorial Gallic homes, villages, and towns were hung all about with evergreens gathered from the local woodlands. People marked these long dark nights with their local firs, pines, and other green, growing things sprouting their leaves, reminders of the greener times to come as the year turns and the days once again begin to lengthen.

Here in Louisiana, the vegetation never really dies off and the pines, oaks, evergreens, and shrubs give up their branches to decorate our homes. The ancient custom of the Yule Log burning throughout the long Christmas nights is also, for many, a fond memory of the Old Country.

Our Rhenish (German) neighbors from upriver even have a custom from their old homeland of bringing a whole tree, smaller of course, into the house. They decorate it with colored ribbons, little keepsakes, and even some candles. These folks from the Rhine valley even had a wonderful custom of lighting bonfires along their rivers and waterways to light up the long solstice nights and some even say it marks the way for St. Nicholas or Pere Noël to pass over and bless their homes and settlements. These also help to light their families' way to Midnight Mass, for after all, this is the main event of the Christmas celebrations.

Treats and hot drinks will be set out for these festivities, cocoa and cookies for the children, mulled wines and rum cakes for the adults. The gathering begins early on Christmas Eve morning, and after the Midnight Mass, all the shopping and decorating come to purpose as the festivities and feasting commence in earnest and proceed through the morning meal and all throughout Christmas day.

I think for breakfast after Mass this year we will have baked glace' bananas, and deviled eggs. Pork chops in orange sauce is one of the seasonal favorites, so that will be on the menu, and several plump chickens stuffed with oyster dressing, along with turnips, carrots and onions baked with the birds. As the great feast day wears on, the celebrations consist of general revelry, dancing, parades, parties, and singing carols. No doubt there will be games and pranks by the youngsters, and probably by a few of the adults as well!

Here in New Orleans, a curious custom has also evolved. To beautify and somewhat humanize the new city as it was being built up, the city fathers planted the streets with orange trees, easily obtained from my home islands. As a consequence, during the Yuletide season, we have oranges everywhere you look, and as such, oranges have become an essential part of the New Orleans Christmas scene. Needless to say, orange cakes, orange jam, candied orange peels, and savory orange sauces are part of the Yule menu. Good children, even in the poorest homes, can usually find oranges among their gifts from Pere Noël.

But for me and my kitchen, the climax of every Christmas season is the Christmas dinner. Customarily, when the Marigny family - extended to include aunts and uncles, cousins from the country, and other close friends and relatives from around town - gather for the feast, the meal is traditionally a sit-down meal with all the trimmings. However, every family has its own traditions. They may have mid-morning brunch, a day-long buffet, or, weather permitting, a picnic in the courtyard!

One thing remains the same, though, all would eat well and be joyful.

RECIPES

PORK CHOPS WITH ORANGE SAUCE

Begin with simple syrup: dissolve 1 cup of sugar into 1 cup of boiling water, stir until it's clear, remove from heat and cool.

For orange syrup: Juice 2 oranges. While the simple syrup is boiling, add the orange peels and pulp (reserve 2 teaspoons of pulp) from the juicing. Boil for a few minutes. Remove the orange peels. You now have orange simple syrup.

For orange savory sauce: Blend one cup of orange syrup with 2/3 cup of orange juice and 2 tsp. of pulp. Cook over low heat. Add 1 tbsp. of cornstarch or flour*, 3/4 cup of chicken stock, 2 tbsp. of cider vinegar, salt to taste, and 1/8 tsp. of cayenne pepper or one half of a dried cayenne pepper. Heat through, stirring until everything dissolves, and set aside.

*Flour (wheat or corn) corn is more authentic to the 18th Century.

Now cook the pork chops, adding the orange sauce about halfway through the process.

Colonial Cooking Methods:

There are only so many ways to cook food. Boucane over smokey wood or charcoal, or grill over an open flame, roast or bake the food in a hearth oven or Dutch oven, boil, braise, stew, or poach in hot water or some other liquid, smother (a variant of braise) in a small amount of liquid and lots of vegetables, like onions, peppers, etc., fry in small amount of fat or deep fry in a lot of fat, or steam over boiling water. The main difference between our 18th Century Creole ancestors and our kitchens is the heat source. All of the above methods are just as doable whether you are using electric heat, gas burners, wood stoves, or open hearth.

Depending on your cooking method, fry, braise, or smother the chops in a frying pan on the range burner. Frying is quick; a regular pork chop takes about 4 minutes on each side, a thin cut or breakfast chop is about 2 minutes on each side. Smothering is slower, since you want the veggies, usually onion or mushrooms, to get tender, perhaps even caramelize a bit, and make a bit of gravy.

Another alternative is to bake the chops in the oven. If you choose this method, bake the chops in the orange sauce for about ½ hour at 350°. Cook the chops on one side, turn them, add more sauce, and let everything cook thoroughly. Check every few minutes so the dish does not burn.

Serve with sweet potato fries and a salad with French dressing.

TANTE MARIE'S DIRTY RICE

Gerard's Noel Tradition: a Recipe of my Wonderful Aunt from the Ardennes Forest. Suzanne "borrowed" this recipe from Frère Gerard, who in turn brought it from his home in France.

- 1 tablespoon + 1 teaspoon lard
- The "Holy Trinity" - 3 onions, 4 green peppers, 5 bunch of celery
- "Plus Two" - 1/2 head garlic and 1/4 cup parsley
- 1 pound ground pork
- Giblets of one fowl, (chicken, duck, turkey, what have you)
- Water
- Salt and pepper to taste
- A *soupçon* (tiny pinch) of cayenne, any other seasoning you like
- 2 cups of rice (before cooking)

Since this is a dressing, use more of the Trinity than normal, say about 3 onions, 3 or 4 peppers, half to one whole bunch of celery, half to one whole head of garlic, a handful of parsley. The amount to use depends on how much dressing you want and the size of the vegetables. Chop the veggies finely and sauté (in butter or olive oil) in a large stew pot for about 5 to 10 minutes.

While they're cooking, chop the giblets until they resemble ground meat. Place the giblets and the pork in the pot and fry them off in the vegetables. Fill the pot with water, add the seasonings and boil away all the water (this takes a couple or three hours).

Again, depending on the amount of dressing desired, cook the rice as you would for any normal dinner. Set aside. Usually 2 cups (before cooking) will suffice to balance the meat and vegetable flavors.

Watch the boiling pot carefully as the water level begins to disappear, do not let the dressing dry out completely. Remove from heat and begin mixing in the rice one big spoon at a time. Correct the seasoning as you go. After two cups (before cooking) of rice have been added, you need to decide whether or not you need to add more. At this stage, you should have a good balance of rice to meat to vegetable flavors, season to taste. It's good to eat now, as is, OR...

The dressing can be baked in separate baking dishes or stuffed into various birds or cuts of meat. Dirty rice cooked in a bird will acquire extra flavoring from the juices of the fowl as it cooks.

Bring the dressing out in bowls or stuffed into the birds, place the birds and dressing on the serving board or the dinner table and have a most . . . JOYEAUX NOËL!

ORANGE AND GINGER COOKIES

Cream together about ½ lb. of butter and 3 large spoons of sugar until mixed well and fluffy. Next with a beater blend in a large egg and 1 large spoon of molasses.

Now take 2 overflowing handfuls of fine flour and stir in 2 small spoons of ginger powder, 1 spoon of soda, a spoon of cinnamon, the pulp of 2 large oranges, some of the juice (not too much or the cookies with be mushy) and 2 or 3 pinches of salt. Slowly mix the dry ingredients into the buttercream to get a good firm dough.

Roll the dough into about 2-inch balls, then roll each around in a plate of sugar and orange zest. Bake in a moderate oven about 15 minutes

Modern Adaptation:
- 3/4 cup butter, softened
- 1 cup sugar
- 1 large egg
- 1/4 cup molasses
- 2 1/4 cups all-purpose flour

- 2 teaspoons ground ginger
- 1 teaspoon baking soda
- 3/4 teaspoon ground cinnamon
- 1/2 teaspoon ground cloves
- 1/4 teaspoon salt
- Additional sugar

In a large bowl, cream butter and sugar until light and fluffy. Beat in egg and molasses. Combine the flour, ginger, baking soda, cinnamon, cloves and salt; gradually add to the creamed mixture and mix well.

Roll into 1-1/2-in. balls, then roll in sugar. Place 2 in. apart on ungreased baking sheets. Bake at 350° until puffy and lightly browned, 10-12 minutes. Remove to wire racks to cool. Serve with wine, coffee, or lemonade.

PEACH SPICE PIE

First prepare a pie shell. Then gather:

- 8 or 10 peaches
- 1 cup sugar
- 1/2 cup sour cream
- 1/4 teaspoon grated ginger
- 1/4 cup wheat flour
- 2 eggs
- 1 teaspoon vanilla

Skin, slice and place all the peaches in the pie shell. Mix everything else together in a bowl and pour over the peaches. B
   Bake in a hot oven for 30 minutes.

While the pie cooks gather together:

- 3 1/2 cups of flour
- 3/4 cups sugar
- 1 cup chopped pecans

- 1/2 cup chopped currants (or raisins)
- 1 teaspoon cinnamon
- 1/2 cup cubed cold butter

Mix everything together, take the pie out of the oven, pour over the baked peaches, bake for another for 15 to 20 minutes. Cool.

YOUR TRICENTENNIAL MEMO

A NOTE ON FRENCH CATHOLICISM

In Catholic French Louisiana, as in all other Christian countries, the two most important holidays on the calendar are undoubtedly Easter and Christmas. It should come as no surprise that the French settlers in the New World should approach these holidays as they do all other aspects of their culture… through the kitchen.

This occurred somewhat more so at Christmastime than at Easter because Gallic celebrations at Midwinter reach deep into the roots of the French mindset. Literally since time out of memory, Midwinter was a time of feasting and fun. When the medieval Church adapted the Midwinter festivals of ancient Europe, it was only natural that the feasting and fun would become part of Jesus' birthday celebrations.

In France especially, and later in Louisiana, culinary Yuletide customs blend right in with the holiday festivities. Coming to mind immediately are the association of Midnight Mass with a long leisurely breakfast that would last sometimes even until dawn. Others await until later, rising from bed late on Christmas day, the entire holiday is one long feast. In midafternoon, if relatives were stopping by, a sit-down dinner may be served, otherwise, the table was laid out in the morning and the family and guests would nibble through the feast all day long.

The foods associated with the celebrations varied from region to region. But no matter what was consumed, it was always a good excuse to enjoy a laid-back day marking the peculiar laid-back Gallic approach to Catholicism.

I recently encountered a quote while reading about the Austrian Emperor Franz Josef that sets the perfect tone for a consideration of French Catholicism: "He was a good Catholic without thinking much about it." Never has there been a better or more succinct description of French and/or Louisiana Catholicism.

As France and the rest of Europe emerged from the Catholic Middle Ages, society was rocked by the tidal wave of Luther's Reformation. While this is not the place to mark all the horrors, injustice, and tragedy of this ridiculous situation when Christians slaughtered each other because they went to the wrong church, it is worth mentioning that it was little different in the European colonies.

In North America, vast distances between the Protestant English, Catholic French and Spanish, and pagan Native Americans minimized this silliness, but it was never far from the surface. Besides, simple survival often trumped philosophical differences.

In Louisiana, this cultural aspect of life was defined by French reaction to the ground-shaking social changes rocking Europe during these centuries. The virtual theocracy of Richelieu's reign during the 1600's, the legacy of Mazarin's influence, and the "divine" kingship of Louis XIV's long rule produced a curious riff on traditional Catholicism known as Gallicanism.

In Early Modern times (1500 - 1800), an ongoing conflict between church and state centered around the appointment of local or regional leaders (e.g., Bishops). The Catholic Church (for better or worse) for many centuries after the fall of Rome had been the only recognizable form of authority in much of Europe. As a result, the local bishop in a given region was usually a political as well as a spiritual leader.

The Reformation in the 1500's threw a wrench into this ancient system. Additionally, as Kings and nobility grew in political power, conflict about these episcopal appointments grew more violent. In France, the 1600's saw the apex of this episcopal power under the reigns of Richelieu and then Mazarin. When Mazarin passed on, young Louis XIV shifted much of the bishops' authority to the throne. As part of this general move away from Roman (that is Papal) influence, a theological movement known as Gallicanism began to take form. The online Britannica provides a succinct description of this slant on the Catholic faith.

> "The most notable champion of parliamentary Gallicanism was the jurist Pierre Pithou, who published his Les Libertés de l'église gallicane in 1594. This book, together with several commentaries on it, was condemned by Rome but continued to be influential well into the 19th century. The best expression of theological Gallicanism was found in the Four Gallican Articles, approved by the assembly of the clergy of France in 1682. This declaration stated: (1) the Pope has supreme spiritual but no secular power; (2) the Pope is subject to ecumenical councils; (3) the Pope must accept as inviolable immemorial customs of the French Church—e.g., the right of secular rulers to appoint bishops or use revenues of vacant bishoprics; (4) papal infallibility in doctrinal matters presupposes confirmation by the total church. Bishop Jacques-Bénigne Bossuet drafted the declaration in Latin and defended it in a conciliatory preamble. Though the articles were condemned at Rome by Alexander VIII in 1690 and were revoked in France by Louis XIV in 1693, they remained the typical expression of Gallicanism."
>
> http://www.britannica.com/EBchecked/topic/224587/Gallicanism
> More details can be found in the Wikipedia article at: http://en.wikipedia.org/wiki/Gallicanism

In far away, isolated Louisiana, all of these factors came together to produce an easy-going, common sense approach to religious matters. Most folks did not ponder the philosophical niceties of the Gallican interpretation of their faith. They were too busy trying to stay alive. Besides, the Pope, and the King for that matter, were literally thousands of miles away, and even priests were few and far between.

It was, to the Catholics of Louisiana, enough to be "a good Catholic without thinking much about it." So, it should be no surprise that customs like Midnight Mass, Mardi Gras, All Saint's Day, and Catholic schools have anchored themselves along the French Gulf Coast. They have become hallmarks of our "Catholic" culture. A recent book title (which is now a popular meme in and around New Orleans) best sums up this outlook, "Who's your Mama, are you Catholic, and can you make a roux"!

23
1740's - THE ILLINOIS COUNTRY

I stood on the levee with Tante Suzanne, along with the other cooks from the New Orleans' households, welcoming the traders. They all came to the levee well supplied with money and local trade items, ready to barter for the best bargains for their respective families. This year, the voyageurs from Illinois were well stocked with wild and domestic meats that had been dried, salted, or cured into hams and sausages. There was wheat flour and cornmeal aplenty, as well as garden produce such as herbs, dried edible flowers, and dried or pickled vegetables.

There had been many years when the quantities of food items were quite small, and even a few when it was next to nothing, but this was not such a year, and everything was plentiful. The harvest was good this year, and the farms and forests of the Illinois Country - Upper Louisiana - yielded a considerable surplus of wheat and the boucheries last fall produced a bountiful supply of hams, sausage, and salt pork.

Trading, bargaining, buying, and selling would undoubtedly go on until after sundown. The next few weeks would be a busy time as the bounty of the north country was processed, cooked, preserved and packed into the kitchens, storehouses, smokehouses, and root cellars of New Orleans. The winter holidays this year would be all the more joyous and memorable for the efforts of the voyageurs.

"Bienvenu, mes amis," I called as Jacques' and Diane's pirogues bumped into the levee just upriver from the Place d'Armes. "What fine delicacies have you brought us this year?" The pair jumped ashore. "Only the finest pate and most delicate truffles from the northern forests!" Diane embraced me in a bear hug, knowing it would both please and embarrass me, then turned and embraced Suzanne in the same manner. Robert's bateau pulled in alongside the pirogues.

"Greeting, Frère Gerard! And Tante Suzanne, *et vous, mon chere!* What sumptuous feast awaits us in your kitchen today?" he called leaping ashore.

"For you, Robert, the finest fresh churned butter on fresh baked soft white baguettes, with steaming hot coffee to wash it down. I do hope that you can replace the last of my finest white wheat flour!" she chided him, smiling a bright smile.

During the last several weeks, Robert, Jacques, and Diane had paddled their small flotilla downstream delivering supplies, foodstuffs, and news to Arkansas, Natchez, and finally, New Orleans. As they guided their bateaux and pirogues down the Mississippi, their motley crew consisted of voyageurs, merchants, a politician or two, the inevitable small group of Natives, adventurous colonists moving on to new land, and the soldiers heading for home or leave in the New World. Today they completed their voyage and now there would be greetings, bartering, and much talk of their adventures on the river.

"Come," Jacques said, "let's find a place under a tree in the square to have lunch, and you can fill us in on the doings down here in the capital."

"But only after you tell us all the news from Upper Louisiana," Suzanne said as we settled down for a long visit.

"And all of your adventures," I added.

"Frère Gerard," Diane said teasingly, "you must shed your brown cleric robes and come with us. Think of the adventures you would have!"

I laughed and shook my head at the jest, but I wondered what would happen if I did join them. In late summer they would take a few small canoes or pirogues and head upstream to the mouth of the Red River or the Arkansas River and then into the forests to join some friendly Natives in their annual hunts. Sometimes they would go a bit further up into the St. Francis River Valley and the eastern slopes of the Ozark's, into a veritable Garden of Eden rich in game and the natural floral bounty of forest nuts, berries, fruits, and herbs. Or, depending on the weather and the mood of the season, they would trap a wide variety of fur-bearing animals and then trade the furs with the those who lived yet further upriver in the Illinois settlements.

Robert was the elder of the group, having come down from New France in the very early years of Louisiana. A courier de bois by trade, he freelanced in furs and forest produce from the Quapaw villages, the Natchez and Tunica settlements, all the way down to the passage through the lakes to Mobile. He had met Jacques and Diane in New Orleans right after the new town was named the colonial capital in the early '20's.

Typical dress of an 18th century French Hunter

Newly arrived from France, Jacques hailed from the Loire valley and Diane was a wild Celt from Brittany. They had both left the Old Country on different ships to escape uncomfortable situations in their hometowns, and then shared the boat trip from Mobile to the new city and became fast - yet platonic - friends. After spending some time in the city, they realized that their fortunes and their freedom would probably best be found in the wilderness. Robert walked into their lives, telling tales of vast forests, wild rivers, quiet streams, and tall mountains. It was inevitable that they would accompany him on his voyages up the river.

Over many years, a routine slowly developed. Late summer would see the trio leave with the annual convoy upriver. Along with the hunters went a company of new soldiers to relieve the garrisons at Fort d'Chartres and the Kaskaskia settlements, new colonists and officials heading north, merchants and tradesmen to do business with the inhabitants of the district. All would travel upriver together for protection. They would be accompanied by a smattering of licensed voyageurs and unlicensed courier-de-bois to deal with les petits nations in furs and food supplies. Robert, Diane, and Jacques would normally split off from the convoy somewhere between the Red River and the St. Francis, depending on their goals for that year, and begin plying their trade.

Filled with wild turkey, bear, deer, and even buffalo, birds, squirrels, and rabbits, the forests were also weighed down with berries, plums, persimmons, cherries, strawberries, grapes, pecans, walnuts, acorns, etc. as well as natural herbs for medicine and flavor. "A trader would have to be pretty green about the ears not to be able to find something eat among such natural bounty," Robert was fond of saying.

The trio would eventually work their way toward Kaskaskia by Christmas. After Mardi Gras, they would begin preparations for the trip back downriver, bringing the goods gathered and processed in the fall as well as however much they could secure of the produce of the northern colony, mainly wheat flour, hams, and maize. It must be hard for them sometimes, dealing so much with the Natives - the sauvages - and spending so much time in those odd cultures on the outskirts of civilization.

But today, we were gathered as friends, talking of adventures and food, as we did each time we met. Today was a good day on the levee.

RECIPES

VOYAGEUR STEW

As the voyageurs and couriers de bois navigated the rivers and tributaries of the Old Northwest (that is the Great Lakes), and the valleys of the Missouri and Mississippi, they generally

lived off the land. There was, however, one staple attested to in their journals* which, more or less, was their staff of life when nothing else was at hand.
It was a sort of stew or soup based on peas and pork. The cooks would ...

> "...hang a tin kettle - eight or ten gallons - over the campfire ... nearly full of water, then add nine quarts of peas (or one quart per man). When the peas were 'well bursted', two or three pounds of pork, cut into strips, were added, and everything was allowed to boil together until daylight. At sun rise, the cook would top the mess with four or five biscuits. The swelling of the peas and biscuit had now filled the kettle to the brim, so thick that a stick would stand upright in it... The men now squatted in a circle around the kettle with their spoons and have at the 'stew' until 'every cavity' was filled."*

*See note 7, p. 4, of the below cited volume

Well stocked with this nutritious albeit plain fare, the expedition would continue. Here is a modern riff on what the voyageurs cooked on their seasonal hunting and trapping expeditions.

Modern Adaptation:

- 1 pound dry split peas
- 6 cups chicken broth
- 1 cup chopped onion
- 1 head of garlic, minced
- 2 bay leaves
- 1/2 teaspoon salt
- 1/8 teaspoon pepper**

Sort and rinse the peas. Add the chicken broth to the peas. Add remaining ingredients to the peas and cook covered for about an hour, adding more broth or water as necessary. Stir occasionally. Remove the bay leaves when finished cooking. Adjust the seasoning.

Mitchell, Patricia B. *French Cooking in Early America.*
Chatham, VA: MitchellsPublications.com, 1991.
Twelfth Printing, 2008.

** 1/8 tsp. of pepper may work in the Illinois country, but not in Lower Louisiana. Black Pepper, Tabasco Hot Sauce, Cajun seasoning mixture, or a combination of these would normally be de rigeur.

YOUR TRICENTENNIAL MEMO

The European (French) population of Louisiana never exceeded five thousand. A somewhat larger number of Africans, six to seven thousand, added to the Old World populations of Lower and Upper Louisiana. As such, voyageurs like Robert, Jacques, and Diane, making their living as hunters, trappers, and traders -had one foot in each of the worlds of French Louisiana.

Spending most of their lives among Native communities up and down the rivers of the Mississippi basin, they would naturally have become as sauvage as the sauvages with whom they shared their personal and commercial affairs. Spending most of their lives outside of "civilization" that is, in the company of their fellow Frenchmen and Canadiens, and yet not completely as part of the Native communities with whom they hunted and traded, these traders were responsible for their own food supply.

While many hunters had years of experience under their belt, newcomers to the trade learned much from their relationships with the Natives along the Lower Mississippi valley. Another aspect of such contact was that most of the locals were more than happy to teach these Europeans how to care for themselves in the wild. Throughout the French colony's time on the mid North American continent, relations, commercial and military, were normally congenial among the Natives and the newcomers. With the exceptions of the Chickasaw (British allies), some major French faux pas with the Natchez, and also some unfortunate misunderstandings early on with the

Madame Langlois' Legacy · 241

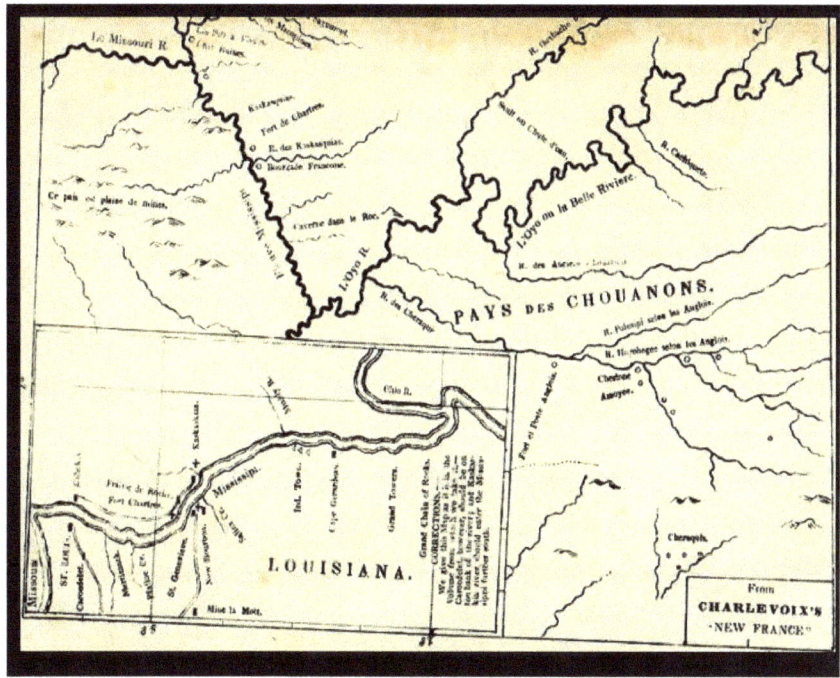

NOTE: The large map is a normal North (up) and South (down) perspective. The insert is East (up) and West (down) perspective.

Chitimacha, French and Indian relationships were normally peaceful and beneficial to both sides.
Hunting and trapping activities were shared with whatever Natives inhabited the local landscape where the voyageurs set up their transient camps. Hunting quite naturally became their chief form of sustenance. The hunters usually carried with them some small supplies of grain, flour, oil, spices, and coffee. These could always be supplemented by trade with local Natives as well as any European settlements they would visit. Catching and preserving (drying, salting, etc.) their kills along their trade routes was also a common practice.

The arrival of the Illinois flotilla of *pirogues** and *bateaux* * in the spring was an exciting affair in New Orleans. Not only was more and different foods entering the market, but news could be had and old friendships renewed. Over the years the three voyageurs had come to know and value the market created by the cooks of the capital, and the cooks of New Orleans were always there on the levee as the Illinois flotillas came into town.

* Bateaux are largish boats, in this case, meant to carry passengers and cargo such as the food and supplies heading down for sale or trade in Lower Louisiana. Pirogues here used were much larger than the two man "Cajun" pirogues familiar from pictures and movies today. These trading pirogues are better described as large dugouts, often carved or burned out of the huge cypress trees that lined the rivers, bayous, and swamps of 18th century Louisiana.

After a season of hunting and trapping in Upper Louisiana, many hunters would winter over in Kaskaskia, the chief settlement of the Illinois Country. A snapshot of life there can be found in Natalia Belting's study of the Upper colony.

> *"A day in Kaskaskia, as in Canada, began at sunup, with breakfast between seven and eight o'clock. Dinner at noon was the principal meal of the day; then there were fresh meats - boiled, roasted, fricasseed, or stewed - soup with bread swimming in it, fruit preserves, tiny round cheeses and sweetened milk. Meat pies were great favorites; on Fridays and Saturdays and other fast days, fish or milk dishes took the place of the meat. Stew was served in a large bowl, a La Gamelle, and set in the center of the table where everyone dipped in with spoon and fork and a sturdy slice of bread. Vegetables of all kinds were raised in the kitchen garden and served on the habitants table - cabbages, peas, beans, carrots, turnips, and parsnips."*

> Belting, Natalia Maree. *Kaskaskia Under the French Regime.* New Orleans: Polyanthos, 1975. pp. 46-47:

Typical French Colonial farm maiden, 1700's

Another work provides a good picture of the French Louisiana diet in the 18th century:

> "Squash (. . . was cultivated by Native Americans before corn and beans."), corn, and beans. "The Oneota culture, from which the Missouri tribe developed, produced excellent hunters of deer, elk, turkey, and bison. Fishing, gardening, and gathering were (also) essential to the tribe's existence." p. 3 ff.
>
> "French farmers and their slaves used a large common field to plant wheat, cotton, melons, pumpkins, and tobacco. Each family owned a strip of land in this field. Farmers also grew fruits, vegetables, and herbs, in small gardens and orchids near their homes. ... farming practices reflected those of their homeland in NW France, where community labor was a tradition." p. 11 ff.
>
> "The French women were fine cooks. They cooked in fireplaces, using iron pots and long-handled skillets and utensils. They used native ingredients and borrowed cooking methods from the Indians and Africans. One example is gumbo, a stew thickened with dried and powdered sassafras leaves . . ." p. 12 ff. ". . . (They) used Indian corn in many ways but preferred to make breads and rolls with wheat flour from France." p. 14.
>
> Matson, Madeline. Food in Missouri;
A Cultural Stew. Columbia MO:
Univ. of Missouri Press 1994. 0826209602
>
> {NOTE: wheat was soon grown in French Louisiana - especially in "Upper" Louisiana from Natchez north to the Illinois Country.}

Regular supplies from Upper (North) Louisiana, sanctioned trade with the Spanish Empire and the West Indies (of various empires), produce and trade in and around New Orleans and Lower Louisiana provide modern observers of the French colony with a much more complete understanding of the life and culture which the European settlers of La Louisiane established and enjoyed throughout the eighteenth century.

24
1747 – THE ENGAGEMENT PARTY

Never had I felt so happy to be the chef of the Marigny household! Not only were the holidays coming, but it had just been formally announced that the Master, Monsieur Antoine, and his lady, Francoise De Lisle, were finally going to get married in the spring. I wanted an engagement party befitting both the Marigny and De Lisle families. I'd raised Antoine since he was eight and was determined to make sure that his engagement party would be the talk of New Orleans.

And what a party it was! The summer of 1747 was hotter than any I remembered, but in late September as we planned the event, the weather finally turned pleasant, and the Marigny household was abuzz with activity. I remember the day we planned the menu. As he often did, 'Toine sat comfortably at the small table by the open window, savoring one of my special cups of coffee, full of fresh, rich cream and spiced with a dash of cinnamon that I had just that morning procured from my favorite trader on the riverbank.

We talked about his childhood, how I often chased him out from under my feet, sending him to that same table with a glass of warm milk and a fresh baked cookie, or chasing him out the kitchen after he had accomplished his thievery of whatever goodies I had prepared for dinner. That day, a man of 25 sat at the table, yet I could not stop myself from teasing him as if he were still a boy.

"So, *mon petite*, Mam'zelle François is finally going to make you an honest man, oui?"

"Now, Tante 'Zu," he said, "you know I've never been one to chase the ladies. "

"Of course not. I raised you right, as a gentleman."

"Anyway, how are we going to make this party? It needs to be very special for my lady."

He smiled and so did I. Even then, we both knew it would be a party to remember, and that when the guests arrived in early November, there would be plenty to eat, with the harvest coming in and the smokehouse full of freshly butchered meats… pork and some beef, a nice fresh side of venison, even elk and buffalo. The problem was choosing what to cook, a problem I delighted in, back then as now.

"Fish for sure," I told him, "pompano with its delicate flavor, with a rich lemon and herb sauce and encrusted with pecans." We talked about ragout de boeuf, stewed in a thick gravy flavored with laurel leaves and sage, and a buccaned pig, with the meat stretched over a bed of hickory branches for their flavor, bathed in honey and thyme, and slow roasted for hours until it nearly fell off the bone. And with oranges so plentiful in the fall, I promised him a rich orange layer cake as the centerpiece of the table.

I remember how his smile grew even bigger. "Tante Zu, you make my mouth water just thinking about it! But please, for me, will you make my favorite? Eggplant stuffed with shrimp like only you can make it! Perhaps, I will even help you out, and I even promise not to nibble while you are cooking."

Antoine had always been interested in everything natural. As a child, he often helped me in the garden, asking a thousand questions about plants, leaves, soil and weather, learning from me just as I had learned from my Maman. And bless him, he brought those skills with him into manhood. Just a few years ago, after the new governor had arrived, Antoine was commissioned to travel south of the city into the swamps between New Orleans and the Gulf and to map what was there.

He learned geography from his father but had surpassed him in mapping skills. When he returned from his travels in Barataria, he began work on a general map of a colony, as well as recording specific notes and maps on the great bay and the waterways between it and the Mississippi. He also began work on his memoir of exploration and the present condition of the colony of Louisiana.

Now, Antoine was ready to settle down into his home, marry, start a family, and pursue the life of a gentleman officer of the colony. He was well respected in the city, and had a good relationship with the governor, who was, of course invited to the engagement fete. I am sure this relationship will blossom into a prosperous one for the Marigny family, probably with quite a few adventures along the way.

It was later that same day when Mademoiselle François made her way to the kitchen, where I fixed her a cup of spiced coffee as I told her of the plans for the menu, which she heartedly approved of, especially the beef.

"Nobody in New Orleans can make the sauces like you, Tante Suzanne," she'd said, "and Mama says she wants you to cook for the wedding as well."

I must admit, I bloomed with pride at the compliment, and I was sure the cook at the De Lisle household would not mind, as long as I agree to share my recipes with her. We, like most folks of color in Louisiana - even those that are free such as me - are almost invisible in society's eyes. Nevertheless, both Antoine and Françoise know my value to the household, and that makes me proud. To these families, I am not only visible, but I am their Tante Suzanne, and the best cook for miles around.

With the menu decided, we sat down together to plan out the rest of event. Although she was only 14 years of age, her Mama had made sure she was trained in the ways of the Creole elite. This was an important event, and not just for the engaged couple. The social and cultural overtones of the marriage were immense! Françoise and Antoine were among the first of the Creoles, as all of their parents had come to Louisiana from France or New France. It was their generation that was building the foundation of New Orleans and Louisiana. Their union, and others like it, would bring about the growth the city needed. It would bring together many of the people from in and around New Orleans.

One of the most exciting aspects of the occasion was the inclusion of Pierre de Rigaud de Vaudreuil de Cavagnial, Marquis de Vaudreuil, the new governor of Louisiana. Just as the first generation of Creole society was coming-of-age, so was the government of the colony and its capital.

The festive evening arrived on one of the first cold days of the New Orleans' wintertime, the carriages crisscrossed the

Vieux Carré and made their way to Ursulines Street, and I remember thinking that we wouldn't fit them all into the house! Family, friends, government officials… all surrounding the happy couple with best wishes.

The party was a splendid affair, but as in almost all parties there was an unfortunate moment. While serving my best ragout ever, a clumsy servant bumped into the Grand Marquis and splashed sauce all over his fine coat. Nobody was very upset, as it was an obvious accident. Nevertheless, something had to be done about the governor's coat. I was also in the dining room at the time and immediately took control of the situation. I prompted the Grand Marquis to step into the kitchen's staging area where it was nice and warm and took his coat immediately to remove the stain.

The coat was still somewhat wet and as I dried it by the warm hearth, he struck up a conversation.
"So, Madame… Tante Suzanne, I believe?" he said to me, "I understand you have been in this household for many years."

I told him how I had come here from Mobile when Antoine was just a little boy and had become the chef de cuisine for the Marigny family, that I had never married and was like an aunt to everyone. He then complimented me on the fine meal I had prepared.

"Madam," he said, "what you do is unlike any other cook in New Orleans. How do you find the ingredients you use to prepare such food?"

We talked about the local farms and suppliers, and his accomplishments in opening markets with our neighbors in Florida, Cuba and New Spain that brought so many wonderful ingredients to our pantries.

"As to the spices," I'd told him, "there are some things that even the Monsieur le Marquis should not ask about." When he returned my smile, I knew he understood about the smugglers and their trade. He then surprised me by asking about my sauces!

"I like to dabble in the kitchen," he admitted, "when I can get away from the chores of governing. It relaxes me and takes my mind off the Indians and the Illinois Country for a while. Tell me then, what is the secret of your sauces?"

I told him that a cook does not reveal her secrets, but for him, I would. We talked about spices and sauces, and our favorite menus. He brought up the condition of the Africans who lived in New Orleans and those that worked the plantations in the surrounding area. He seemed surprised to learn that I was not a slave, but had been born free in San Domingue, had come to New Orleans on my own and found a place in the Marigny household. He was very fascinated by that situation, even more so when he learned that my brother Romulus, who was in charge of a Marigny stables, was also a free person of color.

For such a high ranking official, the Grand Marquis was most gracious and surprisingly down-to-earth. I was almost sad when his coat was dry, and our conversation ended. I helped him put it on, brushed him off, and sent him back to the party. It was not every governor who would have taken time to spend a few moments with a member of the household.

Ah, yes, it was a wonderful party!

RECIPES
EGGPLANT/PEPPERS/MIRLITONS

We used eggplant in this version, but one can use the stuffing for any vegetable of choice.

- 2 medium eggplants, split lengthwise
- 2 cups water

- 1 teaspoon salt
- 4 tablespoons vegetable or olive oil
- 2 cups white or yellow onions, chopped
- 1 pound large (16-20 count) uncooked Louisiana shrimp, peeled, deveined, coarsely chopped. Option: replace shrimp with ground beef or pork
- 1/4 teaspoon cayenne pepper
- 1 cup plus 2 tablespoons dry breadcrumbs
- 1/2 pound Louisiana lump crabmeat, picked over for shells
- Salt and black pepper to taste
- 2 tablespoons hard white cheese

Prepare the vegetable shells by splitting the fruit in half lengthwise.

Preheat oven to 375° F. Preheat broiler. Arrange split eggplants flesh side down on large baking sheet. Pierce with fork. Broil 4 minutes, turn, broil an additional 4 minutes.

Scoop out eggplant pulp, leaving ½ inch thick shell intact. Place pulp in heavy medium saucepan, cover with 2 cups water, add 1 teaspoon salt and bring to boil. Reduce heat, cover and simmer 15 minutes. Uncover and simmer until eggplant is very tender and liquid evaporates, about 5 minutes. Remove from heat.

Brush eggplant shells with 1 tablespoon oil; place, cut side up, on a rimmed baking sheet. Do not over-crowd. Bake until shells are tender but still hold their shape, approximately 20 minutes.

While shells are baking, heat 3 tablespoons oil in heavy large skillet over medium-high heat. Add onions; sauté until tender, about 5 minutes. Add boiled eggplant pulp, shrimp (or meat) and cayenne; sauté until shrimp are cooked through, approximately 4 minutes.

Remove from heat. Stir in 1 cup breadcrumbs and crab meat, and season to taste with salt and pepper. Fill eggplant shells with shrimp and crabmeat mixture. Sprinkle stuffing with grated white cheese and remaining 2 tablespoons breadcrumbs. Bake stuffed eggplants until heated through, about 30 minutes.

Let stand 5 minutes. Serve hot.

CANE SYRUP CAKE

This cake will remind you of gingerbread minus the spices. The batter is thick and produces a moist, flavorful cake. I tried substituting all-purpose flour with self-rising and omitting the salt and baking soda, but the center of the cake collapsed. I would recommend sticking with the ingredients as listed. This cake travels well and is great to take along on picnics.

- 1 stick butter, softened
- 1/2 cup sugar
- 2 cups cane syrup \
- 2 eggs
- 2 cups flour
- 1/2 teaspoon baking soda
- 1 teaspoon salt
- 1/2 cup buttermilk
- 2 teaspoons vanilla extract
- 1/2 teaspoon lemon extract

Grease and flour a 13 x 9-inch baking pan. Cream butter and sugar in a mixer until light and fluffy. Add syrup and eggs to creamed mixture and mix in well.

Sift baking soda and salt into buttermilk. Alternately add flour mixture and buttermilk into creamed mixture mixing well after each addition. Begin and end with flour.

Add vanilla and lemon extract. Stir.

Pour batter into prepared pan. Bake in a 350° oven for 50 minutes or until inserted toothpick comes out clean.
Dust with powdered sugar or serve with whipped cream and chopped pecans.

YOUR TRICENTENNIAL MEMO

HOW THE GRAND MARQUIS CAME TO LOUISIANA

Bienville had come to Louisiana when he was 18 years old. It wasn't Louisiana then, it was just beaches, piney woods, islands, and lots of mushy ground. He and his brother, Pierre Lemoyne, Sieur d'Iberville, entered the Mississippi a few weeks after his 19th birthday. A few days later they stood on the spot where his city would be built. Forty years later, the city was built and thriving. Other settlements peppered the coast to the east and controlled strategic spots up the river valleys to the north.

Bienville, now approaching 60, realized it was time for him to retire and pass the baton on to a new soldier/diplomat.

Le Grand Marquis

As things would have it, when Minister Maurepas in France received Bienville's resignation, almost simultaneously the man who would succeed him appeared at court. Like Bienville and Iberville, this man was a French-Canadian, but from a higher echelon of the Canadian aristocracy. His father had been governor of New France, nominally all of the French possessions in America, but in reality, the extent of territory that would become Canada.

The Grand Marquis, as this gentleman would be called, ushered in the greatest days of French Louisiana. During his tenure as governor of Louisiana, Pierre de Rigaud de Vaudreuil de Cavagnial would preside over the society and the culture that would dominate Louisiana and its politics from his governorship until after the Civil War. Well into the 20th century, this Creole society of New Orleans would linger on and permeate New Orleans' idea of itself. The Grand Marquis, in essence, created Creole Louisiana.

Well, here it is, that word Creole. Few other words create such a stir in the breast of a New Orleanian as Creole. I believe the emotions arise from the insistence on any number of parties that Creole applies to them and them alone, when in fact, it applies to any number of cultural and racial types to be found in those states and countries bordering the Gulf of Mexico and their hinterlands. So, before we get too deep into any controversy in a book about Creole cuisine, let us define our terms.

Those interested may dig a little deeper on the Internet and go back to the Portuguese word crioulo. For our purposes, today along America's Gulf Coast let us make a simple statement. Creoles are people and cultures that were born in the New World of parents and cultures from the Old World, essentially Europe and Africa.

To the colonists of Louisiana in the 1740's, Creoles were those descended from the French settlers, and ironically the French-Canadian settlers, of Louisiana. Creoles were also those people descended from the Africans who found themselves in Louisiana during the 1740's, although nobody wrote much about them. The governorship of Vaudreuil coincided with the coming-of-age of that first generation of Louisiana Creoles. During those first 40-odd years of Louisiana's existence, the primary focus of everybody there had been survival.

By the 1740's the population had grown considerably. The settlements, such as they were, had been established, and certain economic, political, and cultural ways of life had emerged. The arrival of the Grand Marquis allowed the elite of the city to flower into the culture that would come to be the very identity of New Orleans and, to a lesser extent, Louisiana. Banquets, dances and celebrations were beginning to become part and parcel of life in the capital. Both trade and expansion of the physical colony, as well as the economy, allowed for a period of good times in the capital.

Vaudreuil managed and oversaw the growth of this Louisiana economy. Almost immediately upon his arrival in Louisiana, the governor was faced with having to deal with the Natives, bringing to an end the almost constant conflicts and restoring the precarious peace. Showing himself a capable administrator, he was able to deal with this over the years, and at the same time making perhaps his greatest achievement in Louisiana by establishing, for the first time in the colony's history, relative economic prosperity.

Through the 20's and 30's in Louisiana, the colony as a marketplace, and sometimes it's very survival, were often in question. Over these decades there were many periods where the OFFICIAL government position in France was 'starvation and woe'. At the same time, however, networks were being created and began growing which allowed the colonists to at least feed themselves, if not produce enough for trade.

The abundance of seafood available in the many lakes, rivers, and streams, the produce of their own gardens, and the establishment of the German Coast agricultural areas allowed survival a few steps above the level of starvation. In addition, trading and smuggling networks were built throughout the swamps south and west of the capital. To a lesser extent, the ports themselves were dealing with contraband shipments of food. The governor's genius immediately recognized this, and he ordered access to markets in the Spanish colonies, including Cuba and Mexico.

The British navy was his unwitting accomplice in this endeavor. Spanish colonial administrators, in the face of severe wartime shortages, were forced to entertain Vaudreuil's proposals to admit Louisiana produce, much of it on their contraband list. La Belize, at the mouth of the Mississippi, became an entrepôt where French goods were picked up by Spanish ships for trans-shipment to Havana, Santo Domingo,

Hispaniola, and Veracruz, Mexico. Vaudreuil estimated the value of this trade in the period 1742–44 to be 750,000 livres.

When the almost constant Continental war paused for a time, this trade fell off dramatically but quickly revived. The Spanish colonies found that they could no longer do without it. This, of course, reflects export trade which built up Louisiana's official resources, but not to be forgotten is the import trade generated by these activities. Food and other goods from the Spanish Caribbean made their way into the Louisiana economy. Times may have been a bit difficult, but they certainly were not starving.

As usual, a growing economy encouraged the growth of culture. It has become almost a historian's cliché that while a region's geography defines its history, it is economy that drives historical events. A corollary to a growing economy is also the growth of cultural activities. The same can be said for the development of New Orleans and Louisiana during this governorship.

The first Creole generation that was coming-of-age when Bienville retired very much fell right into step with the administration of an unquestioned aristocrat. It was still the Old Regime in French society and the values of the elite or aristocratic values, for better or worse set the tone, both socially and culturally, and Vaudreuil enjoyed his position as Marquis.

He was noted for his lavish banquets and social events, and even expanded the local traditions of the Mardi Gras. All of this encouraged the elite of the Capital to imitate the manners of a French aristocrat. He was definitely one of the more interesting characters to grace the history of colonial New Orleans.

25
EARLY 1740's – SHRIMP, ALLIGATORS AND TURTLES

Christmas and Mardi Gras were now fond memories, and Lent has arrived, it was time for seafood again. Traditionally, abstaining from meat in our daily diets is one popular method of performing our sacrificial duty. Most laypeople normally abstain on Wednesdays and Fridays throughout the year. Abstinence is also the usual practice throughout the Lenten season.

While fasting altogether is the most desirable of sacrificial practices, for one reason or another - usually dealing with age or health - abstaining from meat in our meals is a common and acceptable substitute.

Now, among the many defining aspects of the new colony and its capital from the Mobile settlement to La Balize at the mouth of the mighty St. Louis (Mississippi) is water. Water of the coast, the lakes, the bayous, and the great river itself is the stuff of Louisiana. In most places in and around New Orleans, the land itself is mostly water.

The watery world of SE Louisiana

From my point of view as a cook, this means seafood. There is always a fresh supply of fish, oysters, shrimp, clams, crabs, and even the little crawfish that swarm our streets and ponds in the spring. Native fishermen, river folk from Canada and France, as well as new migrants from southern France, bring their nautical expertise to our shores and keep the markets full of these creatures to compliment the game from the hunters, and the produce and domestic beasts and fowl from our ever-expanding farms and gardens.

In Europe, for centuries, fish and other seafood (relatively rare in inland areas), have become the traditional meat substitute. Now here in Louisiana, it is possible to substitute fish and other seafood for meat virtually every day. Combine this with the variety of cooking styles and techniques we have learned from our Indian and African neighbors, as well as our own - not inconsiderable - French culinary heritage, it is hardly a sacrifice for us to consume these delicious meals as a method of honoring our religious convictions and practices. All of this being said, it is not the place of this humble kitchen friar to question the wisdom of Holy Mother Church.

Recently, I have been recalling my visits to the local Indian villages when we had first arrived in New Orleans. The Natives had taught me much about catching and cooking seafood (see Ch. 17) and I have put this newfound knowledge to good use.

This particular morning Suzanne and I headed down to the levee market, enjoying the pleasant spring day - especially since it would not be long before the heat descended on us - I told her about my visit to the Tchoupitoulas village just up the river as well as my extended stay in the Houma camps down Bayou Lafourche.

"The Tchoupitoulas showed me how to catch river shrimp from the Mississippi," I told her, "and how to catch and cook the huge catfish which they caught in the ponds and backwaters of the river. The Houmas taught me what riches can be found in the swamps and bayous. Freshwater fish by the boatload were gathered on trot lines, or by using walnut hulls to paralyze the gills, and fish traps (weirs) were set down in the faster moving waters of the bayou as it swerved and meandered through the swamp."

Fresh off the boat

I mentioned some other missionary stays among the Chitimacha and the Tangipahoa, where I was introduced to the art of catching turtles - especially the big snappers that could easily twist their necks far enough back to snap off a finger or two - along with crawfish, huge bullfrogs, and even alligator and snakes.

By this time, we were in the square before the levee, I was telling Suzanne, "I learned all the basics of cooking all of this, but I wasn't too fond of preparing snakes, though I must admit they made a tasty meal."

Just then, a young Indian boy came running up and was chattering excitedly in the market patois about his mother's wares. While I continued talking to the boy, Suzanne, mystified, continued across the Place d'Armes to the levee, hollering over he shoulder that we would meet up later.

While Gerard was busy elsewhere in the market, I approached the stalls to see what was available. Being raised on the Caribbean Island of San Domingue, and then coming of age at Mobile Bay, I was more familiar with ocean seafood.

Whereas Gerard was a master of crawfish, catfish, and alligator, I outdid him with pompano, redfish, speckled trout, oysters, and drum. It was a friendly competition though, after all, seafood basics are pretty much the same. One seasons it, then fries it, bakes it, or puts it down in sauce. It was the spices and sauces used that made the dish special.

As we arrived at the market, I was intrigued and most interested in learning more about the Mobilian pidgin with which Gerard comfortably conversed with the Natives as we shopped for their watery wares, an area in which he was much more comfortable than me. The Mobilian trade language is only vaguely related to the Natives around the Mobile Bay. When the LeMoyne brothers arrived on the lower Mississippi, there were dozens of small Native groups living from the river's mouth all the way up to the mouth of the Arkansas. As to be expected, they each had their own dialect, only loosely connected to each other.

As such, long before we French arrived, the various tribes developed a common slang through which they communicated when trading with each other. By the time Frère Gerard and I had arrived in New Orleans, the LeMoynes and other French traders had added a measure of French patois to the mix and Mobilian had become a truly international commercial pidgin for most of the Mississippi valley.

Today, the conversation and bargaining would no doubt be about seafood. Displaying their wares on the levee this morning were some of the Bayougoula nation from upriver. From the coastal regions, women of the Chitimacha tribe were selling oysters, crabs, and a selection of fish from the Gulf and lower bayous.

Gerard and I met up again in the center of the market. "I tire of cooking fish all the time in Lent," Gerard said, as he searched the traders for something different. I followed as he approached the Bayougoula group and asked about other things which he could possibly use to literally "flesh out" his meals of bread and gruel. Listening closely to the conversation, I began to pick up some oft repeated words and make sense of them by context.

In the French kitchens of Mobile, it was not unusual to consume ecrevisses, la grenouilles or tortue - crawfish, frog legs or turtle - so I was familiar with these things and had some small understanding of the questions he was asking the Bayougoula ladies. He also asked about alligator, and although these would have been non-existent in his native country, he had adapted his recipes to include this tasty meat.

The Native women were excited by these unusual requests and eager to share their knowledge and skills about these animals. One of the ladies had even brought to market some freshly caught and cleaned frogs of immense size. Frère Gerard snapped them up to surprise his brothers at their next Sunday meal and shared them with me to cook for the Marigny family. As to the other delicacies he asked about, the ladies promised to be sure to include them on their next market trip. Meanwhile, some of the Chitimacha traders had drifted by to see what the commotion was and were soon taken up in the excited taletelling and promises of unusual species on their next trip.

Even I joined in on the trading, seeking out pompano, oysters and redfish. Thrilled at being able to use some of my new vocabulary, however mangled, I had a fun time, and with Frère Gerard's help, I ended up with a few fine pompanos and some nice oysters. All-in-all, both the newcomers and the Natives "passed a good time" and left with some fine acquisitions.

I badgered Frère Gerard to continue his language lessons on the way home. In a mix of French and Mobilian, our discussion led to a tiny bit of enlightenment for us both regarding the absurd sense of Lenten sacrifice among these riches of the water.

"Is it really a sacrifice to eat so well and so deliciously during this season of doing without?" I asked.

He grinned and shook his head. "Perhaps not, so you must find something else to sacrifice, no?"
We parted at Royal St., Frère Gerard heading back to the Presbytere, and I making for the corner of Ursuline St. and the Marigny residence, both of us thinking of how to prepare our finds for dinner.

References about the seafood and the gathering thereof by Louisiana Indians were drawn from:

Kniffen, Fred B., Gregory, Hiram F., & Stokes, George A. The Historic Indian Tribes of Louisiana: From 1542 to the Present. Baton Rouge, LA: LSU Press, 1987.

Folse, John . The Encyclopedia of Creole and Cajun Cuisine. Gonzales, LA: Publishing Division, Chef John Folse & Co., 20XX.

RECIPES

SEAFOOD GUMBO

First you make a roux! (see Chapter 4) But, in addition to the standard "Holy Trinity of vegetables add one pound of sliced okra OR one or two cans of cut okra.

- 2 or 3 bay leaves
- 1 pound Andouille sausage, sliced into discs
- 1 pound of gumbo crabs
- 1 pound crab meat
- 1 pint oysters w/ water
- 1 pound alligator meat
- 1 pound 31-40 count shrimp
- 1 tablespoon crab boil seasoning
- Water
- 1 cup of rice, steamed or boiled, makes about 3 cups cooked rice.

Put the roux and vegetables back onto the fire and begin slicing the andouille. When the roux sizzles, fill the pot with water add the bay leaves (you don't have to be exact here, you will be adding water several times). After the sausage has been sliced, add to the gumbo mix as it heats up. Bring to a boil and cook the mixture for 15 minutes.

Next add the gumbo crabs and the crab meat, add some more water and boil again for 15- or 20-minutes. Cube the alligator meat and fry it off for about 10 minutes. Add the alligator and oysters to the gumbo. Add the crab boil seasoning and boil the gumbo for another 15 to 20 minutes. Correct the seasoning now by adding more water to the boil. Finally bring the gumbo to a boil again and add the shrimp.

Seafood in general, and especially shrimp, cook quickly. When the gumbo boils again, cook the shrimp for no more than 5 minutes. Remove the gumbo off the fire and let it all settle down. Serve over a large spoon of rice with hot French bread on the side.

YOUR TRICENTENNIAL MEMO

When the French, including our mythological Gerard and Suzanne, arrived on the northern Gulf Coast at the beginning of the eighteenth century, they encountered a rich and fertile land which had sustained a significant population of Natives for centuries. Unfortunately, this population had suffered a severe setback in both terms of numbers (both people and settlements) and agricultural production primarily due to the introduction of European diseases.

Beginning with DeSoto's march through the south in the mid-1500's and all the through the colonial era (and beyond) in North America, Native American populations were depleted in vast numbers. Only a small percentage of this decrease was due to warfare or sporadic fighting with the European settlers or among themselves. Smallpox and other diseases to which Native Americans had no immunity did more to eventually push the Indians onto the reservations than any cavalry regiment ever did.

Despite our Hollywood version of Indian/U.S. relationships, most encounters between Natives and European settlers were peaceful and productive, and so it was between the French and the American natives of the southeast. Indeed, during the first thirty or so years of Louisiana's existence, the "nations" of the lower Mississippi made significant contributions to keeping the settlers alive.

During the several centuries prior to 1700, the Southeastern Woodland Indians developed a mixed agricultural and hunter-gatherer economy. The lower Mississippi valley, with its tributaries, deltas, lakes, and network of bayous along with America's South Coast, provided an immensely rich resource from which the natives could draw a stable and ever-present supply of dietary protein. The newly arrived French and Canadians, bringing their own coastal and riverine methods and memories became apt students of the woodland Natives.

Indeed Iberville, almost as a premonition, wrote in his journal the night before he and his crew of explorers entered the mouth of the Mississippi, of having "some rather tasty oysters" as part of his dinner. Some 30 years later, folks very like our fictional cooks Gerard and Suzanne, were able to develop a new Louisiana-based tradition drawing on native food supplies and blending it all together with influences from maritime Canada, the Caribbean, and France thus beginning the traditional Creole way of cooking seafood that has made New Orleans famous.

A freshly opened Louisiana oyster

Similar to blending these culinary traditions in South Louisiana, an equally important blending of communication between "les petits nations" and the French enabled the establishment and growth of the trade economy in the new colony. As depicted in the story above, the Mobilian Trade Language allowed markets to be established up and down the Mississippi valley for exchanges not only of foodstuffs but also the animal hides and pelts that were the staple goods of the Indian trade.

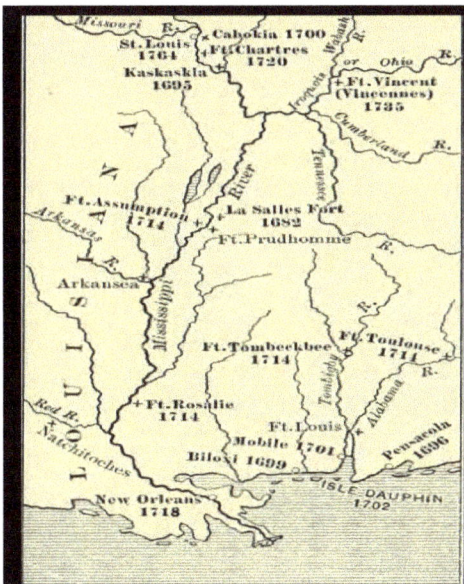

The north central Gulf Coast floodplain and
the Lower Mississippi Valley

What follows is the author's paraphrase of the Wikipedia article on the Mobilian language:

>{Mobilian (a misnomer, as it has little to do with the language of the natives around Mobile Bay) is a pidginized or "corrupted"/"complex" form of Choctaw and Chickasaw (both Western Muskogean) that also contains elements of Eastern Muskogean languages such as Alabama and Koasati, colonial languages including Spanish, French, and English, and perhaps Algonquian and/or other languages. The accepted view of it's origin is that it developed from contact with the French in the eighteenth-century. However, certain factors seem to indicate that the language had a pre-European origin.
>This notion is supported through its well-established use in diverse native contexts, as well as geographic overlapping with that of Southeastern Indian groups formerly associated with the ancient chiefdoms of the pre-Columbian Mississippian Complex. For two centuries (1700-1900) it was the socially accepted lingua franca with outsiders, such as traders and settlers. It is presumed that the fur traders and couriers-debois carried this pidgin language throughout the Mississippi Valley.
>Another idea that supports the pre-Columbian theory is while Mobilian was used to communicate to outsiders, the Europeans did not have a full understanding of the special nature and functions of the language among the Natives. This created a cultural barrier, preserving

their cultural integrity and privacy from non-Indian groups. Its pervasiveness among Native groups, as a result, created its longtime survival.

Indian groups that are said to have used it were the Alabama, [Biloxi](), Chacato, Pakana, Pascagoula, Taensa, Tunica, Caddo, [Chickasaw](), [Choctaw](), [Chitimacha](), [Natchez](), and Ofo. Such a linguistically diverse environment in the lower [Mississippi]() basin drove the need for a common method of communication prior to regular contact with Europeans.

The Native Americans of the Gulf Coast and Mississippi valley have always spoken multiple languages, mainly those of the other nearby tribes that inhabited the same area. Mobilian seems to be a natural response to this situation. Such a language would have provided an efficient survival technique among the nomadic lifestyle shaped by the lower Mississippi environment. }

[https://en.m.wikipedia.org/wiki/Mobilian_Jargon]()
accessed November 2, 2017)

26
1750's - A COLONIAL MARDI GRAS

Frère Gerard remembers…

Winter was fast passing. With the coming of spring, much work needed to be done around the Presbytère, especially in the gardens. There is so much to be done…turning the soil, preparing the seed for planting, deciding what to plant and where it would be most productive. But as a prelude to all of this activity, we had to deal with Mardi Gras.

Since anyone can remember, the beginning of Lent - a very solemn time of the year as all good Christians prepare for the great founding feast of the Resurrection on Easter Sunday - has been marked by one last debacle before beginning the spiritual exercises of fasting, repentance, and sacrifice. In homage to this most solemn season, our Gallic ancestors, quite naturally, turned this "Fat Tuesday" into a day of parties, processions in the streets, dancing, wild music, feasting, and crazy commemorations of the day.

In our little community at the New Orleans Presbytère, we certainly keep such activities to a minimum. It mostly depends on the Father Superior; some are more convivial than others. It usually takes the form of some extra leisure time, and perhaps a few sweets with our meals. Sometimes during this pleasant break in our everyday routine, the brothers would fall to sharing remembrances from the Mardi Gras of their youth in France.

The tale I would share from my early days on the lake in the middle of the great Ardennes Forest was the particular time a companion of mine was seriously injured in the mock trial of Mardi Gras which was held on Ash Wednesday as Lent commenced. It was, and probably still is, the custom to burn an effigy which is supposed to represent the personification of Carnival, while the villagers sang appropriate verses round about the blazing figure.

The effigy was usually fashioned in the likeness of a reputed philandering husband in the village, or some other bounder, or a youngster who was overly spirited in the celebration of Carnival and caused more than his share of trouble. The neighbors would set up a powerful chorus of caterwauls, groans, and melodious sounds, bearing public testimony to the opinion which his friends and neighbors thought of the "effigy's" private virtues.

On one occasion, my companion, a lad named Thierry, dressed himself up in straw, and acted as the personification of the Carnival. Brought before a mock tribunal, he was summarily condemned to death and placed with his back to a wall, like a soldier at a military execution. His execution was to be by pretend firing squad, but on this day, one of the simpletons had left a wad in his musket when cleaning it. Thierry was struck in the upper leg by the errant paper bullet and to this day still limps about the village while pursuing his work.

I have been told since that these mock executions in the Ardennes have been seriously discouraged by the local authorities, and I should hope it is true, but here in New Orleans, we seek only a bit of fun.

As the storytelling among the brothers continued, my thoughts began to drift to how Tante's Suzanne's Mardi Gras was progressing and whether she was having as pleasant a day as I was.

> *The above story has been paraphrased from an account by:*
> *Frazer, Sir James George. The Golden Bough. Vol. 4, The Dying God.*
> *London: Macmillan & Co. Ltd. New York: St. Martin's Press. 1955.*
> *pp. 226 & 227. 1936 Edition of Thirteen Volumes.*

Suzanne Remembers…

As long as I can remember, my family always celebrated Mardi Gras. On San Domingue, Mardi Gras was a village-wide community event. There were outdoor games, processions, contests, music, and dancing. There was much feasting, as much as possible at the end of winter… perhaps a roasted pig, some chickens, some remaining vegetables from the root cellar, cakes of rice, or oats.

In our New World homestead, we all had some local foods, such as Indian corn with honey or sugar mixed in. After we moved to the big farm north of Mobile, we learned of, and then participated in, the public celebrations held in the town surrounding Fort Louis. Some of the gentry in town would hold processions, marching through the streets singing and dancing, and generally turn the town streets into a block party.

Mardi Gras was always time for some of my favorite treats… crawfish beignets, shrimp boucannier, and chicken etouffee, with small pecan crunch cakes for dessert. Instead of eating and drinking in the comfort of our own yard or home, the feast would be moved outside in picnic fashion. These more public celebrations gave folks an opportunity to meet neighbors and friends or renew old acquaintances. The end result of the day, whether public or private, was always the same - too much to eat and drink, too tired from dancing, too hoarse from shouting and singing - and as is often said, a good time was had by all.

On Ash Wednesday, the day after Mardi Gras, the fasting would begin, convenient at this time of year, since there wasn't much left to eat anyway until the first harvests of the spring came in. This time of year was especially interesting and challenging for the cook and the kitchen staff. Making a meal from next to nothing is always fun.

RECIPES

PECAN BEIGNETS

- 4 cups flour,
- Baking powder, baking soda. \
- 1/4 cup sugar,
- 1 egg

- 6 ounces milk
- 2 tablespoons butter, melted
- 8 ounces pecan halves, smashed into chucks
- 2 ounces pecan liquor or brandy
- Powdered sugar

In a large bowl mix 3 cups flour, 1 teaspoon each of baking powder and baking soda and sugar. In a smaller bowl, mix the liquids - egg, milk, butter, and pecan liqueur. Slowly add the liquid mixture to the dry ingredients, mixing until smooth. After the batter is well mixed, begin stirring in the pecan chunks and enough remaining flour to form a soft dough (dough will be sticky). Do not knead.

Turn onto a floured surface. Roll into a 16" by 12" rectangle pan. Cut into 2-in. squares.

In a deep cast-iron or electric skillet, heat 1 inch of oil to 375°. Fry squares, in batches, until golden brown on both sides. Drain on paper towels. Roll warm beignets in confectioners' sugar.

Pecan beignets and coffee

YOUR TRICENTENNIAL MEMO

To understand the French/New Orleans meanings of Mardi Gras and put all the silliness, frivolity, and nonsense in some kind of perspective, one has to look inside the mindset of and the human condition in the Old World prior to the Industrial Revolution, that is until about 1700 or so. During most of human history, life was, as has often been noted, "nasty, brutish and short", except for those in the lucky one or two percent at the top of the economic scale. Scratching a living from the soil is no easy task, and this was the living for 98% of humanity until the last few centuries.

Even though the concept of ' holiday' goes back to Greek and Roman times, here in the West, our holidays are inherited from European religions traditions - mostly Christian - from the Middle Ages. Of course, days or weeks which marked the agricultural seasons of the year were primary candidates for a bit of holiday time. All of these (and more) factors played into the holiday culture created by and inherited from the Medieval Church. And this brings us back to Mardi Gras.

The most important of the European Christian holidays was the Resurrection (Easter). The month and half leading up to this celebration is also a hard time agriculturally. Basically, everybody is starting to run out of food. Because of this simple fact of agricultural life, and for other more philosophical reasons, the Medieval Church declared this the season of Lent, and Christians were expected to fast, make sacrifices, and repent in preparation for the great founding feast of Easter.

The Latin territories of Europe (Italy, France, Spain, and Portugal, then later, expanding to Bavaria, Poland, etc.) declared that the Tuesday before Lent was to be a day of wild parties, feasts, and merrymaking, since all of these activities would be forbidden for the next 40 days. And so, Mardi Gras made its appearance in the holiday calendar. To say when the Mardi Gras celebrations began in France is mere speculation. There have ALWAYS BEEN late winter festivals as long as there has been a France and even a region marked on the maps of Europe as Gaul.

One of the earliest references to the Mardi Gras comes from a nobleman's journal. Nicolas de Baye wrote in his journal in 1411:

> *"Monday, the 22nd of February, the royal household, in order to observe the Lenten fast, which is tomorrow, will be rising before dawn [to prepare]".*

Regular mentions of Carnival time come down through records of the Early Modern period in France. In 1690, in his Dictionary, Antoine Furetière wrote these words:

> *"CARNIVAL, masculine noun: time of rejoicing lasting from Epiphany until Lent. Dances, feasts, and marriages are mainly held at Carnival time."*

In 1752, the Encyclopedia of Denis Diderot and Jean le Rond d'Alembert confirmed this impression with almost the same words Furetière used. In fact, so close is the correspondence that, it seems, Furetière might have been Diderot's source.:

> *"The carnival begins the day after Epiphany, or the 7th of January, and lasts until Lent. Dances, feasts, and marriages are mainly held during carnival.*
> *"https://en.m.wikipedia.org/wiki/Paris_Carnival*
> *#History_of_Carnival_in_Paris*

Paris, too, has its own traditions about Mardi Gras. One such is an ancient and unbroken tradition of "festive and carnival societies" and the organized involvement of civic groups, corporations, and trade unions. Always a celebration of the people, the middle or working classes have always been, in the Paris celebrations, central to the Mardi Gras revelries. This can be seen by an eighteenth-century poem from France:

> *Always at these kinds of masquerades,*
> *Workers take their special pleasures.*
> *They wail, "We must watch our parades!*
> *This is something we've all treasured!*
> *Tomorrow we'll return to the usual grind,*
> *When Mardi Gras is, sadly, over,*

Food and drink will be hard to find
And we'll do our best to recover.

This sounds pretty familiar to anyone growing up in New Orleans even today. Rex, Comus, and the other old-line parades are illustrative of the "secret societies," while parades like Endymion and the truck parades of Crescent City and Elks represent the middle and working folks of the region. The variety, the multi-class composition of the revelers, tradition, and the involvement of diverse segments of the population are essential.

Mardi Gras in Louisiana

By 1699, Iberville and company stumbled into the mouths of the Mississippi in early March. By happy coincidence, Mardi Gras that year fell on the 3rd of the month. Thus, the first night that the first "permanent" French settlers spent in Louisiana was Mardi Gras night. Today the spot where Bayou Mardi Gras emptied into the river and the point of land still today called Pointe du Mardi Gras is still marked on maps of the lower Mississippi delta. The Mardi Gras traditions in the minds of the Le Moyne brothers that evening would have been based on memories of the Paris Mardi Gras strained through their Canadian upbringings.

Mardi Gras in Mobile

Being the first French settlement and capital of Louisiana, Mobile (now in Alabama,) claims that its Mardi Gras is older than the New Orleans celebration. Mobile, as a French town, is sixteen years older than New Orleans. Founded in 1702 by Bienville, with the building of Fort Louis de La Louisiane, the settlers and soldiers living there held their first Mardi Gras in 1703.

Nicholas Langlois, one of the prominent original settlers began the first "secret society" in Mobile, which became the forerunner of all carnival-related mystic societies, krewes, and carnival clubs around the globe. Their activities set the tone for the Louisiana Mardi Gras' through the centuries. The feasting and revelry included the Boeuf Gras (fatted ox), inherited from the Paris and Provençal celebrations of the old country. Masked balls, such as the Masque de la Mobile, began in 1704.

"The first known parade was in 1711, when Mobile's Boeuf Gras Society paraded on Mardi Gras"
(https://en.m.wikipedia.org/wiki/Mardi_Gras_in_Mobile,_Alabama:)

Whether at Mobile, Biloxi, or New Orleans, Mardi Gras was firmly ensconced in Louisiana culture from the beginning. Although New Orleans was founded in 1718, and experienced severe growing pains until at least 1722. Until then the city was basically mud and huts, when the hurricane in September of '22 wiped the site of the town clean. As the Vieux Carré was laid out and building began, almost simultaneously the capital was transferred to New Orleans. With the growth of the city's population, including officials and staffers of the Company, the growth of French culture naturally accompanied the French settlers.

The first reference we have to a New Orleans' Mardi Gras can be found in a recently translated journal of one young man sent over by the Company of the Indies as a clerk. The excerpt quoted below is worth reading from the source. The officer in question is Marc-Antoine Caillot. His journal entry for February 25, 1730 teaches us that the wild happenings at present day celebrations are far from original. And while sporadic over the centuries, Mardi Gras along the Gulf Coast has changed little in intention or practice.

A PARIS/NEW ORLEANS MARDI GRAS
(In "The Company Man" p. 134 ff) is described as follows:

> "We were already quite far along in the carnival season without having had the least bit of fun or entertainment, which made me miss France a great deal. The Sunday before Mardi Gras, upon returning from hunting, I found a friend waiting for me in order to invite me to a supper he was giving for a few people. He told me that I would have all the diversions there that one could partake of in the city. I began to savor the first pleasures in the colony, where I had already been for a few months. We spent not only an evening but the whole night, too, singing and dancing. When I returned home, I was certain that those would be the last pleasures I would partake of during the carnival season, since it was already quite near the end, but no matter the sadness one feels, it seems that those days are dedicated to pleasures and to having fun. The next day, which was Lundi Gras, I went to the office, where I found my associates, who were bored to death. I proposed to them that we form a party of maskers and go to Bayou St. John, where I knew that a lady friend of my friends was marrying off one of her daughters. They accepted, but the difficulty of finding appropriate clothes made us just talk about it."

{NOTE: Later that afternoon, having gathered some musicians, Marc got a party together to take a trip to Bayou St. John. As they were dressing, they also shanghaied some others to go along with them.}

> "… but since we had our faces masked, it was impossible for them to recognize us until we took them off. This made them want to mask too, so that we ended up with eleven in our party. Some were in red clothing, as Amazons, others in clothes trimmed with braid, others as women. As for myself, I was dressed as a shepherdess in white. I had a corset of white dimity, a muslin skirt, a large pannier, right down to the chemise, along with plenty of beauty marks too. I had my husband, who was the Marquis de Carnival; he had a suit trimmed with gold braid on all the seams. Our postilion went in front, accompanied by eight actual Negro slaves, who each carried a flambeau to light our way. It was nine in the evening when we left."

> "When we had gone a (short) distance . . . into the woods, our company was soon separated at the sight of four bears of frightful size .

> .. *These animals, at the light of the flambeaux, went running, just like we did from the fear we felt, without knowing where we were going or what we were doing. Nonetheless, after our first movements, they went away, and we continued on our way, laughing about the little comedy we had just seen, which had really given us a fright."* (p.135)

The story continues with a description of the party. Here I will insert a paraphrase with quotes of these pages; the passage is much too large for inclusion as an excerpt.

Mardi Gras Party
New Orleans & St. John's Village, 1730

The group arrived at the bayou village when the party was just getting started and the dancing had begun. After joining the dancing, they were welcomed in earnest and urged to unmask. Most of the group were recognized, but as Caillot had only been in New Orleans a short while, he was as yet unknown to many. Dressed "coquettishly" as a shepherdess, he...

> ..."*had shaved very closely that evening and had a number of beauty marks on [his] face, and even on my breasts, which [he] had plumped up.*" As such, he succeeded in gaining "*admirers unable to resolve themselves to extinguish their fires, which were lit very hotly, . . . In fact, unless you looked very closely, you could not tell that [he] was a boy.*"
>
> This situation did not last long, for shortly thereafter, he was soon "*reduced to the most pitiful state in the world*" by one young guest's "*delicate and well-formed figure, her snow-white skin, her beautiful rosy cheeks, her incomparably blue eyes. In short, she seemed perfect . . .*"

The rest of the party was passed with Caillot wooing his lady love. As the festivities came to a close about four in the morning, "she was kind enough to let me know that there would be a tomorrow." That tomorrow, Mardi Gras day, was a "a day made for lovers." The day was spent at the bayou plantation, dancing the minuet and the passepied, and having brought to the affair some four dozen bottles of Frontignan, a muscat wine from Languedoc, a good time was had by all. The party came to a close at 5:30 am on Ash Wednesday, after a night of "endless pleasures" that Marc-Antoine described as "nothing under heaven could compare to the charms of that adorable girl."

      One cannot play down the importance of Mardi Gras in the European "Latin" cultures, no matter what else is going on (Caillot's carnival narrative shares the same timeframe as his coverage of the then recent Natchez "massacre"). Whether in Mobile, Paris, New Orleans, indeed anywhere in French Louisiana, Mardi Gras served as a vital corrective to this "vale of tears" and "nasty, brutish, and short" stay upon the mortal plane. As it still does down to this very day.

27
300 YEARS AGO - EVERYDAY EATING IN NEW ORLEANS

Suzanne:
    As I did most mornings when the weather allows, I was wandering in the gardens thinking about what to cook today, when I noticed a lovely patch of mushrooms growing in a shaded corner. Thanks to my friend, Frère Gerard, and everything he had learned from the local Natives, I knew them to not only be a safe species, but also quite flavorful.
It's a small thing such as this which provides inspiration to a chef, and I knew immediately the best way to use these delicate mushrooms… a chicken and shrimp dish in a simple butter and garlic sauce, spiced with cumin and parsley, just the thing after the recent spell of bad weather.
    Leaving the bloody work of butchering the chicken and cleaning the shrimp to the kitchen helpers - one of the benefits of being chef de cuisine - I returned to the kitchen to supervise the daily activity of managing the tasks at hand. Once the chores of scrubbing pots and pans, washing dishes, cleaning work surfaces, doing the laundry, and tending the fire were well underway, I turned to my favorite pursuit - preparing the herbs, spices, and vegetables for today's meal - but it was the sauce that occupied most of my thoughts.
    For the chicken, I would need thyme, salt, pepper, flour, fresh cream, of course, a few shallots and parsley, and a bit of garlic for flavor… and maybe some cardamon, just to spice it up a bit.
    By the time the plucked chicken and peeled shrimp arrived in my kitchen, I had a heavy iron skillet on the burner,

with the bear grease sizzling hot, to which I added the chicken. I let it render as I set about mixing the other ingredients and making a roux. Into melted butter, I carefully added the flour, stirring until I had a light tan béchamel.

Museum replica of an 18th century hearth (author's photograph)

 After adding the other seasoning, I slowly added cream until I had a lovely white sauce.

Setting the sauce aside, I turned to preparing the shrimp. I layered them in a large pan, with the mushrooms on top to add a deep, woodsy flavor. The spices were added to the melted butter and poured over the dish, and it went into a hot oven to bake.

I drained most of the rendered juices from the chicken, and prepared to pour the béchamel over the chicken, then paused. I thought of my Maman, and wondered how she would have made this dish, what she might have added to the pot. On a whim, I hurried to the spice cabinet and took out the ground nutmeg, cayenne, and the precious bit of paprika I had just gotten last week, then added just a dash of each to the dish. The final sauce - light, creamy and full of flavor - was a delight.

Within the hour, a delicious and satisfying chicken dish would grace the table, and I created a new recipe to share with Frère Gerard. As for him, the turkey he was cooking today would be well on its way to perfection about now. I will save him some chicken and shrimp, just as he would save some turkey for me, and later tonight, we will have a quiet feast of our own.

Frère Gerard

The turkey was one of the largest birds I had ever seen. Its full chest alone would fill the bellies of every frère in the Presbytère, and there would be much left over to make a gumbo the next day. I had hoped to have couple of geese, or even a brace of wild pheasants or partridges, but with turkeys so plentiful and so big, I could not resist the huge bird offered to me by the hunters.

"See, Frère Gerard," the hunter had said, holding up his prize catch, "I saved this one just for you and the good fathers, good for your belly and good for your purse, no? So much more meat than a bit of quail or partridge."

"You don't fool me, you old pirate," I teased. "You are keeping the other fowl for the richer families, where you can charge more for them." But for all his finagling, he was right. The turkey did cost less and will feed more people, and of course, provides a very tasty meat.

As I set about cleaning the turkey, I planned the best ingredients to stuff inside the bird as it cooked. Onion, parsley, bell peppers, celery for sure, just to make a good gravy to pour

on the rice, with a few spoons left over for dipping our bread in the next day. There would even be enough meat left over to boil with the bones for a turkey and sausage gumbo.
Simple fare, but delicious and filling.

RECIPES

SHRIMP AND MUSHROOMS IN GARLIC BUTTER SAUSE

- 1 pound shrimp 31-40 count
- 8 toes garlic, crushed & pressed
- 2 sticks butter
- 1 cup mushrooms
- 1 teaspoon dill weed
- 1 stalk shallot
- 1 cayenne pepper
- 2 tablespoons flour
- 1/2 cup heavy cream

 Crush and press garlic. Melt the butter in a large iron skillet. Sauté the garlic, sliced mushrooms, dill weed, chopped shallot, and one whole dried cayenne pepper in the butter until all the vegetables are soft and well blended.
 Add the shrimp and let cook for about five minutes until shrimp begin to turn pink. Stir in the flour (like you are making a roux), and then blend in the cream. Let cook for another five minutes or so. Serve over grits.

CHICKEN STEW IN BECHAMEL

- Thyme, salt, pepper
- Flour
- One chicken - quartered
- Fresh cream

- A few shallots and parsley,
- A bit of garlic
- Cardamon, ground nutmeg, cayenne, paprika

Use the same method as the shrimp dish above.

ROAST TURKEY AND MIREPOIX STUFFING

- 10 to 12 pound turkey w/ giblets
- 2 medium bell peppers
- 3 celery stalks
- 8 shallot -individual stalks
- 8 toes of garlic
- 2 parsnips
- 15 2-inch carrot sticks
- 2 cayenne peppers
- Salt, pepper, parsley, oil

In this recipe, we are working with a small turkey and CHUNKS of vegetables, no chopping necessary. A traditional mirepoix is made up of onions, bell peppers, celery, and carrots. To this mix, onions were replaced with shallots then parsnips and garlic were added.

Place the turkey in the roasting pan in a bit of water. Put the giblets in the pan; they will form the base of the gravy. Put the two whole cayenne peppers into the gravy mix. Chunk up the vegetables to your preference, about one-inch square or 1 x 2 inches depending on the shape of vegetable. Using the stalks and sticks, begin stuffing the bird's cavity, fill in with the other veggies as you go. Whatever does not fit into the bird, let fall into the roasting pan, again adding to the incipient gravy.

Once filling the turkey with vegetables is complete, rub the bird down with salt and pepper, and some sage if you have it. Dribble with a little oil, add some seasoned (or plain) flour. Sprinkle with chopped parsley.

Cover the roasting pan, place in a slow oven 300° F for 2 hours.

YOUR TRICENTENNIAL MEMO

NEW ORLEANS, THE ENLIGHTENMENT, AND THE RISE OF THE BOURGEOISE

In our story, Suzanne and Gerard set about preparing meals in what would become a hallmark for the future interpretations of the Creole cuisine they were helping to create. They and other New Orleans' cooks of that first Creole generation were laying a foundation for future generations, originating a world class cuisine simply from what was on hand around the kitchen.

Reiterating the theme of this work, "They Had To Eat," the cooks and chefs of the colonial city did much to establish an integral component of New Orleans culture as the city came into existence. The birth of New Orleans has been seen by some scholars as an attempt by the enlightened bourgeois of France to create an urban space, modeled on the principles of the Enlightenment.

There, in a New World, on the blank canvas of a wilderness, they could plant the seeds of a bourgeois powerhouse designed to dominate the North American continent. Except for some success in the 1740's, the experiment did not really work, largely due to the inept policies of the French government. The designers of the city along with its founder and builders, did what was needed to create the potential physical space for such a goal. The powers at home in France did not support their efforts materially and sent to the colony not a bourgeois workforce but the destitute, the prisoners, and the most immoral population available from the streets and "hospitals" of Paris.

Most of these forced émigrés died in route or could not adapt to the sub-tropical climate or ran away into the vastness of North America as soon as they had a chance. The few who remained, blending with the original French-Canadian settlers and those French emigrants who came on purpose and decided to stay in Louisiana, created the next generation, the first Creole generation. Along with the descendants of the African settlers (slave and free), and the Germanic Rhinelanders, together they bequeathed to the modern world that Creole culture whose 300th anniversary we celebrated in 2018.

Those sometime hungry, but always resourceful and inventive settlers in French Louisiana managed to create the first examples of the Creole cuisine in the city that is celebrated by Lawrence N. Powell's The Accidental City, 2012:

> ... {*New Orleans*}" ...*was fast becoming a veritable African market town ...For game and grain, and kindling wood, no market came close to New Orleans.*"

> ...*African slaves, "hawked their handicrafts" local Indians sold, "spices and basketry ..." (p. 96)*

> "*The creation of a hybrid culture - a Creole culture, whose whole was always greater than the sum of its ethnic parts - is one of the Atlantic World's most vital contributions to modernity.*"

> "*The charter generation of French colonists, the settlers who carried across the Atlantic that "peculiarly French way of viewing or relating to the world - by cooking it" quite naturally preferred traditional French foodstuffs. (p.97)*

> "*But by the second generation, the Creole generation, those French-descended people began spicing up their diets with local grains, fruits, fish, and wildlife, not to mention domestic livestock and imported crops transforming them into something pleasurable to the palate. The kitchens may have been French, but the cooks were slaves, tossing into the same kettle culinary ingredients plucked from three continents. Not only did they cook the food, but they purchased the groceries ... from Illinois convoys, they bought the wheat flour that arrived (in the winter). From Indians, they might purchase sassafras and maize, as well as the bear fat used in cooking. From African hucksters, they snapped up rice, as well as the okra to make the roux that thickened the gumbo. And from the frontier came wild pheasants, partridges, turkeys, and quail, grapes surpassing in size anything seen in Europe, not to mention colossal catfish 'and an infinity of other fishes that (were) unknown in France '...In other words, African slaves not only stirred the pot; they filled it, too." (p. 98)*

Consumption of food also underwent an evolution of sorts during these two centuries. By the end of the nineteenth century, "foodways" in post-bellum Louisiana and the South would have only dimly reflected eighteenth and nineteenth century culinary customs. By the turn of the twentieth century the meal triumvirate of breakfast, luncheon, and supper had become well established. The Early Modern era in Europe (1500-1700) provides a slightly different picture. Prior to the settlement of the Americas, most people ate whenever they could, while meals prepared in kitchens tended to be two times a day.

Dinner, the main meal of the day, was taken in the middle of the day (anytime between 11 am and 3 pm). Supper, which generally tended to be a light meal, was eaten at 5 or 6 pm. More often than not, supper was leftovers from the earlier midday dinner. Breakfast, as a meal, did not become institutionalized until the mid-1800's. Prior to that, it was usually some porridge or bread, and something to drink, and was usually eaten between the morning chores.

Another point to consider is that mealtimes are culturally based. That is, eating (as well as timekeeping itself) in an agricultural society (pre-1850) is a lot different than eating in a post-1900 urban culture. Meals also varied according to the relative wealth of the household, the time of sunrise and sunset as well as from season to season. The best we can say regarding colonial cooking is that two meals a day was a general norm, with the main midday meal being the largest calorie intake of the day.

The timing of meals is never a hard and fast set of guidelines, but always based on common sense and the availability of food. As the centuries went by, certain logical patterns and customs arose in any given culture.

The above consideration of foodways among European and early American populations is based on evidence supplied in:

> *The Rule of St. Benedict, The Picayune Cookbook, and early cookbooks such as Massialot,* etc. as well as http://www.foodtimeline.org/food-colonial.html#colonialmealtimes

The development of Creole and generally American foodways during the colonial and revolutionary centuries coincided with the rise of the modern middle class, aka the bourgeoisie. This cultural evolution was a centuries-long and drawn-out process. Beginning with the development of agriculture some 10,000 or more years ago, a small group of any village population were the few people who created and supplied the required "tools of the trade" to the farming majority. These craftspeople - blacksmiths, weavers, cooks and brewers, wainwrights, etc. - slowly evolved to answer the needs, and the desires, of village, town and city.

By the European Middle Ages, this class - separate and apart from the triumvirate of rulers & clergy, warriors, and workers (peasants/farmers) - began to coalesce into a distinct population. As governments developed from tribe/clan to district to region to states and finally into nations, another group (scribes, lawyers, lower clergy, and accountants) emerged and joined the mixture.

At the beginning of the Early Modern Period (c. 1500), the middle class, or bourgeoisie, had begun to flex its economic and political muscles. The exploration, colonization, and settlement of the Americas, in large part, is a story of the middle class coming of age and infiltrating, if not creating, what has become the dominant political, moral, and economic structure of today's world.

For a thorough examination of the rise and moral effects of the bourgeoisie, see:

> *McCloskey, Deirdre N. The Bourgeois Virtues;*
> *Ethics for an Age of Commerce. Chicago & London:*
> *U. of Chicago Press, 2006.*

During the eighteenth century in France and in her colonies, political, social, and even culinary norms were undergoing monumental shifts. The thousand plus years between the fall of Rome and the rise of America, the peoples of Europe and Africa cobbled together systems of survival and eventually of civilizations (always based on some sort of economic surplus).

New factors such as colonial expansion, and the Columbian Exchange brought about new ideas and methods of food consumption, even at the level of the humble household kitchens. In noble households - the never changing 1% - meals usually happened twice a day. In the morning, folks of all economic levels grabbed some bread, maybe some cheese, perhaps some leftover meat from yesterday's cooking and washed it down with water or wine or beer.

The Columbian Exchange added coffee, tea, sugar, and maize (as cornbread) to the mix. There was, during this era of Enlightenment, usually just one big meal a day. As the eighteenth century progressed, an evening meal evolved into the souper (Yes, s-o-u-p-e-r, a shared root word for supper and soup).

In Suzanne's kitchen at the Marigny household, or Gerard's kitchen at the Presbytère, such cuisines (French word meaning kitchens as well as food) as these and others throughout the city, the colony, the Americas, and in Europe, Africa, and Asia all reflected and embodied these traditions of the past and embraced the new developments of the modern world of the eighteenth century. New Orleans' cooks like Suzanne and Gerard, however, added that pinch of cayenne and the soupçon of file', that led to one of the world's greatest culinary traditions… Creole Cooking

28
1790's THE EMERGENCE OF A CREOLE CULTURE; GISELLE'S KITCHEN

The Marigny plantation is buzzing like an angry beehive. So much to do, with royalty coming tomorrow. Louis-Philippe and his two brothers, in exile from France, will be our guests, and every table must be set just right, every meal cooked to perfection, to please their royal palates. It is an exciting time, and I should feel more excited than I do.

As it is, today I feel a bit old. Perhaps it is because I have so many young women around, hustling about the kitchen, one end to the other, much faster than I can move these days. They are practicing the kitchen skills learned from me as I learned them from Tante Suzanne when I was a young woman. It does not seem like that many years past, but now, in 1798, at the ripe old age of 46, I feel my sorrows in my bones.

Truth be told, I felt old even at the age of just sixteen. Thirty years ago, there was not much in the way of work for a young widow with a babe in arms. I wish I had never married Josef. I should have waited until a better match than the reckless trader who came along. I knew before our marriage that he loved trapping and hunting more than he would ever love me, but back then I did not have any other offers.

Sometimes I wish I had stayed at the convent and become one of the good Sisters. I would not have become a widow at the age of sixteen, nor would I have felt the agony of burying my daughter's twin brother, who took no breath when he arrived with great difficulty, several hours after his sister. But then, I would not have my lovely daughter or my precious grand-children, all of whom married well, and all are some of the best cooks in New Orleans, having learned from me all the tricks and recipes that Tante Suzanne taught me.

I still miss her and Frère Gerard, even though they passed on years ago. They were not only culinary masters, but good friends as well, who never hesitated to share their knowledge. But I will do right by them and pass on their legacy.

There is one young woman here who has a passion for cooking, and somehow, I sense that she is special. I will teach this new young Creole the chef's art, as Suzanne and Frère Gerard taught me, and I will make sure that she, in turn, teaches others.

Her name is Mimi, and she is a strange one, to be sure, obsessed not with men or marriage or fancy clothes, but with cooking. Her mother is an odd mix of Spanish, French, German and Choctaw, and her father is a French trader much like my Josef was. Unlike me, however, Mimi is a Creole beauty and could easily make a good marriage and well-to-do life for herself, but very much like me, her passion is cooking, and she cannot be swayed from it. At fifteen, she already knows much, and even dares to suggest new ideas and recipes for the increasing variety of foodstuffs that now flow into the city.

From an early age, Mimi would desert her mother's side at their trading post near the river and seek me out in the kitchen, always wanting to know what I was about, how I knew which spice to use on which dish, how to make such a flaky croissant. Mimi is quite a beauty. Even young Bernard, who is only thirteen, has noticed her beauty and sniffs around her like a pup. She could possibly even marry into the Marigny family but pays no attention to Bernard. So, I teach her, and I have chosen her to take my place in the kitchen as the head chef when I am ready to pass on my position. In all things food, Monsieur Pierre trusts me completely, just as his father, Antoine, had trusted Tante Suzanne, and I am sure he will approve of Mimi.

Pierre is a good man, possessing elegant of manners and a polished tongue. He is the kind of man that shines in conversation, particularly at the banquet table. It is my duty to be sure that all meals at the Marigny household reflect his elegance. To be sure, tomorrow's banquet will do just that, not just for the sake of making Pierre and the family proud, but to show the French royals our wonderful array of Creole cooking.

Just as Suzanne and Frère Gerard taught me, I will use the finest herbs and spices, broil the beef and venison over hickory wood for extra flavor, bake the ducks with sage and a wonderful orange glaze, stuff the goose with a spicy, meaty rice mix, perfectly fry crab cakes and top with a parsley and butter cream sauce. I will bake a rich cocoa cake and pecan pies, and of course, pralines and candied citrus peels to go with the coffee. There is much work to do before tomorrow, and I am so looking forward to it.

How lucky I am that I can spend my days in pleasure, doing what I love to do, with people that I care about and that care about me. Yes, I may feel my sorrows in my bones, but I also feel much joy, deep in my heart, at what the years have brought to me... good food, friends and family to share it with, and a good life in New Orleans.

RECIPES

CREOLE STUFFED PEPPERS

Creole Stuffed Pepper with Corn Bread

- 1 medium onion
- 2 stalks of celery
- 6 toes of garlic
- Pot-au-feu or seafood stock
- 4 large bell peppers
- 2 pounds cleaned shrimp

- 1 pound plain breadcrumbs
- Butter
- 2 tablespoons of fine herbs, dill and/or sesame seeds

Modern Adaptation Additions:

- Creole seasoning
- 1/2 teaspoon of crab boil
- 1/2 teaspoon of Filé
- Celery salt

Finely chop all the vegetables, then sauté in olive oil. Add one and a half cups of stock, stir well, bring back to a boil, add shrimp. Cook for two minutes or until the shrimp turns white remove from heat add seasonings. Mix the sautéed vegetables the shrimp and the seasonings. Slowly blend in breadcrumbs. Add more stock if needed to make the breadcrumbs blend evenly. Cut four large bell peppers in half longwise.

Blanch in boiling water for 3 to 4 minutes, then arrange in a baking pan. Overstuff each bell pepper half, top with one pat of butter, a little bit of dill weed, and a teaspoon of sesame seeds. Place the pan on the lower oven rack, carefully pour 2 cups of water into the pan (not on the peppers) and bake in a 320° oven for about an hour.

YOUR TRICENTENNIAL MEMO

CREOLE CUISINE - CREOLE CULTURE

"A cuisine is not shaped so much by its consumers as they, again in the most literal sense, are shaped by it."

(Root, The Food of France, p. 4.)

Antoine and Francoise's marriage in 1748 marked but one incident in the rise of the first Creole generation. Their generation in Louisiana, both of French and/or African descent, would lay the foundations of that unique American sub-culture bearing their name.

This generation's children grew up to become the namesake for a culture known for fine manners, hot-blooded honor, the fabulous frivolity of Mardi Gras, and one of - if not the - most distinctive cuisine in the United States. This should come as no surprise when one considers the life and careers of the descendants of Antoine and Francoise (née de L'isle) de Marigny de Mandeville.

Their son, Pierre de Marigny de Mandeville, was born in New Orleans in 1750. He married Jean Marie d'Estrehan. Their names alone echo down 300 years through eponymous streets and towns throughout the New Orleans region. Pierre served as Colonel of Militia and Commandant of the new Spanish town of Galvezton, near Baton Rouge. He went on to make a fortune in real estate, soon becoming the richest citizen in New Orleans.

Taking advantage of his opportunities, Pierre added to the concessions obtained from France by his father Antoine, also gaining large concessions as well through Spanish grants. He bought up plantations around New Orleans including today's Faubourg Marigny and the land on the north shore of Lake Pontchartrain that has become today's Mandeville. His home "across the lake", Fontainebleau, is now a state park.

At his death in 1800 his fortune was reputed to be seven million dollars, but none of this equaled his greatest claim to fame. At his home on the river near today's Esplanade and Elysian Fields Avenues, Pierre entertained a future King of France, then in exile from The Revolution and Napoleon.

A few years earlier (1798) in Boston, Louis-Philippe, Duc d'Orleans (great-great grandson of the prince for whom New Orleans was named), learned of the coup of 18 Fructidor (September 4, 1797) and of the exile of his mother to Spain. He and his two brothers - Antoine Philippe d'Orleans, Duc de Montpensier, and Louis Charles Duc d'Orleans, Comte de Beaujolais - then made a decision to return to Europe. They traveled to New Orleans, planning to sail to Havana and then on to Spain. While in Louisiana, Louis-Philippe and his two brothers were entertained by Julien de Lallande Poydras in the town of Pointe Coupèe before arriving at Pierre's home in New Orleans, where the royal visitors were entertained in grand fashion.

One tale recounts that elaborate gold dinnerware was made especially for the occasion of the Duc d'Orleans' visit. Supposedly, it was tossed away into the Mississippi after the lavish event with the idea that no one would be worthy of ever using it again. Louis-Philippe went on to later rule France as King from 1830-1848. He was the last Roi de France in history.

Pierre's son, Bernard was 13 at the time of the royal visit. Following in father's footsteps, at the tender age of 18, Bernard was instrumental in the transition of Louisiana from Spain to France and then from France to the United States, planning and implementing the ceremonies of cession. Recognizing political reality and being ardently American in sympathy, as soon as Louisiana was given over to Claiborne he volunteered for the staff of General Wilkinson. He served the general until 1808 when his first wife passed away. In 1810 he was elected to the Legislature at age 25, and in 1812 he was elected a member of the first constitutional convention of Louisiana. He gave the bride, Michaela Almonaster, away at her wedding, representing Napoleon's Marshall Ney, to the Baron de Pontabla who was his godfather's son.

At the Battle of New Orleans Marigny distinguished himself by his courage and activity. In 1824 he supported General Jackson for the presidency. He was also an ardent duelist and an expert with sword and pistol and has been credited with 15 or more encounters. When General Lafayette came to the United States in 1825, he paid homage to the family's royal connections and honored the Marigny family with the only visit to a private family by the Marquis.

The above paraphrased from:
King, Grace. Creole Families of New Orleans.
Baton Rouge: Full citation below.

Grace King, historian to the New Orleans Creoles, continues Bernard's story:

> *"Bernard passed more and more of his time at his father's old summer home of Fontainebleau, on the northern shore of Lake Ponchartrain, not for the sake of the seclusion and quiet offered . . . but for the greater liberty it granted for the enjoyment of his favorite pleasures-the table and the convivial intercourses with friends. Here it is that his standards of both enjoyments attained the height of perfection that has resulted in his gastronomic apotheosis in Louisiana's traditions and romance.*
>
> *A more favorable spot for the pleasing of an epicure can hardly be imagined; a beautiful lake ever rippling on the gentle breezes, or scintillating at the hour of dinner with the glitter of the setting sun; a white beach shaded by magnificent oaks, draped with hangings of moss; luxuriant flowers disposed like jewels on the greensward; hedges of Cherokee roses; vines of wild honeysuckle; the unlimited pine forest behind, fragrant and balmy, traversed by slow meandering bayous; the forest teaming with game, the bayous and the lake with fish. For service he had a retinue of accomplished, devoted slaves and a luxurious city within easy reach to draw upon for wine. Could a crowned head ask for more?*
>
> *Pleasure loving friends from New Orleans flocked to Fontainebleau as pilgrims to a shrine. There they found fowl that fed on Magnolia berries; turkeys fattened on pecans; songbirds and snipe kept until they ripened and fell from their hangings; terrapin from his own pens; soft shell crabs from the beach; oysters fresh from his own reefs; green trout and perch from the bayous; sheepshead and croakers from the lake; pompano, redfish, snappers from the Gulf; vegetables from his own garden; cress from his own sparkling Forest Spring; fruit from his orchard; eggs, chickens, capons from his fowl yard. These, with Sherry, Madeira,*

> *Champagne, and liquors, were the crude elements of repasts that he combined into menus that Brillat Savarin would have been glad to have composed.*
>
> *It is not surprising that the little town of Mandeville is as redolent of good cooking as some other little towns elsewhere are of religion and piety, for Fontainebleau had begotten the most beautiful, most charming, picturesque little Lakeshore town without a doubt in the United States. One can still find there seclusion, cool breezes, green shade of century old oaks draped with moss, a lovely view, and liberty of enjoyment in the good cooking as not the least of its attractions."*
>
> King, Grace. Creole Families of New Orleans.
> Baton Rouge: Claitor's Publ. Div., 1971 (Reprint)
> Originally published by The Macmillan Co., New York, in 1921.

It is important to note here that Grace King's effusive language and phraseology in telling this history of Creole Families is also part of the whole notion regarding the creation and continuance of the Creole myth that permeates the culture, social mores, and public face of New Orleans.

The 1830's and 40's saw Bernard's fortunes began to dwindle. Failed harvests, poor business deals, and the coming of age of the American sector in Louisiana commerce began to tell on the famous man's lifestyle. Nonetheless, even in poverty Bernard maintained his composure, his style, and his reputation. He passed away with the Old South during the reconstruction era after the Civil War in 1868. He left a public career and a very public lifestyle that cemented the notion to future generations of what it meant to be a Creole Gentleman.

RECIPE INDEX

French & Indian Bread	p. 12
1718 Sagamite	p. 19
Flan (Caribbean)	p. 30
Pork Chops w/ Acorn Dressing	p. 31
Basic Roux	p. 41
Okra Gumbo	p. 43
Corn & Pork Stew	p. 54
Cajun Macque Choux	p. 56
Classic Red Beans & Rice	p. 57
Okra Pecan Casserole	p. 64
Yam, Onion, Sweet Pepper Casserole	p. 65
Grits & Grillades	p. 71
Les Sausses:	p. 75
Sausse Espagnole p. 80	
Sausse d'Allemandes p. 82	
Le Glacé p. 82	
Tchoupitoulas Succotash	p. 88
Pecan Pralines p. 95, Pecan Rice	p. 96
Persimmon Bread	p. 101
Royal Saucissons	p. 112

Alligator Sausse Espagnole	p. 123
Cattail Side Dish	p. 130
Creole Calas (Rice Cakes)	p. 140
Turkey Boucannier	p. 147
Fried Fish or Shellfish	p. 155
Herb/Spice Chicken	p. 163
Baked Green Beans in Citrus	p. 165
Simple Chicken Marinade	p. 166
Chicken Le Balize	p. 166
Crawfish Pie	p. 167
Colonial Buffalo Stew	p. 185
Natchitoches Buffalo Roast	p. 200
Buffalo Meat Pies	p. 201
Coffee, Cocoa, Spiced Wine	p. 215ff
Pork chops w/ Orange Sauce	p. 225
Tante Marie's Dirty Rice	p. 226
Orange & Ginger Cookies	p. 228
Peach Spice Pie	p. 239
Voyager Stew	p. 238
Shrimp Stuffed Veggie Shells.	p. 249
Cane Syrup Cake	p. 251
Seafood Gumbo	p. 262
Pecan Beignets	p. 271
Shrimp and Mushrooms in Garlic Butter	p. 284
Chicken Stew in Bechamel	p. 284
Roast Turkey & Mirepoix Stuffing	p. 285ff.

Creole Stuffed Peppers					p. 293

BIBLIOGRAPHY:

Arnold, Morris S. The Rumble of a Distant Drum; The Quapaw and Old World Newcomers, 1673-1804. Fayetteville, AR: Univ. of Arkansas Press, 2000.

Baker, Vaughn, Simpson, Amos, & Allain, Mathe'. "Le Mari est Seigneur: Marital Laws Governing Women in French Louisiana." In LPBS, Vol. I, pp. 470 – 478.

Barnett, Jim. The Natchez Indians. Natchez, MS: Mississippi .Department of Archives and History, 1998 (revised) 2002.

Baudier, Roger. The Catholic Church in Louisiana. New Orleans: A.W. Hyatt Stationery Mfg. Co. Ltd.,1939.

Bienvenu, Marcelle "Rice : A Brief History of this Cajun Staple" in Louisiana Cookin'.   April 2012, pp. XXX.

Brasseaux, Carl A. A Comparative View of French Louisiana, 1699 and 1762. The Journals of Pierre Le Moyne d'Iberville and Jean-Jacques-Blaise d'Abbadie. The USL History Series # 13. Lafayette, LA: Center for Louisiana Studies, University of Southwestern Louisiana. 1979. Revised edition, 1981.

Brown, Margaret Kimball & Dean, Lawrie, Cena. The French in the Mid-Mississippi Valley. Second Edition. St. Louis, MO: Center for French Colonial Studies, Willian L. Potter Publication Series, Number 9, 1995.

Campanella, Richard & Marina. New Orleans, Then and Now. Gretna, LA: Pelican Publishing, 1999.

Campanella, Richard. "Geography of a Food, or Geography of a Word? The Curious Cultural Diffusion of Sagamité." in Louisiana History: the Journal of the Louisiana Historical Association. Fall, 2013, Volume LIV, No. 4. pp. 465-476.

The Christian Women's Exchange (ed.) The Creole Cookery Book. New Orleans: T.H. Thomason, Printer, 1885.

Clark, Emily. Masterless Mistresses; The New Orleans Ursulines and the Development of a New World Society, 1727 – 1834. Chapel Hill N.C.: University of North Carolina Press, 2007.
 ISBN 978-0-8078-5822-6

_____ (Ed.). Voices from and Early American Convent. Baton Rouge: LSU Press, 2007.   ISBN 978-0-8071-3237-1

Colten, Craig E. Bayou St. John: Strategic Waterway of the Louisiana Purchase. In LPBS, XIV, pp. 23 – 30.

Costa, Myldred Masson. (Tr.) The Letters of Marie Madelieine Hachard, 1727-28. New Orleans: Laborde Printing Company, 1974.

Dawdy, Shannon Lee. Building the Devil's Empire: French Colonial New Orleans. Chicago: University of Chicago Press, 2008.   ISBN: 978-0-226-13842-8

Dawdy, SL and Matthews, Christopher N. "Colonial and Early Antebellum New Orleans" in Rees, pp. 273 - 290. 2010.

Dawdy, Shannon Lee and Hartnett, Alexandra. "The Archaeology of Illegal and Illicit Economies" Annu. Rev. Anthropol. 2013. 42:37–51. First published online as a Review in Advance on July 24, 2013

Dawdy, SL. 2011. "Why pirates are back." Annual Rev. Law Soc. Sci. 7:361–85.

Dawdy, SL and Bonni J. 2012. "Towards a general theory of piracy." Anthropol. Q. 85(3):673–99

De Conde, Alexander. This Affair of Louisiana. New York: Charles Scribner's Sons, 1976.

de La Harpe, Jean-Baptiste Bénard. The Historical Journal of the Establishment of the French in Louisiana. (Joan Cain & Virginia Koenig, Tr.) (Glenn R. Conrad, Ed.). The USL History Series #3. Lafayette, La.:University of Southwestern Louisiana, 1971.

{Note} Written in the mid 1720's either by de La Harpe or the French royal geographer, Chevalier de Beaurain, but signed by de La Harpe. A French original was published in New Orleans in 1831.

de Villiers, Baron Marc. (Tr. Warrington Dawson) A History of the Foundation of New Orleans (1717 - 1722). The Louisiana Historical Quarterly, Vol. 3, No. 2, April 1920. http://www2.latech.edu/~bmagee/louisiana_anthology/texts/de_villiers/de_villiers--new_orleans_founding.html Accessed 7/24/2018, and many other times earlier.

Doyle, Leonard J. St. Benedict's Rule for Monasteries. Collegeville, MN: the order of St. Benedict, Inc.,1948.

Dufour, Charles L. Ten Flags in the Wind. New York: Harper & Row, 1967.

Du Pratz, M. Le Page. The History of Louisiana ; Translated From the French of M. Le Page Du Pratz. Baton Rouge: Published for the Louisiana American Revolution Bicentennial Commission by the Louisiana State University Press, c. 1975.
ISBN: 9780807101568

W. J. Eccles, "RIGAUD DE VAUDREUIL DE CAVAGNIAL, PIERRE DE, Marquis de VAUDREUIL," in Dictionary of Canadian Biography, vol. 4, University of Toronto/Université Laval, 2003–, accessed April 16, 2014, http://www.biographi.ca/en/bio rigaud_de_vaudreuil_de_cavagnial_pierre_de_4E.html.
Elliot, Jack D. Jr. The Fort of Natchez and the Colonial Origins of Mississippi, Natchez National Historical Park. Eastern National, 2013.
Fichrer, Thomas Marc. "The African Presence in Colonial Louisiana: an Essay on the Continuity of Caribbean Culture." in Macdonald, Kemp, & Haas, pp. 3-31.

Folse, John. The Encyclopedia of Creole and Cajun Cuisine. Gonzales, LA: Publishing Division, Chef John Folse & Co., 20XX.

_____. After the Hunt. Gonzales, LA: Publishing Division, Chef John Folse & Co., 2017.

Fortier, Alcée, A History of Louisiana; in Five Volumes. 2nd Edition (ed. Jo Ann Carrigan, LSU History Dept.) Baton Rouge: Claitor's Book Store, 1966. First Published, 1903.
     Volume One: Early Explorers and the Domination of the French.

Frazer, Sir James George. The Golden Bough. Vol. 4, The Dying God. London: Macmillan & Co. Ltd. New York: St. Martin's Press. 1955. pp. 226 & 227.
1936 Edition of Thirteen Volumes.

Freiberg, Edna B. Bayou St. John in Colonial Louisiana. New Orleans: The Harvey Press, 1980.

Gayarré, Charles. History of Louisiana: Volume I. The French Domination. 4th Edition. New Orleans: F.F. Hansell & Bro., Ltd. 1903.

Gehman, Mary. The Free People of Color of New Orleans; An Introduction. 5th Edition (2009). Donaldsonville, LA: Margaret Media, Inc. 1994-2003.

Giraud, Marcel. A History of French Louisiana, 5 Volumes.

Vol. 1. The Reign of Louis XIV, 1698-1715. Presses Universitaires de France, 1953. Tr. Joseph C. Lambert. Baton Rouge: LSU Press, 1974.

_____ Vol. II. Years of Transition, 1715-1717. Presses Universitaires de France, 1958. Tr. Brian Pearce. Baton Rouge: LSU Press, 1993.

_____ Vol. V. The Company of the Indies, 1723-1731. Presses Universitaires de France, 1953. Tr. Brian Pearce. Baton Rouge: LSU Press, 1991.

Hachard, Marie-Madeliene. Relation du Voyage Des Dames Religieuses Ursulines de Rouen a la Nouvelle-Orleans. Gravier, Gabriel (Ed.). Paris: Maisonneuve et Ce, Quai Voltaire, 15. 1872.

Hall, Gwendolyn Midlo. Africans in Colonial Louisiana. Baton Rouge: LSU Press, 1992.

_____. The Formation of Afro-Creole Culture. In LPBS, XIV, pp. 88 – 110.

Hauck, Philomena. Bienville, Father of Louisiana. Lafayette, LA: Center for Louisiana Studies, University of Southwestern Louisiana, 1998. Second Printing, 2006.

Hearne, Lafcadio. La Cuisine Creole: A Collection of Culinary Recipes. New Orleans: F.F. Hansell & Bro., Ltd. 1885. (2nd Edition)

Holtman, Robert B. and Conrad, Glenn R. (Eds.). French Louisiana: A Commemoration of the French Revolution Bicentennial. . Lafayette, LA: Center for Louisiana Studies, Univ. of Louisiana at Lafayette, 1989.

Iberville, Pierre LeMoyne. Iberville's Gulf Journals. McWilliams, Richebourg Gaillard (Ed. & Tr.). University, Alabama: U. of Alabama Press, 1981.

Ingersoll, Thomas N. "Fatal Golden Dreams": The Founding of New Orleans, 1718-1731. In LPBS, XIV, pp. 53 – 87.

_____. "The Slave Trade and the Ethnic Diversity of Louisiana's Slave Community.". In LPBS, XI, pp. 61 – 81.

Jefferson, Thomas. Writings. 2 volumes. Norwalk, CT: The Easton Press, 1993. Copyright © 1984 by the Literary Classics of the United States, Inc. Vol. 2, "Letters", p. 1105.

King, Grace. Creole Families of New Orleans. Baton Rouge: Claitor's Publ. Div., 1971 (Reprint) Originally published by The Macmillan Co., New York, in 1921.

Kniffen, Fred B., Gregory, Hiram F., & Stokes, George A. The Historic Indian Tribes of Louisiana: From 1542 to the Present. Baton Rouge, LA: LSU Press, 1987.

Kunkel, Paul A. "The Indians of Louisiana, About 1700 – Their Customs and MAnnr of Living." In LPBS, Vol. I, pp. 248 – 268.

LaBorde, Peggy Scott and Magill, John. Christmas in New Orleans. Gretna, LA: Pelican Publishing Co, 2009.

Leavitt, Mel. A Short History of New Orleans. San Francisco: Lexikos, 1982.

MacDonald Robert R., Kemp, John R., Haas, Edward F. (Editors). Louisiana's Black Heritage. New Orleans: Louisiana State Museum, 1979.

Martin, Francois-Xavier. The History of Louisiana: from the Earliest Period.
3rd Edition. Gretna, LA: Pelican Publishing Co., 1975 (Second Printing).
Originally published 1827 in New Orleans.

Massialot, Francois. Le Cuisine Royal et Bourgeois,
Qui apprend à ordonner toute sorte de Repas, & la meilleure manière des Ragoûts les plus à la mode & les plus exquis.
A Paris: Chez Charles de Sercy, au Palais, au sixiéme Pilier de la Grand 'Salle, vis-à-vis la Montée de la Cour des Aydes, à la Bonne-Foy couronnée. Seconde Edition, revûë & augmentée. M DC XCIII. AVEC PRIVILEDGE DU ROI.

McConnell, Roland C. Louisiana's Black Military History, 1729-1865.in Macdonald, Kemp, & Haas, pp.32 - 62.

Meyers, Rose. A History of Baton Rouge; 1699 – 1812. Baton Rouge, LSU Press, 1976.

McWilliams, James. The Pecan; A History of America'sNative Nut. Austin: University of Texas Press; 2013. First Edition.

McWilliams, Richebourg Gaillard, Ed. Fleur de Lys and Calumet: Being the Penicaut Narrative of French Adventure in Louisiana. Tuscaloosa, AL: University of Alabama Press, 1953, renewed 1981.

Miller-Surrey, N.M. The Commerce of Louisiana during the French Regime, 1699-1763. Tuscaloosa: Univ. of Alabama Press, 1916. Reprint 2006.

Mitchell, Patricia B. French Cooking in Early America. Chatham, VA: MitchellsPublications.com, 1991. Twelfth Printing, 2008.

O'Neill, Charles E. Church and State in French Colonial Louisiana. New Haven: Yale University Press, 1966.

O'Neill, Charles E. (Ed.). Charlevoix's Louisiana; Selections from the History and the Journal (of Pierre F.X. de Charlevoix). Baton Rouge: LSU Press, 1977. Charlevoix's works first published in 1744.

Phares, Ross. Cavalier in the Wilderness. Gretna, LA: Pelican Publishing Co. Inc., 1976. Orig. © 1952, LSU Press, © Ross Phares, 1971. Third Printing, June 1976.

Podruchny, Carolyn. Making the Voyageur World: Travelers and Traders in the North American Fur Trade. Lincoln and London: University of Nebraska Press, 2006.

Rees, Mark A. (Ed.) Archaeology of Louisiana. Baton Rouge: LSU Press, 2010.

Revel, Jean-François. (Tr. Helen R. Lane) Culture and Cuisine: A Journey Through the History of Food. New York: Doubleday and Co., 1982.

Saxon, Lyle. Fabulous New Orleans. New York: D. Appleton-Century Co., 1939.

Shepherd Jr., Samuel C., Ed. The Louisiana Purchase Bicentennial Series in Louisiana History. 19 Volumes. Lafayette, LA: Center for Louisiana Studies, Univ. of Louisiana at Lafayette, 2005. Herein cited as LPBS.

Vol. I. The French Experience in Louisiana. Glenn R. Conrad (Ed.)

Vol. XI. The African Experience in Louisiana; Part A, From Africa to the Civil War. Charles Vincent (Ed.)

Vol. XIV. New Orleans and Urban Louisiana, Part A, Settlement to 1860.

Shepherd, Verene & Beckles, Hilary McD. (Editors) Caribbean Slavery in the Atlantic World; A Student Reader. Princeton N.J.: Markus

Weiner Publishers, 2000. This is a revised and expanded edition of the work previously published as Caribbean Slave Society and Economy. Herein cited as Shepherd & Beckles.

Smith, Andrew F. The Tomato in America. Urbana & Chicago: University of Illinois Press, 1994. (Paperback Ed., 2001)

Soniat, Meloney. "The Tchoupitoulas Plantation." In Louisiana Historical Quarterly,
Volume 7 #2, 1924. p. 314 ff.

Stein, Robert Louis. The French Slave Trade in the Eighteenth Century; An Old Regime Business. Madison, Wisconsin: The University of Wisconsin Press, 1979.

Sublette, Ned. The World That Made New Orleans; From Spanish Silver to Congo Square. Chicago: Lawrence Hill Books, 2008.

Symons, Michael. A History of Cooks and Cooking. Champagne, IL: U. Of Illinois Press, 1998,2000.

The Picayune. The Picayune's Creole Cook Book. New Orleans, LA: Picayune Job Print, 1901. (Reprint, Kansas City: Andrews McMeel Publishing, LLC, 2013. American Antiquarian Cookbook Collection.)

Tucker, Susan. New Orleans Cuisine, Fourteen Signature Dishes and Their Histories. Jackson, MS: Univ. Press of Mississippi, 2009.

Thomas, Daniel H. Fort Toulouse; The French Outpost at the Alabamas on the Coosa. Tuscaloosa: Univ. of Alabama Press, 1989.

Usner, Daniel H. Jr. Indians, Settlers, & Slaves in a Frontier Exchange Economy. Chapel Hill and London: University of North Carolina Press, 1992.

Vella, Christina. Intimate Enemies: The Two Worlds of the Baroness de Pontalba. Baton Rouge: LSU Press, 1997.

Wall, Bennett H. et.al. Louisiana: A History; Third Edition.

Watts, David. Early Hispanic New World Agriculture, 1492-1509. In Shepherd & Beckles, pp. 136 – 152.

Zecher, Carla, Gordon Sayre, and Shannon Lee Dawdy, eds. Dumont du Montigny: Regards sur le monde Atlantique. (Quebec, 2008)

ABOUT THE AUTHOR

    Jon G. (Jerry) Laiche has spent most of his life immersed in local Louisiana history and genealogy. Before retiring to compose and publish Madame Langlois' Legacy, he served twenty-years teaching courses in Louisiana, American, and World History. In addition to his background as a historian, he taught Religious Studies in the High Schools of the Archdiocese of New Orleans and in Computer Ethics and Internet Technology at Tulane University.
    A native of New Orleans, he and his wife, Elizabeth, also provide Editorial Services for local, regional, and international writers. They currently reside at Beltaine Grove, 45 miles north of New Orleans' Lake Pontchartrain.

www.ingramcontent.com/pod-product-compliance
Lightning Source LLC
Chambersburg PA
CBHW051543010526
44118CB00022B/2559